Underground Angel

"A Slave of Love on the Railway to Freedom"

BY SHERYL D. WHITE

Copyright © 2013 by Sheryl D. White

Underground Angel
"A Slave of Love on the Railway to Freedom"
by Sheryl D. White

Printed in the United States of America

ISBN 9781628398649

All rights reserved solely by the author. The author guarantees all contents are original and do not infringe upon the legal rights of any other person or work. No part of this book may be reproduced in any form without the permission of the author. The views expressed in this book are not necessarily those of the publisher.

Unless otherwise indicated, Bible quotations are taken from the King James Version of the Bible. Copyright © 1611.

www.xulonpress.com

Introduction

Laura Smith Haviland was a tiny little lady whose heart was greater than her body. At 4'9" this "Underground Angel" stood tall for her convictions of human dignity and respect to all, black and white. Haviland lived in the 19th century American pro-slavery era, during the Civil War, and the post-war reconstruction era. As a Christian she took on the role of a servant, a slave, and an angel to those in the bondage of slavery. Both Quaker and Methodist, Haviland tirelessly aided slaves to freedom through the Underground Railroad, hiding them in her home as well as leading many personally through these secret passageways from the Northeastern States into Canada.

One of her stories is captured in Harriet Beecher Stowe's *Uncle Tom's Cabin*. Protecting Haviland's identity during a very dangerous era of the 1850 Fugitive Slave Act, Stowe tells the story of George and Eliza Harris being rescued by a Mrs. Smyth, who in reality was our Laura Smith Haviland. Wanted dead or alive with a $3000 bounty by slaveholders who had held her at gunpoint, Laura traveled deep into the South as an undercover spy to understand slavery and assist slaves to freedom. During the Civil War Laura trudged her way alongside the Union army. She challenged generals, the United States Congress, and presidents in order to assist those dying and in desperate need of care during and following the war.

Singlehandedly, she labored to secure the release of 3,000 Union soldiers held by unjust sentences at the hand of an ex-Rebel judge in 1864. Of note she successfully engaged with President Andrew Johnson for the release of sixteen ex-slave prisoners in 1866; and she also negotiated with Congress and President Arthur for the reimbursement of funds to pay for Columbus Institute supplies and support of Kansas refugee families in 1883.

Haviland's claim to fame in Kansas came after the war providing much needed relief for the Exodusters, 60,000 refugees pouring into the state of Kansas from 1879-1881. She worked alongside John Brown's half-brother, J.R. Brown (1864) and Sojourner Truth (1879) while in Kansas. In Washington D.C., Haviland received her marching papers from General C.R. Howard, who had charge over the Freedmen's Bureau well as General Edwin Stanton, the esteemed Secretary of War under Abraham Lincoln. Yet, her fame stems from her servant's heart in feeding the poor, providing warm clothes and bedding, praying for and nursing the sick, visiting those in prison, and starting many schools for the refugee orphans.

Haviland's continued signature saying was "Thine for the oppressed." A small town, Haviland, KS, named their Quaker settlement after her in 1886. Next to the life size statue and memorial of Laura Haviland located in her hometown of Adrian, Michigan is a water fountain that has inscribed on it, ". . .I was thirsty, and you gave me drink." Matthew 25:35.

Acknowledgements

Dr. Carol Vaughn
Dolores Williams, Rodney Hannan
Shari McAfee, Marlene Lofgren
Barclay College Library, Haviland, KS
Marlieta Davis and the Third Grade Class
of Haviland Grade School,
Anne Loomis and Jack Ewing

In Loving Memory of
Shirley Dowell, Lucymae Meireis,
and Dorotha Giannangelo

Prologue

Underground Angel is the life story of Laura Haviland, framed as historical fiction. None of the known facts of her life work have been altered or changed in any way. Fictional stories have been woven together to bring her character alive and to emphasize her substantial contributions to serve others. All of the facts have been taken from Mrs. Haviland's autobiography *A Woman's Lifework and Labor* (1889), and *A Quaker Pioneer,* Mildred Danforth (1961). Pictures, many quotations from Mrs. Haviland and portions of slave testimonies have been copied from the 1889 text. These now reside in the public domain and are free from copyright infringements. The purpose for doing this is to emphasize Mrs. Haviland's autobiography and its historical significance.

Laura Smith Haviland, 1808-1898, has been credited for her amazing work in securing assistance and freedom for tens of thousands of slaves. Mrs. Haviland gave her life completely and freely in leading slaves to freedom and a new way of life before, during and after the Civil War.

Two of Mrs. Haviland's friends, Sojourner Truth and Elizabeth Comstock, worked with her to make great contributions to the work of abolitionism and reconstruction following the Civil War. Elizabeth Comstock, an abolitionist from England, is known for the special prayer meeting she held with President Abraham Lincoln in 1862.

Her spirit of philanthropy assisted in bringing $70,000 dollars to the Exodusters, also known as the Great Exodus into Kansas between 1879-1881. Sojourner Truth is a national treasure and legend in American History for her escape from slavery, her diligent work for assisting her brothers and sisters in need, and her lectures, in particular *Ain't I a Woman?* The story of Truth and Haviland's overturning the segregation rules of the public street cars in Washington DC can be found in Olive Gilbert's *Narrative of Sojourner Truth.* Battle Creek, MI: 1878.

The Emancipation Proclamation by President Abraham Lincoln contains the message that motivated all three of these women. "All persons held as slaves. . .shall be then, thence forward, and forever free."

Table of Contents

Introduction v
Acknowledgements vii
Table of Contents xi
Prologue ix

PART ONE: Abolitionists, Underground Railroad,
Pre Civil War Era xvi

Chapter   1 – Truth 1
Chapter   2 – 50 Years Earlier- 1829: Life on the
                Michigan Frontier 24
Chapter   3 – Logan Anti-Slavery Society 39
Chapter   4 – Chandler & Change- 1833-1834 58
Chapter   5 – The Raisin Institute &
                The Underground Railroad 74
Chapter   6 – Joys: Underground, School
                & Children 93
Chapter   7 – The Sorrows of My Heart 101
Chapter   8 – Life Goes on at Gunpoint 114
Chapter   9 – Cincinnati Underground –
                John & Jane White 137
Chapter 10 – George & Eliza Harris 149
Chapter 11 – Maria's Free! 158
Chapter 12 – Fugitive Slave Law: 1850 170
Chapter 13 – Beaten Slaves, Bloodhounds &
                Backdoor Spies 192

**PART TWO: Service During the Civil War
& Reconstruction Era** 215

Chapter 14 – Enlisted 217
Chapter 15 – The Call to Natchez 239
Chapter 16 – 3,000 Soldiers 252
Chapter 17 – Red Tape 265
Chapter 18 – Kansas 1864 284
Chapter 19 – Needed in the Northeast! 300
Chapter 20 – Down Trodden, Down River 316
Chapter 21 – Forging Forward for Freedom 330
Chapter 22 – Bless the Children 338
Chapter 23 – Jolt 356
Chapter 24 – Tragedy & Triumph! 372

Postscript 389
About the Author 391

The Emancipation Proclamation
January 1, 1863

By the President of the United States of America:

A Proclamation

Whereas, on the twenty-second day of September, in the year of our Lord one thousand eight hundred and sixty-two, a proclamation was issued by the President of the United States, containing, among other things, the following, to wit:

"That on the first day of January, in the year of our Lord one thousand eight hundred and sixty-three, all persons held as slaves within any State or designated part of a State, the people whereof shall then be in rebellion against the United States, shall be then, thenceforward, and forever free; and the Executive Government of the United States, including the military and naval authority thereof, will recognize and maintain the freedom of such persons, and will do no act or acts to repress such persons, or any of them, in any efforts they may make for their actual freedom.

"That the Executive will, on the first day of January aforesaid, by proclamation, designate the States and parts of States, if any, in which the people thereof, respectively, shall then be in rebellion against the United States; and the fact that any State, or the people thereof, shall on that day be, in good faith, represented in the Congress of the United States by members chosen thereto at elections wherein a majority of the qualified voters of such State shall have participated, shall, in the absence of strong countervailing testimony, be deemed conclusive evidence that such State, and the people thereof, are not then in rebellion against the United States."

Now, therefore I, Abraham Lincoln, President of the United States, by virtue of the power in me vested as Commander-in-Chief, of the Army and Navy of the United States in time of actual armed rebellion against the authority and government of the United States, and as a fit and necessary war measure for suppressing said rebellion, do, on this first day of January, in the year of our Lord one thousand eight hundred and sixty-three, and in accordance with my purpose so to do publicly proclaimed for the full period of one hundred days, from the day first above mentioned, order and designate as the States and parts of States wherein the people thereof respectively, are this day in rebellion against the United States, the following, to wit:

Arkansas, Texas, Louisiana, (except the Parishes of St. Bernard, Plaquemines, Jefferson, St. John, St. Charles, St. James Ascension, Assumption, Terrebonne, Lafourche, St. Mary, St. Martin, and Orleans, including the City of New Orleans) Mississippi, Alabama, Florida, Georgia, South Carolina, North Carolina, and Virginia, (except the forty-eight counties designated as West Virginia, and also the counties of Berkley, Accomac, Northampton, Elizabeth City, York, Princess Ann, and Norfolk, including the cities of Norfolk and Portsmouth, and which excepted parts, are for the present, left precisely as if this proclamation were not issued.)

And by virtue of the power, and for the purpose aforesaid, I do order and declare that all persons held as slaves within said designated States, and parts of

States, are, and henceforward shall be free; and that the Executive government of the United States, including the military and naval authorities thereof, will recognize and maintain the freedom of said persons.

And I hereby enjoin upon the people so declared to be free to abstain from all violence, unless in necessary self-defense; and I recommend to them that, in all cases when allowed, they labor faithfully for reasonable wages.

And I further declare and make known, that such persons of suitable condition, will be received into the armed service of the United States to garrison forts, positions, stations, and other places, and to man vessels of all sorts in said service.

And upon this act, sincerely believed to be an act of justice, warranted by the Constitution, upon military necessity, I invoke the considerate judgment of mankind, and the gracious favor of Almighty God.

In witness whereof, I have hereunto set my hand and caused the seal of the United States to be affixed.

Done at the City of Washington, this first day of January, in the year of our Lord one thousand eight hundred and sixty three, and of the Independence of the United States of America the eighty-seventh.

By the President: ABRAHAM LINCOLN
WILLIAM H. SEWARD, Secretary of State.

PART ONE

Abolitionists, Underground Railroad, Pre Civil War Era

Chapter One

Truth

A bright, beautiful fall morning was dawning as the sun crept over the horizon. A brilliant red sky draped the eastern horizon and graced the landscape with green, looming trees tinted with the yellows and oranges of fall. They still drooped with tears on this lovely day after the turbulent storms of the night. A flight of birds flew in perfect symmetry above chirping with great joy for the coolness that had recently swept across the land. The fall foliage with its burnt colored wild flowers glistened under the morning dew with the sun brilliantly beaming against the metal of "The Pacific Island" railroad.

Against this backdrop a spry, small elderly lady climbed on board the railway car, and if you had been close by you could have heard her sigh. She looked tired from her many travels; the little wrinkles across her face were visibly framed by a neatly-tied, gray Quaker bonnet. Suddenly, she heard a familiar female voice breaking through the cool, crisp air in a tone of frustration and anger. Laura Haviland winced. She would never want to face the anger of this woman, one who had endured much humiliation and suffering throughout her lifetime. Laura had never needed to deal with her in this way. Yet, her heart went out to her. The voice belonged to her dear friend, known by all as Sojourner Truth.

"I'se saying to thee. I have permission to ride this here train from Kansas City to Leavenworth! I am an ambassador for the Kansas Freedmen Bureau. My papers were just right here."

The ticket salesman showed no pity to the tall, large, clumsy black woman. "Ma'am, you're going to have to go to the back of the line. I am here to sell and take purchased tickets for this rail trip" he said with an edgy voice.

"But I'se saying to thee, that. . ."

Interrupting Sojourner, the rude sales attendant called for assistance from one of the train's crew. "Can you get this nigger lady out of the way? She has no ticket and no money to buy one."

Overhearing this through the window of the rail car, Laura almost lost her Quaker bonnet in the rush to jump out and assist her friend. Running straight towards the ticket booth, Laura almost tripped over the wire fence that was supposed to keep people in line. She could hear Sojourner ranting and raving, "Excuse me, Mister Sales Man, I want to speak with thy boss man. Don't be spewing that vile lack of respect my direction!"

Suddenly, Sojourner, not so young in age herself, swung around and saw Mrs. Haviland bounding her direction. Sojourner, dressed in her best Quaker gray, let out a whoop of joy across the railroad station. "Sister Laura!"

"Sister So. . . Stay there!" Laura called out breathlessly though her voice trailed off. Yet she kept up her quick pace. One could hear the joy and endearment in her voice. She was elated as she raced towards her tall, lanky, dark skinned friend. Laura ran the distance of a hundred feet in a fleeting moment to rescue her dear friend, Sojourner Truth. That was quite a feat for a seventy year old in a long skirt.

What a great reunion! These two Quaker ladies embraced in a moment of joy! "Oh, it's so good to see thee! How ist thee?" Laura asked trying to catch her breath. They had not seen one another in several years.

"For an old lady, I'm trooping along just fine. How are thee, Sister Laura?"

"So, thee' ist a legend!" Laura laughed. (So was her affectionate name for Sojourner.) Thou knows how it is, So—so much to do. Who would have dreamed that we would meet again in Kansas?"

Sojourner exclaimed, "Well, I'se been looking for thee. I can't seem to find my bureau papers, and this here Mister Sales Man has no heart."

Approaching the ticket window Laura said calmly, yet sternly, to the salesman. "Sir, this fine lady is with me." She flashed her Kansas Freedmen Bureau railway pass to the rude clerk inside the ticket station.

The unwavering salesman, condescendingly looked at the pass over his glasses, and said in a very detached yet kinder voice: "I just don't have time to deal with these do-gooder private citizens who think they are going to save the country. Just get on the train and present your pass to the conductor."

The ladies moved on without any further word to the salesman. They quietly walked to the train, climbing the steps onto the railcar. Once they were in their seats, they looked at each other. Sojourner broke out into that booming chorus of "Nobody Knows the Trouble I've Seen," and they bust into gales of laughter.

"O, Sojourner, I have missed thee," Laura said still laughing.

Sojourner calmly reflected, "There is still much work to be done; and I couldn't have picked a better woman to carry the yoke by my side."

"We've been working side by side many years, we just didn't know it." Laura continued. "Yes, So, we've been through a lot." The ladies kept talking like birds chirping happily.

"Yes, Laura, we has!" she said as she rattled through her hand bag and finally found the pass that she had been unable to present a few minutes earlier.

Sojourner laughed heartily. "Remember our day on the streetcar, an' how thee gave that street car driver a great big dose of the truth? Thee said, 'My Sista here' (pausing and pointing to herself) 'she belongs to humanity.'"

"Of course," Laura remembered. "That old driver thought he could push thee around by literally shoving thee off the streetcar."

"Yes, but thou let him know that he was out of line, Sister Laura."

"That was easy enough. I just told the truth. But thee was thinking ahead to have me get that streetcar number."

"Sure 'nough. Who could have dreamed that the Washington Freedmen's Bureau would send us to court to battle this out in front of a judge?" Sojourner exclaimed.

Laura responded with as much pride as a humble Quaker could evoke. "Well, it was a great thing, opening the doors for black Americans to experience the privilege of riding the same streetcars as all other Americans in Washington D.C."

"Don't forget," Sojourner reminded her, "It was because of thy testim'ny that the judge found on our behalf."

Laura laughed aloud and said, "All I did was speak the truth."

"'The truth,'" Sojourner mimicked her, "yes, the truth. . . .That's what our lives are about. Right?"

"Absolutely, why else would we be here together again, risking life and limb, Sojourner Truth"

Startled by a young, black railroad man who asked for their tickets, they paused to show him their passes. They were the only ones in the car at the time and the railroad man tipped his hat speaking courteously, "Pardon me ladies but I was curious. Did I hear you say something about riding the streetcars in D.C.?"

"Why yes," Mrs. Haviland cheerfully responded.

He continued. "I don't have such great memories of my time in the capital of our country. Times were tough. No jobs to be had. I hung around and was depressed. I remember being told how the law on the streets had changed regarding blacks riding streetcars several years ago. Do you mean to tell me that you are the ladies that had something to do with this change towards justice?"

Sojourner blushed, though it was a bit hard to see the crimson flame through her dark coloring. She quickly recovered and leaned back to say. "Young man, what is your name?"

"John Carver Livingston, ma'am"

"John Carver Livingston, does thee have time to hear our story? It will take a few minutes to tell."

John smiled and responded, "Yes, ma'am. We have just been informed that our trip has been delayed for a time."

"Well, then let me tell thee!" Mrs. Truth cleared her throat and began to speak in her dignified, oratorical voice.

"It was several years ago, I believe it was 1865. . .Is that right Mrs. Haviland?"

"Yes. That is right, Mrs. Truth." Haviland concurred. She noticed that a small crowd of onlookers began to board the train and were headed to their seats.

"In 1865 While in Washington D.C., my friend here, Mrs. Haviland, accompanied me about the city shopping for necessities of the sick folk at the Freedmen's hospital. We were on a mission for the Washington D.C. Freedmen's Bureau. On this day, Mrs. Haviland suggested we take a streetcar back to our hotel, although she knew white and black folk were generally separated on the streetcars." Sojourner remembered.

"Yes, that's right," Haviland confirmed.

Sojourner recalled, "Mrs. Haviland signaled the car, I stepped to one side as if to continue my walk and when it stopped I jumped aboard. The conductor pushed me back, saying, 'Get out of the way and let this lady come in.' 'Whoop!' said I, 'I am a lady too!'"

"Yes, that's what thee said!" Laura Haviland affirmed and then added, "We went with no further problem until we had to change cars. Then a man close by quizzed the conductor and asked, 'Are niggers allowed to ride on this car?' Those were his words."

Sojourner with eyes ablaze like a scorching rod said, "Yes, and that's when that conductor grabbed me by the shoulder, jerked me around and ordered me out. I told him, 'I will not leave!' Mrs. Haviland stood her ground beside me and said, 'Don't put her out!' The conductor growled, 'Does this lady belong to you?'"

Jumping in Laura exclaimed, "I indignantly stated, 'No, She doesn't belong to me, she belongs to humanity.' Then he retorted, 'Take her and go.' The conductor was brutal. He gave Sojourner another push slamming her poor shoulder against the door."

Sojourner chimed in, "I said, 'I will not let thee shove me about like a dog!' Then I told Mrs. Haviland, 'Get his streetcar number.'"

Both Quaker ladies were quite animated at this point. Laura continued. "I wrote down his number and the conductor didn't say another word."

Truth groaned. "When we arrived at the hospital, the surgeons were called in to examine my shoulder and found that a bone was misplaced and my shoulder disjointed. It was very painful."

"I remember well," Laura sympathized.

"We complained to the president of the road and were advised to have the man arrested for assault and battery. The Bureau furnished me a lawyer, and the conductor lost his job. We won our case." Sojourner paused, sighed and continued. "A great swell of fear swept throughout streetcar operators in D.C., and even before the trial was ended, the inside of the cars looked like pepper and salt. I felt like Polly Parrot calling out, 'Jack, I'm a-riding.'"

"Wonderful!" John Carver Livingston responded with a tone of deep respect in his voice.

"The best part of this adventure was the great change that came in just a few weeks because a few were bold enough to challenge the system. Not long after, some colored women looking wistfully toward a car, were told by the conductor, 'Walk in, ladies.' Now they who had so lately cursed me for wanting to ride could stop for black as well as white, and could even address them courteously," Sojourner cooed.

John replied. "That is such a great tribute ladies. It is obvious you are doing great work helping our people. I hope to see great changes here in Kansas. We need the likes of you here."

"Young man, this is the fulfillment of a dream for all of our people to come find land and opportunity during this Exoduster era. . . ." Sojourner's voice dropped off.

"We have been praying for this 'better day a-comin' for many, many years." Laura concurred.

A crowd around them continued to grow as the train filled with people. Many listening with great interest, moved on to their seats. Many were black, some white. Others seated in front would glance back at these unique Quaker ladies distinguished by their apparel and their mission. Several had listened intently as the two had told their story, and smiled appreciatively. Some just stoically looked straight head and chose to ignore everyone around them. Most of these folks were poor, indigent people, young and old.

To everyone's surprise several passengers began clapping and nodding in approval, having heard the ladies' story. Some recognized Sojourner from her many travels, and came to get her autograph signed on her shadow picture.

Sojourner had made copies of this shadow picture originally taken from her autobiography. She carried her shadow cards everywhere she traveled.

Just then, the whistle sounded, and young John Carver Livingston, tipping his hat, hurried to the front of the train. Once the train was on its way, Truth and Haviland walked up and down the aisles of the cars, from the front passenger car to the caboose, handing out fliers, encouraging everyone to take advantage of the supplies and opportunities offered them by the Kansas Freedmen's Bureau.

"Yes, get out of the city, put down roots on a farmstead and provide for thy family," Laura quipped. Sojourner followed close behind, saying, "Mrs. Haviland is right. Thou shouldn't languish thy talents on sweat-filled, around the clock, industrial labor with no fresh air. Thy children deserve better." They were most persuasive, and many smiled and agreed to examine these opportunities and follow through with their advice.

Thousands of people were sweeping into Kansas during the Great Exodus of late 1879. They were called Exodusters, fleeing from southern states and the hateful brutality of slave owners. Kansas had become the land of hope for the freedmen in the late nineteenth century. Sojourner's great hope was to help her people find their Canaan land, their home of promise. This was the trip of a lifetime for this 82-year-old ex-slave using every last ounce of strength to see the fulfillment of this dream. Mrs. Haviland looked at her admiringly. Sojourner, her senior of eleven years, was an inspiration to everyone, but in particular to Laura Haviland, whose life had been dedicated to a similar cause, but for many different reasons. Laura's life had also been one of hardship, though never wasted on self-pity or indulgence. Thus, these two continued to share their message and persuade every individual along their way. It was a unique relationship, white and black working side by side in equality for the cause of resettlement of the freed refugees.

As the engine roared and the train moved on through the rolling hills of eastern Kansas leaving smoke in its wake, the two old friends continued to chat and laugh about their many special memories and adventures. They reminisced about the good ole'days of the mid-sixties and their lives working together in Washington D.C. Actually, they really weren't such "good ole days." Working to relieve the indignities and atrocities, found in the hospitals and soup kitchens following the Civil War, was an endless, thankless job. Yet these ladies possessed that contagious spirit of joy that would carry them through any time. They discussed the long, arduous journey of the freedmen searching for places to live and jobs to support families. For the many years they had served these poor blacks through soup kitchens and the hospitals, they had come to recognize the shiftless look in young men's eyes.

"Sojourner, thy life story is such an incredible journey," Haviland continued. "I always love hearing thy story about President Lincoln." Everyone within ear range turned their eyes on Sojourner as she began to share that very special encounter. Her "once in a lifetime" experience was to meet the President who set her people free.

"Yes, President Lincoln. He completely befuddled me. I says to him, 'I never heard of thee before thee was talked of for President.' And he says to me with a smile, 'Well, I heard of you, years and years before I ever thought of being President. Your name was well known in the Middle West.' I tried to tell him that he was the best president the country ever had, but President Lincoln would not accept my compliment. He mentioned several other presidents, who, he thought, were at least as good, including George Washington. I looked at him quietly, looked away, shrugged, and said. 'They may have been good to others, but they neglected to do anything for my race.' Yet, President Lincoln insisted. 'They would have done just as I have done, if the time had been ripe.'"

Sojourner turned away, glancing out the window of the train, staring aimlessly, as though she was a million miles away, before she completed her thoughts. "Perhaps so, I dunno. . .what a great man. . . ." Those sitting within earshot on the train listened intently, and many of these had tears flowing down their cheeks.

The train ride, though long, passed quickly with such deep and meaningful discussion between two dear friends. As the train rolled into the station in Leavenworth, KS, the ladies hurried off the platform to gather the barrels of supplies that awaited them in the storage cars. They were greeted by another dear coworker, Elizabeth Comstock, an English Quaker sister. After a short joyful greeting, the three workers turned the front walk of the train station into their headquarters for the day. With a sign that said "Free Staples, Come & Get It," the three ladies worked tirelessly handing out rations, ten pound bags of potatoes and flour, blankets and warm clothing so desperately needed for the bitterly cold Kansas winter ahead. Each person needed an authorized order to get these supplies, but Mrs. Haviland had the authority to give to all as she deemed necessary. There was no doubt in her mind that each family arriving had great need.

The three Quaker refugee workers handed out fliers, and reminded each individual regarding the opportunities available for land. They explained in detail how a family could claim 160 acres free of charge if they promised to farm and set up a home for five years, owing only ten dollars at the end of these years. This was a great opportunity to the many families looking for home and work. These women were passionate and painstakingly clear as they patiently answered questions to educate those who approached them.

Haviland, Comstock and Truth were not hired by the government. They worked on behalf of the Kansas Freedmen's Bureau, a relief organization which provided a small stipend to take care of their needs. Both Sojourner and Laura had previously worked for the Washington D.C. and Michigan Freedmen's Bureau supervising soup kitchens, food and clothes pantries, as well as relief work in prisons. No work was too menial for them. They had worked in hospitals as nurses and given oversight of the rations to the poorest of the poor in D.C. Elizabeth Comstock, originally from England, had settled at Rollins in Lenawee County, MI, not far from Mrs. Haviland's hometown of Adrian. She was a spiritual leader, a Quaker minister, an organizer, delegator and a superb fundraiser who alone raised $13,000 from her Quaker friends in England, and $90,000 overall to provide for the destitute in the mass exodus to Kansas. These three women would do everything in their power to help those in desperation and poverty.

As the sun began to wane in the west, the ladies closed their make-shift shop of rations and headed across the street to the boarding house where a good meal and a good night of sleep awaited them. They chirped away, reminiscing about special memories and common interests. One of these was their encounter with the famed author of *Uncle Tom's Cabin,* Harriet Beecher Stowe.

Sojourner's deep voice could be heard growling across the alley, "Can thee believe it? Mrs. Stowe wrote in her latest article that I am dead! Doesn't that beat all, Mrs. Haviland? She only changed thy name to Mrs. Smith in *Uncle Tom's Cabin* so's to protect thee. She killed me off in her articles." Laura's laughter filled the air with a needed sense of fun and as they walked across the way. She concluded, "So, it does not matter. Thou art a legend!"

Mrs. Margaret Brown welcomed the three rosy cheeked women into her home. After pleasantries and introducing Sojourner to Margaret, the ladies continued to banter back and forth as they entered the dining room for the evening meal. Elizabeth countered, "Well, say what thee wants, Laura, but I believe it is just splendid that the two of thee were acknowledged by Mrs. Harriet Beecher Stowe's pen."

Sojourner laughed heartily, quipping, "Elizabeth, thee would have been, too, if thee had not lived on the wrong side of the pond."

Laura agreed, "That's right, Elizabeth, if thee wouldn't have taken so long to make the big leap across the Atlantic, thee, too, would have been included in *Uncle Tom's Cabin,* or at least the subject of one of her abolitionist articles."

After a good laugh, Mrs. Brown offered the evening blessing. Following the "Amen," she hastily returned to the kitchen to check on the fresh biscuits ready to come out of the oven. The delicious aroma of homemade bread was tantalizing to everyone's taste buds.

"Margaret, everything smells wonderful!" Elizabeth interjected. "Can we help thee?"

"Oh no," Margaret responded from the kitchen. "You have worked hard all day. Please, just enjoy."

Warmth and friendship filled the room as the ladies partook of a delicious, late evening meal leaving the long day of work behind them. There was a quiet hush as everyone had their fill of the most delicious, steaming chicken and dumplings. Finally, Mrs. Brown walked in with a beautiful, golden-crusted peach pie.

"Mrs. Brown, what a gorgeous looking pie!" Sojourner exclaimed.

"Everything is simply delicious, Margaret." Laura added. The ladies heartily agreed.

Following the meal Mrs. Brown and the ladies retired to the parlor for a time of relaxation, conversation and a cup of hot tea. This gave Margaret Brown the opportunity to learn more about the ladies' latest activities. It had been over a decade since she had visited with Laura and Elizabeth in person. And of course, she had just met Sojourner.

"Sojourner, I have heard much about your spirited speeches, and most recently, your influence upon Congress to open up land for this Exodus migration. You have done such good for the cause of reconstruction. I would just love to have a copy of your book," Margaret initiated.

Sojourner responded, "I have a book for thee, Margaret."

"Oh, thank you, Sojourner, I will treasure it. I hope you don't mind signing it, as well. I will love to share it with my family."

"That's mighty kind of thee. I try to explain to people that comin' up from slav'ry, then movin' on up to servanthood, and now movin' on up to being a celebrity is so diff'rnt to me. I'm used to doin' it all, never had no special perks in life. Thy kindness speaks to my heart."

"Oh, Sojourner, you are a treasure and a legend. Margaret and Laura are so right about that. Thank you."

Turning towards Elizabeth, Margaret mentioned, "Elizabeth, I understand that money is pouring in from England for our relief efforts thanks to your influence."

Elizabeth replied, "No, not really my influence, Margaret. The Quakers in England have always cared deeply about the plight of the slaves in America. They continue to give and share their resources for this important mission work. My Quaker friends were delighted when our President Lincoln issued 'The Emancipation Proclamation.' They have been quite supportive ever since."

"Oh yes, and how thankful we are that your English friends' provisions have helped secure so many needed supplies for our freedmen," Margaret continued.

Laura interjected, "Margaret, we have come a long way since Elizabeth and her friends, Joseph Grinnell and Mary Bradford, met with our dear President Lincoln and spent time on their knees in prayer, 'proclaiming liberty to the captives.'"

"Indeed we have, Laura," Margaret concluded.

"God bless our dear President Lincoln's soul," Laura ended as in prayer.

The ladies nodded in agreement, and Sojourner whispered reverently, "There's no one better."

"None of us shall ever forget the great loss our country suffered with his untimely death." Laura spoke with emphasis.

Silence followed.

Margaret Brown brought them all back to the present by saying, "And, if my memory serves me right, Laura, the last time I had the chance to visit with you, you had a choice meeting with General Bank's wife. Do I understand it right, that as a result of this meeting 3,000 Union soldiers in Louisiana serving unjust military sentences were set free?"

"Yes, indeed. That was one of my happiest moments. What a great celebration they finally had when they were released!" Laura gushed.

Smiling, Margaret continued. "Is it true that you met with President Johnson to obtain pardons for slaves in prison? I read something about that, as well."

"Yes, that was the year following President Lincoln's death," Laura remarked.

"I can't imagine your encounter in the rabid White House of Confederate-friendly President Andrew Johnson was a pleasant one," Margaret interjected.

"Thee is right, Margaret. There was no friendliness there," Laura concurred. "It was very disappointing to me. Yet, quite honestly, I was surprised that Johnson actually did pardon the dozen ex-slaveprisoners for whom I interceded."

With a sigh, Margaret concluded, "My dear ladies, each of you is to be commended and admired for your great service towards freedom from slavery. How can I sit here in the present company of God's dignitaries?"

Sojourner immediately piped in, "Oh no, Margaret we are mere servants. Yet, if the truth be told, thee is a dignitary being married to the brother of the infamous Captain John Brown."

Peals of laughter rolled across the room. Our hostess, Mrs. J.R. Brown laughed, and replied lightheartedly, "I'm not sure if John's celebrity status is helpful or not."

"Well, I should say it is! It was a great help in obtaining the mass of supplies we desperately needed. John Brown is very popular among the masses," Elizabeth emphasized.

"Yes," Margaret Brown sighed.

"Also, I remember how thy husband, Mr. Brown, donated his brother's sharp-shooter fifteen years ago, gaining a timely amount of funds for our labors here," Laura reminisced.

"What better use could it have than to alleviate some of the suffering from the two border-ruffian Kansas conflicts at Lawrence? So many scars and heartaches still remain from the horrific events when Quantrell and the Confederate soldiers raided the poor folks in Lawrence near my brother-in-law's headquarters." Margaret sighed.

"That was certainly a terrible time for the citizens of Lawrence," Laura consoled.

"Yes," Margaret sighed.

"Mrs. Brown, I know that thee misses thy wonderful husband. How long has he been gone?" Elizabeth queried.

"It will be five years this winter," Margaret noted.

"We always miss those we've lost. It don't matter how long, I say," Sojourner sympathized.

"Thank you, Sojourner. Your words are kind. It was Mr. Brown's and my hope to do what we could to help the freedmen who were suddenly thrust into our state, and thanks to the three of you, this hope has not been lost," Margaret concluded.

"Margaret, it was such an honor and privilege for me to work alongside thy husband in the Kansas relief work those years ago. He gave me the office right next to his, and I learned so much from him of what I now know about Kansas and its people," Laura remembered.

"Thank you, Sister Laura." She sighed, unconsciously, wiping away tears.

"We are blessed with thy wonderful hospitality and these lovely accommodations," Elizabeth said with a grateful heart.

"Yes, indeed!" Laura added.

"Well, the pleasure is mine. I understand that you are traveling to Columbus tomorrow," Mrs. Brown commented with a smile through her tears.

"We are!" Elizabeth perked up with enthusiasm. "We are going to see my daughter, Caroline DeGreen, and help her organize for the great work that she is doing for our cause. She and her husband, Edwin, have started an industrial school, the Columbus Institute, for the freedmen and women in the Columbus, Kansas area."

"Caroline is a dedicated young woman. Thee can be mighty proud, Elizabeth," Laura boasted. "And I mean that in sincere Quakerly humility." The ladies shared a great laugh at the idea of a proud Quaker. Such a thought was completely foreign in their theology, but somehow found its way into such delightful conversations.

Finally, after they had offered their assistance for kitchen cleanup to no avail, they were shooed up the stairs to their room for the night. After settling into the two beds pushed together to accommodate three for the night, Elizabeth said. "Seriously, ladies, the road we have traveled is weary and tiresome. There is so much suffering among the freed slaves. There is so much work to be done."

"Yes, it seems as though we accomplish one feat only to be surrounded by more insurmountable tasks," Laura acquiesced.

"Yes, but my dear sisters, never forget that taking that step up out of slavery is the greatest accomplishment, and it's been accomplished!" Sojourner passionately stated.

"Thee is right, Sojourner. We just see the enormous tasks that lie ahead in providing for paramount needs," Elizabeth continued.

"Ah, yes! One day at a time. . ." Sojourner mumbled, beginning to drift off to sleep.

Elizabeth continued to ramble. "I think we will desperately need that tenacious and fighting spirit of both, thee and Laura. Think about it, all thee has overcome stepping out of slavery. And then there is Laura; she is fearless against fierce opposition, even if she has to climb the chain of command to get there. Really, who else could make her way so naturally and easily among all of the major Union generals. I mean, there's General Curtis, General Butler. . .help me out here, So!"

Sojourner could not resist, and joined in sleepily. "Let's see, General Hunter, General Banks. . .any general we're missing here?"

"Girls!" Laura cried. "Why are thee both torturing me?"

Laura could not help but laugh at them in spite of herself.

"Now, I know we've been carrying on with this silliness. Seriously, both of thee would have done just exactly what I did given the same circumstances," Laura reprimanded.

"No, Laura. Sojourner is right. Thee made thy way tirelessly through all of the red tape, walking fearlessly up the ladder in the chain of command of the military to confront that Rebel Judge Atocha's atrocious sentences for the innocent Union soldiers. Had it not been for thy tenacity chasing down general after general, and making inroads to General Banks sharing information with his wife, those men would still be in prison or dead," Elizabeth emphasized with a yawn finally beginning to unwind.

Laura, who had been quite fatigued, was now wide awake. "If either one of thee had been there, thee would have done exactly the same. I felt very passionate that these men had been given military sentences of thirty to forty years for the most trivial offenses, and they did not deserve such severe hard time. We were fortunate to receive that reversal," Laura emphasized.

There was complete silence in the room.

"All right, let's get some real rest, lest we forget the real purpose we have been commissioned to this downtrodden race here in this desolate state. We know what the good Book says, 'The greatest among thee shall be thy servant.'" Having said this Laura snuffed out the lamp for the night.

As quietness rested over the darkness in the room, Laura sat up straight in bed, looking out the window next to her. As she sat there admiring the beautiful harvest moon and the twinkling stars of the fall night, she shared one final thought with her co-laborers. "I just want to say how blessed I am. . .how blessed I feel to serve with the two of thee. Thank thee both." The snores of her friends snoozing peacefully were her only response. Chuckling to herself, Laura rolled over and drifted off into a deep, peaceful sleep, as well.

The next morning, the ladies bid Mrs. Brown farewell quite early, following a quick breakfast, in order to catch the train headed for Columbus, Kansas. Columbus was a new community in the far southeast part of the state. It was nice to have a day to catch their breath. They drank in the beauty of the fall foliage and hilly landscape on both sides. The other personnel on the train assured them they were in the most beautiful part of Kansas, and that if they were to travel further west, they would find Kansas like the ends of the earth, flat as a pancake. All three of them smiled at this word picture. It was such a pleasant journey.

It was a treat to have time with dear friends and share personal stories. These types of journeys gave the abolitionist girls the opportunities to remember "old times." Telling story after story, they shared one another's joys and celebrations, as well as hardships and sorrows. Intermingled with tears and gasps of laughter, these sisters of the soul found solace in this healing bond. Through the most difficult, traumatic situations, they found a way of looking at the bright side, the way upward as their response to God's call, their life work. Each served in the role of caring for the needs of ex-slaves. Laura shared the hardships in opening two much needed refugee orphanages, the private Haviland Orphanage and the Coldwater Orphanage, operated by the state of Michigan. In the process Laura experienced her own personal trauma, falling eight feet headlong into her cellar. This accident almost killed her, but after two years of recuperation she finally returned full force to her work for the orphanages. Laura had a way of bringing levity into her hardships, especially if it included a good dose of Quaker humility.

So it was with a wink of the eye, Laura stated. "Hmm, had I known I would have received such great comfort and support from my fall, I would have fallen for it much earlier."

"Mrs. Haviland!" Elizabeth burst into laughter. "Thou wouldst not! A good and honest Quaker tells the truth and does not exploit circumstances for thy own favor."

"Well, I must confess," she responded, still laughing herself, "I dislike pain way too much to choose such a path of desperation and destruction!" Everyone laughed at dear Mrs. Haviland. Her humor always contained just a hint of self-deprecation, making her a most excellent Quaker, though she had served as an excellent Methodist for 42 years, as well. No one could believe that these somber-looking women in the drab Quaker gray could laugh at themselves so easily and have quite so much fun.

"But I almost forgot to tell thee about my delightful lunch date with our good sister, Susan B. Anthony!" Laura gushed.

"O Laura, do tell!" Elizabeth exclaimed.

"As I was traveling with 75 orphan children to my home in Michigan, our train made a stop at St. Louis. And as planned, Mrs. Anthony met us there with a delightful basket lunch," Laura explained.

"Yes, St. Louis is Mrs. Anthony's home," Sojourner remembered.

"And she is such a good friend to our Exoduster cause," Elizabeth joined in.

"She is related to our Kansas Governor St. John who cares deeply about the reconstruction cause," Laura quipped.

"She probably knows better than many what a formidable task it is to assimilate the thousands of Exoduster refugees as they stampede their way across the state of Kansas." Elizabeth sighed.

"Yes, indeed," Laura concurred. "We were most thankful for the picnic basket filled with delicious cookies, crepes and other sweet treats for our trip home."

"Oh, that's making me hungry, Sister Laura," Sojourner cooed.

"Yes, but the wonderful part for me was having a heart to heart with Mrs. Anthony. It was indeed an inspirational time," Laura continued.

"Susan has such a heart of compassion. I think we all admire her for the graceful and articulate way she has in communicating her dream and passion. The dream that one day all women will have the right to vote right alongside their male counterparts," Elizabeth sighed.

"Yes, women should have the right to vote. But our friends of color are not even accepted as humans! Forget the thought of being equal, my hope is that they will be treated humanely," Laura agonized.

Sojourner passionately agreed. "Yes, neither of thee has had to stand up to the one and only freed statesman, Frederick Douglass, with a challenging question, 'Is God Dead?' Nor would either of thee need to cry out at a woman's convention, 'Ain't I a Woman?'"

Laura conceded to her sister sympathetically. "No. Thee is definitely right! But Sojourner Truth, 'Ain't I a Woman' is thy signature speech. And, I guarantee thee that neither Frederick Douglass nor any of those women at that convention will ever forget that."

Sojourner clapped and laughed with tears in her eyes.

"What an honor to upstage a statesman and a whole convention of women," Elizabeth chimed in.

"Oh Heavens! No!" Sojourner sighed. "I'se never want to upstage anyone of that stature."

"I don't know," Elizabeth continued. "Sojourner, all of thy hard labors with that national petition to Congress opened the way for the freed slaves to make their way through to Bleeding Kansas, the first free state of the West."

"Well, that's mighty kind of thee to say, Mrs. Comstock. I'm of the mind that there were so many people squashed together in these Southern States that they would have been spewed to the West, no matter what the Congress did."

"Miss Sojourner, thee's not getting off that easy! Thou worked long and hard to see thy dream come true. That's why we're all here today! We're here because thou acted on thy convictions, thy love for thy people and the dream that colored folks could start a new life in a new land!" Laura passionately praised.

"Mrs. Haviland, thou does have a way with words. Thou speaks from thy heart! Perhaps thee should write a book," Sojourner said as she brushed a tear from her eye.

"No. Dear, Sojourner, I couldn't think of it!" Laura blushed.

Elizabeth, siding with Sojourner, responded. "But why not? Thee has so much to share of thy travels through the Underground Railroad and thy work with the generals during the Civil War. I, for one, think that thee could turn thy journal into a book."

Laura reflected thoughtfully, "Oh, I don't think so. Yet Sojourner has written a beautiful book of her freedom from slavery. Sojourner, thy book is a treasure! Elizabeth, I've seen thee with a journal, as well. Will thee turn it into a book?"

"Well, yes, I have seriously been thinking about doing just that. Certainly, I think thee should write thy story, Laura."

Sojourner bantered back, "I agree with Elizabeth, Laura, it's all settled. Thee should write a book."

Laura squirmed uncomfortably. "Oh, thank thee. But I don't think so." Yet, in spite of herself, her mind began to wander. What would she say in a book? She did have a journal that she could follow. The ladies were right about that.

Instantly Laura snapped back to the conversation at hand. "Just think this discussion came about because of Laura's lunch with the 'one and only' Susan B. Anthony." Elizabeth smirked.

Sojourner laughed and said, "I must tell both of thee one more story. This is a story our Sister Susan would appreciate." She continued, "I would never want it publicized. A few years ago I went to the polls in order to place my vote in the ballot box. I just walked right in, grabbed a ballot and went behind the curtain only to have a group of four rude bullies pull the curtain open, walk in and take hold of me. They picked me up and carried me out of the election office and over to the sheriff's office with my arms and limbs waving and me screamin'."

Both ladies gasped and cried out, "Oh Sojourner!"

Sojourner put up her hand to continue. "The sheriff was a bit nicer than my bully escorts. However, he condescendingly said, 'Sojourner, Sojourner, you know the law. You's a woman, and that means you can't vote.' And of course, I retorted, "I don't care what the law is sheriff. I'm telling thee, it ain't right that women can't vote!'"

Elizabeth began to clap her hands for joy, and Laura couldn't stop laughing.

Sojourner concluded with this: "One day ladies, it will happen. We will have the vote. I just feel it in my bones. I believe Susan B. Anthony is right."

"Well, maybe thou can feel it in thy bones, but the only thing I can feel in my bones is the weather beginning to change. I believe Kansas is in store for a big storm," Laura declared, and they all laughed.

"Yes," Sojourner conceded. "But I tell thee, one day women shall have the vote."

As the ladies had grown silent, Elizabeth thoughtfully responded, "Yes, one day, Sojourner, just not in our lifetime."

"Yet, Sojourner, thou hast certainly done thy part towards securing the woman's vote," Laura quipped back with a smile.

"Indeed." Sojourner groaned.

The sun was hiding somewhere behind the clouds as the Quaker ladies finished a delicious lunch of chicken sandwiches and crème puffs. Moving over to their sleeping car, Laura sat with her journal and pen in hand. Could she write a book of her many adventures? She looked over at her friends and they had both dozed off for a bit of a nap. Slowly, she, too, began to nod off, all the while thinking, "What would I say about myself if I wrote a book?" Before Laura realized it, she had fallen fast asleep into a dream world of life as she once knew it.

Chapter Two

Fifty Years Earlier- Life on the Michigan Frontier–1829

Stretching my arms and legs, I jumped off the bumpy wagon after it had finally come to a complete standstill. It seemed my whole being was still jolting back & forth. My body ached from the many days and endless miles of being jerked around over the difficult terrain from Niagara County, New York, and all the way west to Southern Michigan. Jumping to the ground, I breathed in deeply the cool fall air, and marveled at the bright orange and yellow foliage framed picturesquely against the beauty of the bluish-green, algae-infested Raisin River. Grabbing my two ruddy toddler boys, Harvey and Daniel, in an arm-lock before they attempted to take off down the river, I corralled them noting that daring look of adventure in their eyes. There would be plenty of adventure for these little ones later on. But right now I reached out for Charles, the love of my life. We embraced in this special moment! The Havilands were finally home!

Gazing across the horizon, our young family stood in silence at the spectacular view as dusk set in and the large, orangish ball of a sun continued to lower across the sky. It was simply breathtaking! For a moment we forgot about the difficult circumstances through which we had just passed and the back-breaking work that

Fifty Years Earlier- Life on the Michigan Frontier–1829

lie ahead and simply basked in our good fortune! We were home. Yes, it's true, we would have to clear the Michigan frontier in order to build our home, and that would take time. Yet, my parents and siblings had made this difficult journey three years earlier; and they would be here to lend us a helping hand. At least we had a place to call home. Life on the Michigan frontier would prove challenging and difficult, at best. But for today we could rest!

The boys gathered the sticks and logs to build the fire. Charles set up camp on our new land while I scurried together a simple supper of beans and cornbread. Exhausted from our long travels, the boys bedded down for the night. Charles and I, cuddling close to the campfire, spoke in low tones so as not to disturb the little ones. Charles whispered. "In the morning, we'll venture out and see if we can get the lay of the land. We'll cross over to thy parent's quarter. If I'm reading this map right, we're on our plot and we are only a couple of miles from them." I could not contain my excitement. It had been three years since I had wrapped my arms around Mama and Papa, and of course, my adorable, seven siblings! Tears welled up in my eyes as I tried to soak in the joy. I choked out the words, "I can hardly wait." Watching the bright Michigan stars twinkling in the night, Charles kissed me tenderly and finally sent me off to sleep next to the boys.

As the fire waned on, Charles listened as he kept watch for the night. His ears strained against the cool fall night's breeze, praying that the good Lord would protect his young family from the harshness of the frontier, the animals of the wild and any attack from Indians. He was all too familiar with the endless stories from many settlers along our journey about the terrors of Indian massacres. Charles knew that our land ran next to the Raisin River, and such land had belonged to Tecumseh, the renowned Indian Chief's hunting ground, until his death just a few years earlier. Charles drifted off to sleep with his hand wrapped around the strap of his gun, one he would never use on another human soul, for he was a devout, pacifist Quaker, a member of the Society of Friends.

As dawn began to break and the sun was creeping up over the horizon, a lone haze billowed forth a promising hope for a new day. What a sweet reunion for the Smiths and the Havilands as we gathered. Being the eldest daughter, I had missed my baby brother Samuel, who was three when my family had moved to Michigan. Sitting around the Smith's simple, hard-wood dining table, laughter rang out as we shared stories of Harvey and Daniel, whom my parents were meeting for the first time. Mama shared baby stories of Samuel. Samuel, now six, scoffed at this mush. He was no longer a baby. Yet it was not to be stopped. How often do a mother and daughter walk through the journey of motherhood at the same time?

After the men had stoked the fire, Papa Daniel announced, "There are several families in Raisin who will meet here in the morning for worship. Thee will join us." Having announced this, Papa and Charles chased the boys outdoors, leaving the mother and daughter to chat.

"Mama, hast thou heard from Harvey?" Harvey Smith, my brother next in birth order, had worked tirelessly pinching every penny to attend Oberlin College in Ohio. Laura understood the political sentiments of the day and she knew that Oberlin would be scorned as a seedbed of liberal thinking.

"Yes, Laura. Harvey had Papa go and speak to Brother Webb for the quarter of land adjoining our place. But it will be a year before Harvey returns to settle on his land."

"I can't wait for him to come home. I want to know more about Oberlin. I received a letter from him, and he said he couldn't wait to tell me about a new organization, one that aided slaves in their escape to freedom. It's called the Underground Railroad."

Fifty Years Earlier- Life on the Michigan Frontier–1829

"Now Laura, don't go getting thyself involved with some radical group. Thou hast children to raise and a husband to care for and think about. Laura Smith Haviland, thee always gets thyself attached to these emotional social issues. Why can't thee just mind to thy own?"

"But Mama?" Laura responded with crestfallen spirit.

The ladies were so intense in conversation that they jumped when the door slammed and Papa Daniel, looking down upon them, bellowed out, "What is going on here?"

Laura, appealing to her dear father, cried out. "Papa, I was just telling Mama that Harvey has written to me about the Underground Railroad, a new group at Oberlin College."

Charles, right behind Papa, chimed in. "Laura says that it's a community of folks who help protect and hide slaves, leading them north to Canada where they become free citizens."

"Oh Laura child, thou hast always been so obsessed with the slaves. I remember finding thee I my library, tears streaming down thy face, reading *The Journal of John Woolman* and his history of the slave trade. What affect has that had on thy mind? A young mind should not dwell on the atrocious treatment of slaves being thrown overboard to the sharks from crowded ships. Thou knowest that we do not approve of slavery. We do not even buy products made by the sweat and tears of a slave. But to get involved in such political issues, it's just not the Quaker way! I'm afraid thy mother and I have failed thee." Papa choked out the words.

Acquiescing, I knew I could say no more. After a brief farewell, Charles guided me and the boys back to our homestead in our covered wagon. Lying awake that night, I struggled to keep my sobs quiet. I felt so dead inside. Was I a failure? Was God really here with me? I remembered a time when I attended special Methodist, evangelistic services with my uncles. I had felt the Spirit of God and poured out my struggles and heartache to the Lord. I loved going to these meetings until Mama and Papa had been told that "if it were not for her parents, Laura Smith would be a Methodist." Papa reproached my actions. "Laura, it is not the Quaker way," Mama would say. "Quakers wait for God to speak. They are moved by settled principle, not emotional excitement. No, Friends would never break out into an enthusiastic version of a song that sounds like a bar tune, even if it is the Doxology. No!" It was reinforced in my mind that this was not God's way according to the Quakers. Their duty was to listen and wait for the gentle nudging of the Spirit of God.

Drifting off to sleep I knew my struggle with faith was far from settled. I felt like one of the slave "untouchables" in my quest for God's presence and touch. The next morning, Charles and I arrived promptly at my parents' homestead for worship. As I sat with the women on their side of the veil, I could hear Papa's voice as he admonished the small group of Quakers gathered in his home. "Dear Friends, do not forsake the assembling together of God's chosen people." The excitement for the day was the decision to purchase a plot of land to build the Raisin Valley Society of Friends Meetinghouse. First they agreed to help our family construct our home. Afterwards, they would build that Friend's meetinghouse on the new plot of land.

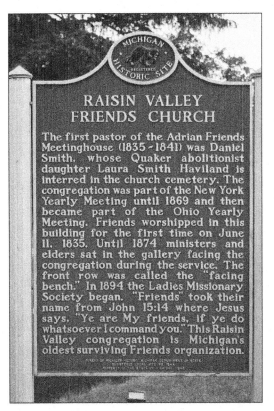

Though I could not see him, Papa's voice always soothed me. As he shared the morning message, my mind began to wander to a meeting from long ago. It was an exceptional meeting, an encounter when I was thirteen. I had been summoned

Fifty Years Earlier- Life on the Michigan Frontier–1829

along with my parents by a note from an old family friend, Caleb McComber. At the appointed Sunday afternoon, he greeted us in a small gathering, saying. "One of thee has passed through an experience far beyond thy years. Thou hast known what it was to ask for deliverance from sorrow and darkness, and thou hast also known what it was to receive the answer of peace from thy Heavenly Father. Hold fast. . .be faithful in little and more will be given. Bear in mind, little things are little, but to be faithful in little things is somewhat great."

I had cherished those words over the years, and I believed without a doubt they were meant for me. Unfortunately I had not been faithful in the little things. Sure, I was a dutiful wife and mother; but something was desperately missing. . . .

"Laura, Laura!" Mama's voice startled me back from my daydreaming. Had I fallen asleep? "Is thee willing to carry supper for the men working on thy house this next week?"

"Oh, oh, yes, of course," I quickly recovered.

"All right, then," Sene concluded, "all of the meals are covered." I sat stunned, and wondered how long I had been lost in my own little world.

Following the service, our families, the Smiths and Havilands, spent a special day together making popcorn, reading poetry and bits of Scripture to one another. The Sabbath was our only day of rest during the week, and it was a great time to play games with the children. The boys were chasing around the barn and house, while the girls knit and crocheted sweaters and hats they were making for the cold season. As dusk began to cover the brightness of the day, Charles and I headed across the land with the boys in our little covered wagon home.

On the way we were lost in the excitement of plans for our beautiful, new log cabin home. We were looking forward to living in a real home instead of the back of a covered wagon. Fall was quickly fading into winter months; and the cold was becoming difficult for the boys and me to withstand. As the family cuddled together, I lay thinking that a whole new world would open before us. I was certain, because of my recent morning sickness, that I was carrying another child. Contemplating these deep thoughts in the dark, I nuzzled my face and tears into the depths of the feather pillow. In spite of this good news, I could not eradicate an agonizing emptiness in my heart. I was bringing children into this world yet, I knew I had a special purpose, a calling beyond the life of a mother and pioneer woman. What could it be?

As if clearing the land, attending to cooking, cleaning, supporting a husband in building a home, and rearing my two little boys and the one on the way was not enough, I was searching for a flicker of light, a hope for something that had been snuffed out long ago. I was haunted by the words of a Baptist preacher from long ago who said to me, "Return to your first love." Strangely enough, after attending the funeral service of a local infant this preacher sought me out of a crowd, took my hand, and asked, "Have you experienced religion?"

"I think I have," I had haltingly responded.

He replied by saying:

> Yes, you have experienced the pardon of sin, and you have rejoiced, as your prayers were answered. Yes, you know your duty, but have not fulfilled it, and now live in darkness. Do not occupy this dangerous ground longer. Return to your First Love. He who is abundant in mercy will again accept you. May God grant his blessing upon you. Good-bye.

Bathed in tears, I remembered his words and felt terribly lost. I could not find this blessing. My faith seemed drained and dead. I felt no hope just eternal loss! Listening to the snores of Charles, I thought, this poor man has no idea of the vacillating condition of his wife's mind. What he didn't know wouldn't hurt him.

Fifty Years Earlier- Life on the Michigan Frontier–1829

Why should he worry about the fact that his wife was a lost soul? Perhaps Papa was right? He said my problem was due to an emotional overload. Of course, it could just be my pregnancy. Who knew? Did anyone care? Finally, sleep stole over my young, small frame.

The Haviland family was up at the break of dawn. Every day was filled with the hard work of the land, planting crops, feeding and caring for the animals, while at the same time the rafters of our home were being raised. Charles, Papa and his brothers spent many back-breaking hours constructing our home. I was happy with my small home, sixteen feet wide and almost eighteen feet long, constructed of hewed logs with a little stone fireplace wedged in the corner by the kitchen.

Once our house was completed as planned, the men turned their energies to construct the Society of Friends meetinghouse four miles north of our home place. Papa Daniel was the first preacher, and my beloved Charles took over when Papa needed to resign. Life was beginning to take shape and fall into a pattern. This life pattern included the birth of a beautiful daughter, Anna, in 1830, and then, yet another little girl, Esther, in 1831.

Yet, in the midst of all of these happy, settling activities, my restless soul continued on in its great despair. I felt like a slave to apathy and disbelief, as though whips were cracking over my very being. Perhaps it was the rigors of my new life on the Michigan plains; churning butter, making soap, scrubbing clothes, catching, killing and cooking fowl and fish, attending to the needs of four babies under the age of five. No one knew for sure why, but my health began to deteriorate. Maybe I was simply depressed. I had found myself a slave in the grasp of whatever it was. With my slight 4' 9" frame, I did not have much weight to spare. Still, I was losing weight and looking very weak. Charles and my parents became very grave as they watched me dwindling away. So often I wished I could just pour my heart out to someone. Just the moment I hoped to share these plaguing thoughts, I would shrink back into my own abyss of self-doubt and guilt, wrapping myself in sorrow and solitude. I took to my bed, yet still cared for my little ones.

My heart cried, "My doom is sealed!" Though I had enjoyed my early experiences of faith in the Methodist revival meetings, I had walked away from God. I couldn't expect that after I had turned my back on God, that He would receive me once again. I had read in the Scriptures, Hebrews 6:4, 6, "it is impossible for those who were once enlightened and have tasted of the heavenly gift. . . .if they should fall away, to renew them again to repentance, seeing they crucify to themselves the Son of God afresh, and put him to open shame." No I was eternally lost! I had committed the "unpardonable sin."

This pit of darkness continued several months. I was a slave to my anxiety and fear. I couldn't talk to Charles or to my parents. The children, pulling at my skirts, could not understand what was wrong with their mother. I couldn't stay in my room forever. So, I did what the Smith/Haviland clan does in times of distress. I got up, continued to care for my children and went out into the community to help others. I found such great joy in helping others.

Mama, of course, continued to voice her worries and concerns, though both Papa and Charles kept their thoughts to themselves. Once in a while, Charles would question me in the proper Quaker address: "It seems to me, Mrs. Haviland, that thee is working a bit too much." Then, occasionally, Papa would take my arm and ask, "Laura Smith Haviland, thee seems to be too busy for thy own good." And I would reply in my characteristic manner: "Thank thee for thy concern, I am thy servant." Then I would trot off to attend to my children and new interests.

One of these new interests was helping at the Lenawee County Home for orphaned children. Another was helping my brother Harvey settle in his new home after he returned from Oberlin. He had purchased a farm. I loved my visits with him as he would share the dangerous stories of slave families who were escaping to freedom through the Underground Railroad.

Mesmerized by this new means of transportation to freedom for those in bondage, my mind could only imagine how it worked. Those in the Underground Railroad would set up safe homes and zones, use disguised voices, signals and symbols in order to move the refugees from one place to another. I delighted in all of his stories. There were a great many slaves who traveled through Ohio on their way to Canada that would stop over in Michigan. The seed was planted in my mind that my home could be such a safe place for the depressed and deprived of this slave race. I began to see these life influences crack a tiny hole in my darkness. A dim light began to penetrate my heart, and I shared these thoughts in my journal.

On a Sabbath day so ordinary that no one would ever believe it to be different from any other, my family and I attended services at the Raisin Valley Society of Friends Meetinghouse. It would have been just another ordinary Sabbath had it not been for a little book lying on the table by the front door. After the services were over and the Sunday dinner completed, the women were knitting, the children playing outdoors and the men were planning their next building site. I found a seat in the sanctuary and read that little book from cover to cover. It was no ordinary book. It contained a message from a young woman who struggled with faith, meaning and hope in her life. One who felt that she, too, had committed the "unpardonable sin." I couldn't believe that there was one like me in the world, carrying my struggle, yet able to articulate it so effectively. It pierced my heart and soul! My heart began to melt as I found comfort, knowledge and the beautiful realization that my sins were completely forgiven! I had not rejected my Savior nor determined that I did not need one. There was no need for despair, as I had so grievously thought. Hebrews 6 spoke to those who continually reject the offering of our Savior's great gift, His sacrifice for us on the cross. I had never rejected the ultimate gift of love by our Savior.

Suddenly, a bright star of hope pierced through my ever-present cloud of darkness. Yes, I was the prodigal! Yes, I was doomed! Yes, I was hopeless and lost and yes. . .a larger truth began to soak into my core being. There was hope! I remembered kneeling as a small girl in our barn at the rear of our corn crib. There I asked the question. "Is it possible that He who created this beautiful world could notice a little girl like me?" Though I had kneeled three times and had repeated the words over and over, "God be merciful to me a sinner," I had never really experienced any great emotion.

As I remembered all of these experiences of truth and faith, it happened. A joyful realization slowly dawned across my heart. I had accepted Christ! I began to realize I am a child of God. I am free! Free to serve as Christ to those whose plight had been to be born of a dark color. Free to serve children and families who had no means for education. With many tears of gratitude, mingled with new hope, new aspirations and the bright rays of dawn illuminating every promise, I could now fully accept the Lord Jesus as my mediator and restorer. . .by faith. . ." by grace ye are saved through faith." Grace, faith, strength and peace became my rich experience.

I sprang with joy from my chair, ran out and played with the children in the beautiful warmth of a sunny spring day in Michigan. The children could not help but notice the lightness of my heart and step. My eldest son Harvey said, "Mother, what's gotten into thee today?" And I glibly replied, "Thou just doth not understand the goodness of the Lord. My soul delights in Him today!" Meanwhile, little Daniel said, "Mother, I wish thy heart would delight in Him every day!" I could not help but laugh and say, "So do I, my child, so do I!"

Returning to the nursery to watch over my little Anna and Esther, both sleeping soundly, my heart rejoiced, and for the first time in many years I felt a great peace. My fingers strummed across their little faces. They were oblivious to the great accomplishment achieved in their mother's heart. But it did not take long for their father and grandparents to recognize the change in my disposition.

"Laura, I do not know what has come across thee, but it serves thee well." These were the words springing from my mother's lips. My husband enjoyed my company much more, and our hearts once again seemed to be joined in the purpose of sharing and serving our Lord together.

Then, one day as our family was shopping in the Raisin Dry Goods Store, the proprietor, Brother Hinshaw, introduced Charles and myself to a lady who would change our lives forever. A beautiful young lady, Elizabeth Margaret Chandler, made our acquaintance. After a proper introduction, Miss Chandler pressed a circular into my hand. "Mrs. Haviland, I would love to have thee join me at my home for a time of reading. I am inviting members of the Raisin Township and Lenawee Community to participate. Will thou come?"

"Certainly." I said, accepting her invitation. Wanting to be hospitable, I asked, "What is the time?"

She responded, "Tomorrow mid-afternoon. I live two miles north of thy brother Harvey's place."

"Gladly, I will be there!"

After she left the store, Brother Hinshaw, a fine birthright Quaker, told Charles, "Miss Chandler is a Hicksite Friend. She and her brother Thomas have recently moved here with their aunt, Ruth Evans. I am afraid she is here to stir up all sorts of trouble in our fine town."

"What type of trouble, Hinshaw?" Charles asked in a concerned voice.

"She writes poetry about slaves." Hinshaw retorted. "Mrs. Evans continues to encourage Miss Chandler in this endeavor. I fear it will only stir up anger and resentment.

"Brother Hinshaw, thou knows most of the folks in Lenawee County are very sympathetic to the abolitionist cause. How can she cause trouble when so many agree with her views?" Charles countered.

"I don't know, Haviland. Thou knowest that our Quaker Meeting does not approve of this type of talk in aiding and abetting slaves. It is out of character for our Society."

Having aroused my curiosity I asked, "Brother Hinshaw, what does Sister Chandler say in her poetry that gives thee cause for concern?"

"Well, just look for thyself! Here it is in black and white. This paper, *The Genius for Universal Emancipation* is the one that Benjamin Gundy publishes. She writes in the Ladies Repository section and passes it to all of the ladies in the county. Her writing calls for an immediate emancipation of all slaves. She began by influencing my wife. This just stirs up angry sentiment among our women folk. It's nothing but trouble!"

I knew exactly what paper Brother Hinshaw was referring to because my brother Harvey and I talked about it frequently. We were excited about the impact it was making around our country educating ignorant and bigoted minds against the atrocities of slavery.

"May I see that paper?" I almost grabbed it out of his hands before he could hand it to me. My eyes fell to a column where the poem, *The Slave Ship,* jumped out from the page. I had to sit for a moment at Mr. Hinshaw's soda fountain to absorb the message. This poem captivated my heart and my thoughts:

Fifty Years Earlier- Life on the Michigan Frontier–1829

The Slave-ship was winding her course o'er the ocean,
The winds and the waters had sunk into rest;
All hush'd was the whirl of the tempest's commotion,
That late had awaken'd the sailor's devotion,
When terror had kindled remorse in his breast.
And onward she rode, though by curses attended,
Though heavy with guilt was the freight that she bore,
Though with shrieks of despair was the midnight air rended,
And ceaseless the groans of the wretches ascended,
That from friends and from country forever she tore.
On the deck, with his head on his fetter'd hand rested,
He who once was a chief and a warrior stood;
One moment he gain'd, by his foes unmolested,
To think o'er his woes, and the fate he detested,
Till madness was firing his brain and his blood.
"Oh, never!" he murmur'd in anguish, "no, never!"
These limbs shall be bent to the menial's toil!
They have reft us, my bride—but they shall not forever
Your chief from his home and his country dissever—
No! never will I be the conqueror's spoil
Say! long didst thou wait for my coming, my mother?
Did ye bend o'er the desert, my sister, your eye?
And weep at the lengthen'd delay of your brother,
As each slow passing moment was chased by another,
And still he appear'd not a tear-drop to dry.
But ye shall—yes, again ye shall fondly embrace me!
We will meet my young bride in the land of the blest:

Death, death once again in my country shall place me,

One bound shall forever from fetters release me!"

He burst them, and sunk in the ocean's dark breast.

(The Slave-Ship was written by Elizabeth Margaret Chandler, age 18, published first in *The Casket*).

I turned away quickly, my eyes filled with tears, so as not to face Brother Hinshaw. I summoned Charles. Handing him the goods I needed to buy, I scurried the children together at the door, and bidding Brother Hinshaw a hasty farewell, I escaped.

On our way home, Charles softly spoke, "What was it that made thee cry?"

"Oh, Charles," I exclaimed. "The poem is called *The Slave Ship*. It reminded me so much of John Woolman's history of the slave trade. It sent chills up my spine."

"Well, it seems to me that thee needs to attend that meeting tomorrow afternoon. Perhaps this is the outlet thou needs to serve those anguished slaves."

Leaning over, I kissed my dear husband. He quickly let out a whistle to the horses and gave them a little sting of the whip as we scurried home. I could not contain my excitement over the prospects of working with this passionate young woman who cared so deeply for these same ones whom I grieved over, as well. My heart once again thanked God for giving me such great peace and contentment.

Chapter Three

Logan Anti-Slavery Society

Arriving at the Evan's home the next afternoon, I was greeted by Ruth Evans, Elizabeth Chandler's aunt, who escorted me into the parlor of this beautiful, regal home. The home was sheltered so completely by a grove of evergreen trees that I had never noticed the beauty of the place before. Once inside, it was obvious the family was affluent and influenced by English customs. The Chandlers and Mrs. Evans were from Philadelphia, and the décor carried with it a patriotic, colonial flair of regent traditions. Elizabeth entered via the spiral staircase with her hooped skirts a-flair and her enthusiastic greeting.

"Mrs. Haviland, I'm so thrilled thee could join us. We are a small group, but a mighty one." Her smile was framed by cute little dimples and a sweetness I had not noticed at Hinshaw's Store the day before.

"It is my pleasure and honor to hear what thee has to say. I must confess Mr. Hinshaw shared thy 'Slave Ship' poem with me yesterday, and it affected me deeply."

"I am glad that it hath affected thee in a positive way. Not everyone shares thy passion," Elizabeth replied.

At that moment, two distinguished Quaker men entered the room and greeted Elizabeth and myself. Elizabeth made the introductions. "I want thee to meet my brother, Thomas Chandler, and my dear adopted uncle, Darius Comstock. Gentleman, this is Mrs. Laura Haviland."

I responded by extending my hand in greeting. "It's my pleasure to meet both of thee."

Brother Comstock, a Quaker from another Society in Adrian, quipped, "Oh my dear, Elizabeth, thee is in honorable company if Mrs. Laura Haviland is in the audience. She is well known for her capabilities in caring for children and the sick, of which we have all been at one time."

Laughing and nodding in agreement, Elizabeth demurely replied. "So I have heard. It is a privilege for me to have finally made thy acquaintance, Mrs. Haviland."

Feeling a slight flush pass across my face, I replied. "Dear Brother Comstock, I was not aware of my notoriety." Laughing together, Mrs. Evans directed the company into the front room, where chairs had been placed for all of the attendees.

I knew no one in the small group other than Brother Comstock before the event began. But I was overwhelmed with the kindred heart and spirit in a common disdain for slavery and the commitment to do something to help these poor distressed humans whose only crime was to be born with dark pigment.

Miss Chandler began the meeting with the reading of the poem *The Slave Ship.* Next, Darius Comstock began to share his dream that an anti-slavery group could begin in the Raisin/Adrian area, Lenawee County. He believed such a group could speak out strongly against the institution of slavery. His sentiments were strong and powerful, but shared by all present. "We can do something. We must do something to influence our community against this horrible way of life that is so debilitating to humans." Thomas Chandler remained stoically quiet, though he nodded his assent to all of the anti-slavery comments presented by his beautiful sister.

Miss Chandler turned to me and asked, "Mrs. Haviland, what has been thy experience with the atrocities of slavery?"

Slowly, I began looking at each one as I shared the awful impressions that cut to the core of my heart. I said, "It is the images of cruel slave-holders throwing humans overboard ships because of the greed that possessed their spirits believing they should be able to gain from these slaves' strength while abusing and murdering them at the same time. This is grievous. I struggle over the cruelty that has been displayed towards the Africans. Let me tell two stories to help thee understand what I can never forget."

> There was an old man, Uncle Jeff. He was frequently employed by merchants to cry off their stale articles on the street. At one time Uncle Jeff, whose head was almost as white as wool, was crying, 'Gentlemen and ladies' black silk stockins of all colors for sale.' Holding them up to view as he passed along the street, he was followed by a group of boys crying out, 'Nigger, nigger,' and throwing grass and clay at him. At length he turned to these half-grown boys, looking very sad, and said, 'Boys, I am just as God made me, an' so is a toad.' At this the boys slunk away. I felt very indignant in seeing the men who were standing near only laugh, instead of sharply reproving those ill-behaved children.
>
> Then there was Ben. Ben came to our town with a family who opened an inn. He was employed mostly in the kitchen, and while Ben was asleep on the kitchen floor, some cruel boys put a quantity of powder in the back of his pants. Placing a slow match to it, they

left the room. They watched the diabolical sport through a window, and soon saw their victim blown up. It was said Ben's body nearly hit the ceiling. His hips and body were so badly burned that he was never able to sit or stoop after this wicked act. He always had to walk with a cane. Whenever too weary to stand, Ben was compelled to lie down as his right hip and lower limb were stiffened. Little notice was taken of this reckless act except to feed and clothe this life-long cripple as he went from house to house because he was of that crushed and neglected race.

After I spoke there was not a dry eye among our small, congenial group. One by one, each individual shared their experience, even the ever-stoic Thomas Chandler shared a touching story of a slave whom he was able to hide from his slaveholder.

Elizabeth closed our meeting with the following words from William Lloyd Garrison, printed in the *Genius of Universal Emancipation*, October 9, 1829:

"Slavery is a monster and he must be treated as such—hunted down bravely, and dispatched at a blow."

After the closing, Darius Comstock interjected, "Sisters Chandler and Haviland, I believe with the union of the two of thee, our cause will be stronger than before. Elizabeth's writings have done much to awaken the hearts of those still in bondage to the ilk of slavery. With Mrs. Haviland's passion against the suffering of slavery, we have in Lenawee County, Michigan, a strong force for the good!"

"Oh dear, Uncle Darius, thou is such an encourager! In Pennsylvania, there are anti-slavery societies started by women across the East Coast. Why couldn't Mrs. Haviland and I do the same thing here?" Elizabeth asked.

"What dost thou say, Mrs. Haviland?" Comstock countered, turning the question my direction.

Hesitatingly, I spouted out the honesty in my heart. "I would love to do just that. But at the present time, as thee knows Brother Comstock, our Raisin Valley Society of Friends would not allow such a proposition from one of its leading members. As my husband, Charles, serves as the pastor, I believe that I must abstain."

Elizabeth Chandler agreed. "Yes, Laura—may I call thee Laura?"

"Please," I replied.

"Laura, I believe thee is entirely correct! From my short tenure here in Raisin Township, I can see that the Quakers are very hesitant to become actively involved," Chandler continued.

"Well, I am a Quaker in good standing," Comstock declared, "And I believe we need to act out of principle, not from the fear of breaking a rule or a man-made law!"

"Exactly! I completely agree," I heard myself say. "But what can we do?"

Elizabeth, once again understanding my dilemma, spoke, "Uncle Darius, thou must look at this from Laura's position. Quakers believe they have done all that is necessary to fight slavery. They do not buy goods made through the sweat of slave labor. They do not hold slaves, and they believe that if everyone did the same, there would be no slavery."

"Yes, that is correct," I agreed. "Yet it is so frustrating. Most do not align with Quaker principles, and slavery is alive and well. I believe strong action must be taken to stop this abominable institution!"

"That is what I love about thee, Mrs. Haviland! It is thy passion for helping the oppressed. Is that not a Christian virtue?" Comstock asked.

"Of course, yet, it is no secret to either of thee, the Quaker way is to wait for consensus. Could that be God's way while so many continue to suffer?"I heard myself thinking aloud.

"Laura, how long dost thou think it might take for the Raisin Valley Society of Friends to reach such consensus regarding the alleviation of suffering by slavery?" Elizabeth questioned.

"Oh." I groaned. "I have no idea. I haven't actually given the question much thought."

"Perhaps five years?" Comstock proposed.

"Oh no, certainly much longer," I assured him.

"Fifty years?" Comstock continued to pursue this line of questioning.

"Oh, Uncle Darius. Don't be so harsh on Mrs. Haviland. How could she know the answer to such a question?" Elizabeth Chandler chided.

"Well, realistically, I think it could take at least twenty years," I responded.

"Twenty years! That is a very long time. How many poor souls will continue to suffer and perish if we do not take action, Mrs. Haviland?" Elizabeth groaned.

As I thought deep and hard about her response, I simply had to agree. Would the God of all humanity want me to stand by and do nothing while so many humans just like me continue to suffer, simply because of the color of their skin?

There was a great silence in the room, and a peace that I cannot explain came over me. I could not help but believe it was the presence of the Almighty composing my heart, and I made a choice that would affect and change my life and my families' lives forever. I heard a voice that sounded strangely like my own speak with conviction. "Yes," I said, "I will join forces with thee and give my influence and heart for the cause if it means I can alleviate the pain for a few."

Elizabeth hugged me and said, squealing for joy, "Oh, Mrs. Haviland, Laura! Thank thee! Thank thee! What a team we will be!"

Brother Comstock, enjoying the moment as well, brought us all back to the dilemma at hand. "But what will thou do about the Raisin Valley Society?"

I thought for several minutes before responding, "Well, I believe, I will have to pray to the Lord for a way to talk to my family and persuade them that I must withdraw from Raisin Valley."

After hastily making a few plans for our next meeting, we covenanted together in prayer with God. As I left, my new friends showered me with the kindness and assurance that they, too, would continue praying. We determined to make whatever difference we could.

On my way home following the meeting, I stopped for a few minutes at Harvey's place full of excitement and "not just" a little bit of trepidation. Harvey, my brother, was a wonderful person with whom I could share my far-fetched ideas and thoughts. Greeting him on the porch, I aired the wild, absurd thoughts of aiding slaves that seemed to clash strongly with my staunch Quaker upbringing. "Harvey, hast thou ever heard of William Lloyd Garrison?"

"Well, of course, Laura. Everyone along the Eastern seaboard knows about Garrison. He is the great abolitionist editor of the *Liberator*. He is very controversial because he boldly proclaims the truth that all slavery should be abolished now."

"Yes, I know he makes some strong statements. I'm not sure these thoughts would be well accepted by our Quaker elders."

Harvey, the Oberlin educated one, belted out his big, booming laugh, looked squarely into my eyes and said, "Laura, not much that happens among active abolitionists will be accepted by our Quaker elders!"

Staring into space, I sat watching the beauty of the day's sun as it dazzled in brilliance, dancing across the horizon. That powerful fireball in the sky felt like the ball of fire burning in my heart. I knew I had a fight ahead. I just didn't know if I was up for it. But one thing was certain—there was no way to go but forward.

"Harvey," I asked. "Will thou stand beside me if I forge ahead with Miss Chandler in this work of abolitionism?"

Harvey had a gleam in his eye when he said, "Forge ahead! I am by thy side!"

Reaching over, I hugged his neck. "We've been through a lot together. This means the world to me!"

"Laura Smith Haviland, thou art a leader! And thou must lead! I would be disappointed if thee were to shirk this issue that affects 'the least of these.'"

Arriving home, I was greeted by a concerned husband who searched my eyes to see if that fire of passion was still lit. Finding it so, Charles took my horse to the barn and then walked into the kitchen for a soup supper. Sitting at the table, I shared my exciting adventure with him from the Chandler's home, and in particular, the comments of Darius Comstock.

"Darius Comstock!" Charles swooned. "He is a man of influence. Laura, it sounds as though thy relationship with Miss Chandler and Mr. Comstock has great potential."

I continued on like an excited schoolgirl. "We are planning to meet again next Tuesday afternoon, same time, same place. We are inviting women from the community, and are planning to create a female anti-slavery society."

"Does that mean that men are not welcome?" Charles groaned.

"Oh, no," I cackled. "Brother Comstock just believes that women will be welcomed more easily and more quickly than men into homes within the community. We are going to take Elizabeth's poems and share them with the women in Raisin Township and also in the new township of Adrian. We will then invite all of the women to a tea at the Chandler home. We hope that we can influence many of these to sign the charter for our society."

"Laura," Charles's voice commanded her attention. "We must go and speak to thy parents. We cannot move forward without first approaching them and the elders of the Society of Friends about our involvement in this cause."

Logan Anti-Slavery Society

"But Charles, what will we do if they reject the direction of moving forwards with our work against slavery?"

"Laura, thou are much more persuasive than thee gives thyself credit. We will take Harvey for reinforcement." Charles comforted her. "The great God above is by thy side. Worry not, my love. Our ever-loving Father will guide thee."

"How blessed I am," I thought, lying beside my loving husband, curled up next to him, covered with his love and support.

Shots rang through the early morning air as I was still oblivious in my bliss. Charles jumped up and went outside to confront the situation.

Charles called out. "Laura, Laura! Get up! Thee must get dressed and prepare breakfast quickly. Two men are at our gate. I will delay them for a few minutes." All the while I was wondering if I was still dreaming. Little Esther's cry coming from her crib at the end of our bed made it clear this was no dream. I wrapped a towel around my body's midsection where baby Esther securely rested. Hurrying into the kitchen, I pulled out dough for biscuits and poured lard into the iron cast skillet to fry eggs. I called out to Harvey and Daniel to start a fire in the fireplace.

Charles brought the men into our home, introducing them to me as progressive businessmen from Tennessee. Shackleton and Jones were their last names. They were requesting permission to hunt. Charles gave me a wink as he directed the men's attention to the thirteen point buck that was hanging above the mantel of the fireplace. After they had admired Charles's buck, we served them breakfast. Soon thereafter, they got down to business.

Jones began. "Mr. & Mrs. Haviland, we are very concerned that this is a prime path that some of our associates might take in trying to escape from their contractual agreements."

Charles inquired with a shocked look at me, "Contractual agreements? I thought we were discussing hunting."

Jones continued, "Well, yes, sir. This is a form of hunting, I suspect. You see there are common laborers who have agreed to serve us in return for room and board?"

Shackleton chimed in. "Yes, and then, of course, they believe they deserve more, a better home, a better life. They want to stay with their families; the list of their so-called rights is endless."

"So they escape," Jones continued. "There is a new means of transportation for many of these folks. It's called the Underground Railroad. We understand it has made its way into Michigan. We have also heard there is support for it among this community."

"Really?" Charles exclaimed, his voice trembling.

"Oh yes. Darius Comstock, the father of Adrian Comstock, a community leader, is very strong in this type of anti-slavery sentiment," Shackleton confidently asserted.

I had remained remarkably quiet through this entire conversation, but could not contain my anger at the subtle, deceitful method by which they had entered our home. "Slavery, thee said nothing of slavery. Thou spoke of a business agreement! That certainly has nothing to do with slavery."

Jones countered, "Why, Mrs. Haviland, I beg to differ. Simply ask the many slaveholders of the South, and you will recognize that these laborers are certainly a very important contractual part of their businesses."

I stood up, taking the dishes from the table, and said, "I bid thee a good day. I have no further interest in a discussion that degrades a race of humans as though their purpose is to fulfill a business agreement while they remain captive in servitude and bondage."

Charles stood and curtly escorted the men to the door. The men threatened on their way out, "We just want to say that, if you should ever join this group of abolitionists, you will regret such action. We plan to press charges against any who harbor a fugitive of the law."

Charles sternly replied, "That is clearly impossible, as Michigan is a free state. Why did thee approach our homestead with this unsettling matter?"

Shackleton quipped back, "We have sources that tell us your wife is very soft when it comes to helping these escapees, and we also hear that she has joined forces with Miss Chandler, a published abolitionist writer. We stopped at their homestead last evening."

Jones replied with a surly scowl. "And of course, we received there the same less-than-cordial response, but without the breakfast."

Charles responded in a very low voice, "Sir, I don't believe thee will find any support in these parts of the country for thy pro-slavery positions. We are not concerned about thy threats. See that as the two of thee leave, neither of thee returns to hunt either deer or men!" With Charles's stinging response still in their ears, Shackleton and Jones mounted their horses and departed.

Charles sent the children into their rooms and embraced me, as I was still shaking from this unbelievably emotional encounter. "Charles, thou ist right. We must go immediately and approach Mama and Papa with our plans." As we had planned to share the Sabbath evening with them, we decided we must express our concerns, particularly because of Charles's position as pastor of our meeting. We could not move forward with this abolitionist movement as long as Charles served as the pastor of the Raisin Valley Society of Friends.

The following day was the Sabbath. As I sat through the Sunday School and service, I dreaded the encounter that was to come later in the day. Perhaps, it was the fact that our meeting of Friends did nothing for the plight of slaves. Though I had often been chastised to be a stoic member of the Society of Friends, I struggled that they could stand by blindly and not act to help those in need. Yes,

Papa was right. We never purchased materials or goods made by slave labor. But what do we do to help them? How could I believe in a God who didn't step into the midst of this struggle within the human race? Could I really serve such a God? My family was concerned about following the proper protocol in the worship of God! Yet how could we stand by and do nothing!

As much as I tried to control these thoughts and feelings running through my mind, they kept recurring. I prayed for calm and a strength that I did not feel. As open worship, our time of silent and corporate meditation, lasted much longer than usual, my spirit grew increasingly impatient.

When suddenly Sister Hinshaw abruptly stood and said,

> I lift my heart to the Lord in praise! Yet, I am concerned about a ripple that is sweeping through our community and fellowship. There are those among us who are violating the ways of the Society. They are willing to break the law in order to aid and abet slaves. I know that we have agreed not to speak openly on these issues, but I believe it is wrong for the good members of this meeting to break the law. Romans chapter 13 tells us that we should 'obey the laws of the land.' God has placed those in authority over us and we are to submit to their leadership. Now, for instance, our Sister Elizabeth Chandler may be a good Hicksite Quaker. She is creating anti-law sentiment by her writings and the meetings she holds in Sister Ruth Evan's home. She is not a faithful attender of our meeting house. That's why I believe our Raisin Valley Meeting should issue a statement of protest against Miss Chandler, sending the message that we will not tolerate such brazen rebellion.

There was a hissing that spread from the women's side of the veil to the men's side. I could not help but wonder if her words had been crafted and rehearsed by her husband. Shaking off this thought, I saw a large, looming figure stand, and I could immediately tell through the veil that it was my brother, Harvey Smith.

With a booming voice unbecoming to Quakers, Harvey dissented quite vehemently.

> I, for one, must disagree with Sister Hinshaw. Everyone knows that the sentiment in Raisin Valley is one of support for freeing those caught in the clutches of slavery. Why, Adrian Comstock, the leader of the Adrian township, stands against slavery. Though I do not believe it is my place to mention names, many other leaders of our community are against slavery; and they are willing to take a stand. Why should the God-fearing servants of Raisin Valley Friends be any different?

It was as though someone had dropped a bomb in the room. Brother Hinshaw stood in defense of his wife's position. Edwin Comstock, who very rarely attended our little Raisin Valley Friends Meeting stood to verify Harvey's testimony regarding his brother, and included himself as a supporter of abolitionist principles.

Our poor church meeting had never seen such an uprising. Sister Moore stood, turned and looked at me directly. As she spoke, I thought my whole being might fall through a hole in the floor. She said, "I understand that there is a push to begin an anti-slavery society here in Raisin. And I understand from my cousin back east that the Hicksite Friends there have merged with many other religious sects where sacrilegious singing and prayers are included in their meetings. I would not want our Friends Meeting to become a victim of such anti-Quaker activities."

Though my hands and body felt like icicles, I diverted my eyes downward, and my heart prayed for my dear husband, Charles, who stood as our moderator and pastor. After everyone had said their piece, Charles simply said, "Lord, please hear these, our petitions. We are divided, but pray that one day we will be united. Speak to our hearts and souls. Lead us in thy way."

Following the meeting many left without the normal friendly farewells. Instead of sharing in our Sabbath meal together, those who were adamantly opposed to an active involvement in abolitionism took their covered dish and went home.

It was such a very difficult day for Charles and me. The only folks left for our Sabbath meal were those from our families, the Smith and Havilands. As we had planned to talk with our families this day, we had not anticipated being in such a spirit of turmoil and flux. I presented my case to my parents. They, in turn, sat silently in disbelief. They knew nothing about my involvement with Miss Chandler. Yet, I believe that I finally convinced them that my meeting with this new group had been so recent that I had not had the opportunity to share my plans with them. Yes, they had heard the stirrings of discontent among the church members regarding Elizabeth Chandler's writings and work. Yes, they were extremely concerned, as well, about my involvement in a group that went against the Society of Friend's principles.

Harvey spoke in my defense. "Papa, Mama, please listen to what Laura is saying! We are not just Quakers. We are Christians! It is not the Christian way to stand by and watch the suffering of slavery and look the other way. As our parents, thee both have taught us to live by the principles of love, 'to love one another as thou lovest thyself.' Charles, Laura and I have taken a stand to live by those principles. How can thou be angry or discontented? We are simply living as thou hast taught us."

My father, Daniel Smith, looked at my husband, Charles Haviland, and asked. "And thou, the pastor of this meeting of Friends, what hast thou to say?"

With complete control and fortitude, Charles responded. "I must stand with my Savior who says, 'if thou hast done it to the least of these my brethren, thou hast done it to me' Matthew 25:40."

Papa responded to the three of us by saying, "Thy mother and I must take a few days to fast and pray regarding this matter. I ask of thee to make no further decision or public statement regarding thy position until we have responded to thee. Dost thou agree?"

We all nodded in agreement. And then, my parents left abruptly. I could hear my mother's little whimper as they left the church building. I felt limp, heartbroken and sick. As we gathered the children from their oblivious, joyful play, I longed to be a child again with no worries or cares. Then again I had been such a strange child I had probably been born with a brow of worry on my forehead. The ride home in the wagon was dismally quiet; and we were in bed before my husband finally asked me, "Is thee all right?"

I sighed, "Yes, but Charles, I'm worried about thee."

He sighed deeply and said, "I know we are waiting upon thy parents for their response. But I plan to resign my post next Sunday no matter their response."

"Yes, my dear. What choice dost thou have?"

He agreed, rolled over and kissed me tenderly. My life could be in complete chaos, but with Charles by my side, I knew that we could conquer it all. He is such a precious gift from God!

My parents' response came much quicker than any of us could have expected. It was the beginning of winter, December 1833, and the grays and pinks highlighted the sky as the snow began to fall in huge flakes. Esther and Anna were delighted to pop popcorn in a kettle over the fireplace. Daniel had been stocking the fireplace all day with wood, and my Harvey was out with Charles mending fence. The house was tidy from our day's work when I heard the clip-clop of horse hooves heading up the drive.

We all went out to greet Papa and Mama. They heartily and lovingly greeted us when suddenly we heard another horse coming up our lane. Here came Brother Harvey just in time for our big, unexpected gathering.

As the girls set the table for a simple supper, Charles and Harvey walked in from the field. They had seen the folk's buggy and had come home to join in the festivities. Charles led our prayer, and we all had our fill of slab ham, vegetable soup, apple fritters and of course, popcorn.

The girls went into their room, and I helped them into bed. The boys wanted to stay and hear what their grandparents had come to share. They were old enough now to understand more of the world around them.

It was Papa who spoke first, and he spoke directly to me. "Laura, dost thou remember, as a child, how I chastised thee for thy sensitivities and sympathies that I believed were harmful to thee?"

"Yes, Papa," I replied.

"It was for thy well-being that I was concerned. That has always been thy mother's and my first thought for all of our children. Yet I have done some thinking over the last few days, and. . ." Papa hesitated.

Mama carried on. "Your father traveled to Adrian yesterday to speak with Mr. Adrian Comstock. He wanted to hear for himself if the testimony that his brother, Edwin, gave in open worship on Sunday was accurate."

Papa, gathering his thoughts, continued, "Yes, thy mother is right. I visited with Mr. Adrian Comstock and his brother, Edwin, as well, and I found that what Harvey said Sunday is correct. We have many leaders and many supporters of the abolitionist movement in the area. Then on my drive home, I thought deeply, oh so deeply, about what Charles said to me Sunday. I believe he is right as well."

Mama added, "Yes, we certainly trained all of our children to love one another and to respect one another's dignity."

"Finally," Papa continued, "I must confess to my dear daughter, Laura, that thee is right! Thou hast been right in thy passionate and loving concern for the oppressed slaves that have been excoriated and despised. I am sorry daughter that I have held thee back for so long in following thy heart for helping those who desperately need it."

At this, I could no longer contain my tears of joy. Jumping up, I threw my arms around dear Papa, who at this moment proved in my eyes to be the most wonderful, loving father! There was joy and hugs all around as the Smiths and the Havilands agreed that they would work together in loving and serving the oppressed.

Papa began to ask Harvey many questions about his association at Oberlin College, and they discussed in detail the work of the Underground Railroad and those persons who were conductors of it. Both Mama and Papa were completely enthralled as Harvey described the men and women, many of whom are Quakers, who wait until the designated time to move these precious human refugees through the Underground Railroad System. Some conductors have false floors in their wagons and generally three men or four women could be squeezed into hiding under these false floors. Others have secret places in their attics or tunnels leading from their basements where slaves can hide and be moved safely. The goal was to see the refugees safely into Canada, where they were free from cruelty of any slaveholder or bounty hunter. The stories were horrific and eye-raising. Yet our families talked late into the night about what we could do in Raisin to help these poor disenfranchised souls.

As a result of this family discussion, Charles sat down with pen and paper and the family composed a letter of withdrawal from the Raisin Valley Society of Friends Meeting. This was difficult for everyone. The members of this church were like family members to all of us. We decided we would leave amicably and with love. Each member of the family signed the letter that would be presented the next Sabbath. There were also others, a few close friends who joined us in this venture. This was just the beginning of an era that drew the family together in an unbelievably tight bond, one it had never experienced before.

On the Sabbath as open worship began, before anyone else could respond, Charles stood and read the letter from the Smith and Haviland families.

> We, the undersigned, do say there is a diversity of sentiment existing in the Society on the divine authority of the Holy Scriptures, the resurrection of the dead, the day of judgment, justification by faith, the effect of Adam's fall upon his posterity, and the abolition of slavery. This having caused a disunity amongst us, and there being no hope of a reconciliation by investigation. As ministers are told by ruling members that there is to be no other test of the soundness of their ministry but something in their own breast, thus virtually denying the Holy Scriptures to be the test of doctrine; we, therefore, do wish quietly to withdraw from the Monthly Meeting, and thus resign our right of membership with the Society of Friends.

Signatures included those of my close family: Daniel Smith, Sene Smith, Charles Haviland Jr., Laura S. Haviland, Edwin Comstock, Ezekiel Webb, Harvey Smith, Sala Smith and fourteen others.

Then in solidarity we stood, walked around shaking hands, hugging one another through tears, and we all walked out together. Before leaving, Charles concluded the meeting by saying, "We love all of thee and still hope to maintain the bond of unity with thee, though we will not be meeting in worship together. One day we pray that we will be reunited in the bond of love and peace."

But that day would be a long time coming. Several months later we began attending a Wesleyan Methodist Church. This church family seemed to be closest to the way we believed and lived and was supportive of our anti-slavery work. They were glad to receive our memberships, though the Raisin Valley Society of Friends never removed our names from their membership roll. Anytime the question arose, the Raisin Friends intimated that we were simply being disciplined.

Chapter Four

Chandler & Change, 1833-1834

Mama, my little girls and I were passing out invitations in Raisin to the "First Tea of the Logan Female Anti-Slavery Society." Mama had never really been involved in this type of activity, and she was rather self-conscious. "Really Laura, I don't understand how all of this fuss will help in the fight against slavery." She was exhausted from making stops at farm houses and businesses, handing out invitations all the way from Adrian back along the main road of Raisin.

"Mama, dost thou not see how we are in a battle for the minds and hearts of these ladies? It is so very important. By doing this we can garner support from many local ladies' groups for our cause. Besides, if we don't teach them, how will they know?"

"Well, I'm not sure I know the answer to that question. Still doesn't it make thee wonder? When thee was just a little girl and we lived in New York, thee thought it was fun to dress up and pretend like we were going to attend social galas. Yet, since we have moved here in the Northwest Territory, we have not entertained such thoughts of frivolous events because we don't have time. After all, we are pioneer women, not to mention Quaker women. But to have a social event tied to such a political cause, I don't know. It seems ungodly, so different from anything I've ever experienced," Sene Smith vented.

"Mama," I exclaimed. "We are doing this because of our godly convictions. We can have a great time and incorporate our efforts into a humane and just cause. I think it's marvelous!"

"Well, of course, Laura, thee would." Sene conceded, watching her daughter admiringly.

We were exhausted, making dozens of stops in Adrian and Raisin. Sene noticed signs of fatigue in her daughter and asked, "Laura, ist thee all right?" She could barely get the words out before Laura jumped down and ran behind the wagon vomiting.

"Laura, what is wrong with thee?" Mama Sene exclaimed.

Gagging, I walked to the other side, and said, "Mama, wilt thou drive the team home?" Mama walked around and took the reins. Leaving town, Sene asked. "Ist thee with child?"

"Yes, Mama I believe I am." I calmly replied. "If this child is a boy, I'm going to name him Joseph after our little Joseph that thou lost!"

Sene said nothing. Watching Mama out of the corner of my eye, I could see a little tear form. We just never talked much about Joseph.

We stopped at the Lenawee County Home as I always checked to see what the orphan children needed. I enjoyed delivering meals and staples such as milk and bread for them. Dropping off invitations for the house mother and a couple loaves of bread I had made early that morning, we were once again on our way. Mama teasingly said, "Laura, thou must believe that thee was an orphan thyself for the amount of time thee invests in these little ones." I just smiled and said. "The truth is, Mama, I received this heart of kindness from thee. Thou is the kindest woman I have ever known."

Back on the road Mama and I talked more about the need for people to get involved with the orphans. Then suddenly I blurted out, "I wish I could adopt all of these children."

"Laura, thou ist beside thyself with craziness! Thou hast four children, and a fifth on the way."

"I know, Mama, but they so desperately need someone to take care of them."

Shortly we arrived at the Smith homestead. I helped Mama unload her goods, thanked her for her help in passing out the invitations and kissed her good-bye.

"Laura Smith Haviland, promise me that thee will take care of thyself and do no more than thee can handle." These were Mama's parting words.

Laughing with joy, I drove off, calling out to her, "Thanks, Mama. I love thee, too!"

The day of the great gala arrived. We called it the Chandler Tea, though the official title was the Logan Female Anti-Slavery Society Tea! Who had time for such verbosity? As Mama and I entered Ruth Evan's elegant home, I was thrilled at the overwhelming response. Women were here from Raisin, Adrian, Blissfield, Madison, Rome and other surrounding communities. Small round tables were placed outside on the lawn of the beautiful home, some on the wrap-around porch, while others were uniquely clustered in the backyard.

There must have been fifty women present in elegant gowns. Many were English-styled with flounce and hoop skirts. Then there were also dresses more like my own – a simple Pioneer muslin-cotton dress with a tad of calico lace and flounce on the fringes. I never wanted life to become too proper, too tedious or too worldly. After all, I was reared a Quaker. But I was not alone; there were many other Quaker women there with similar gowns and flounces, including our dear Sister Hinshaw. Yes, Sister Hinshaw, the one who spoke out against Elizabeth and Hicksite Quakers that ominous day in the Raisin Valley Friends Meetinghouse!

I stopped by her table to give her a special greeting. "My, Sister Hinshaw, thee looks lovely this evening. It is nice to see so many of our Quaker sisters here, even though some of them are from the Hicksite church." I moved by quickly, thinking she would not have time for a response, as I knew my comment was sarcastic, certainly not very humble for a godly Quaker.

Yet, Sister Hinshaw was ready for me. She stood up, tugging at my arm, "Sister Laura, I want thee to know that after listening to our dear Miss Chandler and taking the time to read her writings in depth, I believe that I spoke out of turn that day at open worship. I apologize to thee for that. If thou ever needs my help in any way in the Underground. . .please know. . .I will be glad to be of service," she said stumbling over many of her words. She had certainly caught me by surprise. So, I turned back to her and responded in all sincerity, "Thank thee."

She continued, "Please forgive me, as well as my husband, for being critical."

"Of course, please also forgive me," I replied with a tear rolling down my cheek. We clasped arms, and the evening took on a much more enjoyable tenor. This was a defining moment, and the only such reconciliation that I enjoyed with someone from Raisin Valley Friends, as we were shunned by the church members for many years to come.

Elizabeth Chandler and her aunt, Ruth Evans, certainly knew how to execute a gala event, with appetizers of scones and sliced apples, the main menu of chicken salad on lettuce and Philadelphia-style cheesecake. The delicacies were delightful.

Following was a beautiful program with Mrs. Evans singing "The Star Spangled Banner." Elizabeth Chandler read her poignant poetry, and she gave a call for women's groups in the county to become involved in the Logan Anti-Slavery Society. Elizabeth asked me to explain the work of the Underground Railroad, and how properties in our county could eventually become a station on the railroad.

Everyone sat spellbound as I discussed the work that was being done across the Northeast United States.

"Thee can see on this map how fugitive slaves are being transferred by many caring white and free black people from the Southern slave states into Illinois, Indiana, Ohio, Michigan and to freedom in Canada. There are many routes, and Lenawee County could be a prime stopping place along the way. If any of thee would be interested in using thy home as a station for the Underground Railroad, please see me. Thy involvement must be completely discreet and anonymous. There are certain passwords and catch phrases that every station uses. The slaves are hidden in attics, barns, tunnels, cellars, anywhere that false doors and walls can easily be erected and constructed. But best of all, thy homes and properties may be used as a sanctuary for those of God's creation who are considered the 'least of these.'"

The evening was exquisitely beautiful. There must have been something romantic and captivating about hiding dark pigmented humans on the run from prejudice and bigotry. The ladies sat spellbound, enjoying the food, music, poetry and the stories. As the evening came to an end and the ladies began collecting their wraps, many of them promised Elizabeth and me that their ladies' groups would collect money and supplies to help with the cause of the Logan Female Anti-Slavery society. A few others slipped an arm around my shoulder to tell me that they were interested in using their homes or barns as a station. Each needed to visit with their husbands and families, but they would get back to me with a response. It was a very satisfying night. Our work had just begun, and yet what a beginning it had been. I was most thankful for my dear friend, Elizabeth Chandler.

As we continued spreading the word about the Logan Female Anti-Slavery Society, it seemed as though God's favor was smiling down on our cause. We had secured over a dozen Quaker, Baptist and Presbyterian homes in our county to serve as stationmasters on the Underground Railroad. Not many slaves were channeled our direction immediately, but our connections with Oberlin College, who coordinated many Underground Railroad groups, began to open up the plan and the time for slaves to head for freedom through Lenawee County.

In January 1834, my son Joseph was born. There was no time to slow down as the momentum was just beginning to build. I carried him in a sling and my other four children followed as we canvassed the areas with our cause and our compassion. It was a busy time for our group of ladies. Elizabeth and I shared the responsibilities of our anti-slavery society. She kept writing powerful poems and articles that were published in both Benjamin Lundy's *The New Century* and William Lloyd Garrison's *The Liberator*. She correctly understood that the battle for freeing slaves was in the hearts and minds of decent, caring citizens. She inspired all of us, though we may not have agreed with all of her liberal theological, Hicksite Quaker views. Elizabeth was loved by all for her compassionate work on this social issue.

At the end of October 1834, a sad day dawned. I was called in to nurse my dear friend, Elizabeth, just as I often was called in to help any of my neighbors with a fever. My home remedies often worked wonders for the sick. I had been called into the Lenawee County Orphanage many times to pray and minister to the sick. So, it was not unusual for me to be called to the great colonial style Evans home to assist Elizabeth in her illness. I labored over my dear friend with love and every remedy and concoction in the reach of my hands. But all to no avail. Immediately, we called for Doctor Sims. Yet as strong as Elizabeth's commitment for ending slavery was, her body carried no such strength. On November 2, my dear sister went to be with the Lord at the tender age of 27. The grief and loss our small anti-slavery society experienced was enough to crush our efforts in the making.

Standing with a large group of mourners on a dismal wintry-looking day, we said our goodbyes. There were many tears and testimonies. No one walked away that day untouched by the life and work of Elizabeth Margaret Chandler. The minister spoke with persuasive urgency challenging each one of us to take seriously the call that would carry forward Elizabeth's passion and spirit of abolitionism. His words continued to echo in my heart throughout the day and for many days to come. I could not shake the thought that if we were to falter now, Elizabeth's efforts would come to a sudden death as well. I was dismayed that we were so close to reaching many more hearts in Lenawee County when suddenly the heart of our leader had stopped beating!

For days I was sad and depressed. Elizabeth and I were close to the same age, and my heart wept for her, as she never had the opportunity to establish a family. Her writings, however, were the heart of the abolitionist movement. Then suddenly it was as though something from deep within me cried out. I knew that the work must go on, and my husband and I would have to be the ones to pick up the slack and lead the way. I am a good organizer, nurse and enthusiast. Fortunately, Elizabeth's writings continued to spread far and wide posthumously, thanks to the two abolitionist publishers, Lundy and Garrison. Due to her influence, at the age of 27 in 1835, I dedicated all of my efforts into carrying on her passion for the abolitionist cause.

Chandler had done much to establish our Logan Female Anti-Slavery Society in 1832. Our society began first within Quaker territory, but it quickly included Presbyterians, Baptists and others as well. We were the first local anti-slavery group established anywhere in the Northwest Territory. We moved quickly to participate with the new American Anti-Slavery Society created in New York in 1834. The goal for the national society was to win over the American people's sense of moral outrage against the injustices and the inhumane nature of slavery. From far and wide, lecturers were sought to persuade and convince our country regarding the evils of slavery.

One blustery winter morning early in 1835, it happened. I was stoking the fire, scrambling the eggs and supervising the activities of my children. Anna was giving Joseph milk. Harvey and Daniel had just come in from their chores of gathering wood and feeding the animals. Esther was stirring my pancake batter by the stove when we heard a wagon approach. I asked Harvey to go find his father, who had started out early that morning mending fence. Daniel, my next to the oldest, took his rightful place, standing by the door. I wasn't terribly frightened, but thoughts of our previous slave-hunting guests had crossed my mind. As Daniel looked out the window, he called out in the deepest seven-year-old voice he could muster, "Woe there! Who art thou looking for?"

A male, sounding more like a mouse than a man, squeaked out the word, "Leprous." This was the infamous password from the beginning of the Underground Railroad rhyme.

Daniel looked at me in shock. I stepped forward and called out the word "Cross"

And the man correctly responded, "Over."

"Hast thou been on the railroad?" I queried.

And he answered, "I have for a short distance."

Next was the line: "Where did thee start?"

"The depot," he said.

"Where did thee stop?"

"At a place called safety."

I continued on. "Hast thou a brother there? I think I know him."

"I know you know," the man continued. "You traveled on the road."

With that I flung open the door to face a scared, scantily clothed, black couple with a newborn baby shivering from the bare elements of winter cold. They openly allowed fear to show on their faces. As I ushered them in, my husband arrived through the back door just in time for introductions. He looked at me hesitantly and then smiled after acknowledging my look of approval.

"I'm Charles Haviland, and this is my wife, Laura, and our children, Harvey, Daniel, Anna, Esther and baby Joseph," he said as he offered his right hand.

The man received Charles' handshake gingerly but gratefully, and introduced himself and his wife, trembling from fear. "I'm Willis, and this is my wife, Elsie, and our baby, Louisa. We are the Hamiltons. We have come from Newport, Indiana, from the Shugart family and protected by the station master, Levi Coffin."

"Ah, yes, Levi Coffin, I've heard he is the respected leader of our movement. Come in quickly. Let's get these wet clothes off of thee. Please come in and join us. . ."

Elsie interrupted. "Excuse me, ma'am, but are you sure it's safe for us to be out here in the open? I mean, I thank you for yur. . . .yur hospitality, but do you really think we're safe?"

"Absolutely!" Charles's booming voice put her troubled thoughts to rest. "As thee knows, there isn't a soul for three miles the direction from which thee came. The same is true from all other directions. If someone approaches, we have at least a good five minutes to hide thee."

"Al-ll right then, if yur sure," Elsie hesitatingly stammered.

Charles helped Willis into some of his clothes, and I did the same for Elsie. Anna and Esther were mesmerized by beautiful Louisa. Providing her a dry blanket, they could not take their eyes off of her. They were so distracted that I had to ask Daniel to keep watch over our little Joseph.

"Missus Haviland, thank you for bein' so kin'. Ya' just can't know what this means for us. We were told where to find yo family, but this traveling on the run jest' causes me a might amount o' fear in my heart!"

"Don't worry. Just come into the kitchen, warm up and we'll serve breakfast shortly. Thee will be safe here," I replied calmly.

Elsie walked into the kitchen and assumed responsibilities as though she was the cook of the house, saving the hot cakes that had been neglected on the griddle. That was a great day, our first one on the Underground Railroad. They were mighty hungry. As they ate, I kept pouring more batter and scrambling more eggs. I could not imagine how long they'd been traveling without a good meal.

Graciously, the Shugarts had sent them forth with a wagon and two horses that Willis had earned by laboring for them last year. They had taken back roads, driven at night only along the Raisin River, and had eaten fruits and vegetables from the bushes and trees along the way. It was obvious they were famished. After they had had their fill, we wanted them to sleep. Elsie was adamant that she could not sleep in the main part of the house. So my boys carried their mattresses into the attic, and the girls and I made up beds for them with blanket upon blanket to keep them warm. Once they were bedded down, we didn't hear a peep from them for almost two days. They were so exhausted, and Elsie would not ask for food. So, Anna and Esther would take turns tip-toeing up the attic stairs and leaving hot plates of food. When they saw the efforts were being rewarded by the return of empty plates, my girls thought it was a fun game. They were sweet to watch. I guess our whole family was becoming acclimated to a new way of life.

Word got out before long that we were harboring fugitives. To my surprise all of that hard work of educating our community began to be rewarded. Farmers would stop by and ask Charles what they could do to help. The ladies at our anti-slavery meetings began to bring clothing and food goods. Of course, there were those that would say, "Oh, Sister Haviland, what hast thou done to thyself and thy family?" Or "doesn't thee know, thee is only asking for trouble?" And, of course, I would smile and respond by saying, "Thank thee for thy concern. We appreciate thy prayers for this good cause."

Charles was glad to have Willis Hamilton on the farm. He was a tremendous help for him. In order to help Willis, Charles leased ten acres of our land to the Hamiltons over a ten year period of time for the improvements Willis would make on the land. It was about that time that I began to take in children from the Lenawee County Orphanage for tutorage. There were nine; and I could take time to teach them the basics of the alphabet, reading and writing along with my own four children, who also needed the education. It was good to have Elsie by my side, as she would take care of the chores and the cooking so that I could attend to the education of these children. With the gifts from people in the community I was able to help the Hamilton family, as well as begin a school. It took time to win Elsie's trust, but it was rewarding. In 1836, we added another baby to our family, beautiful Laura Jane. It was a blessing to have Elsie close by with our school, household chores, and two children under two years of age. The horror stories of their escape from Tennessee with swollen and blistered feet, and the fear of being captured by their Southern persecutors, made a great impact on my young children and the other students in our school.

In spite of our success, our school tutorage with the orphans came to a crashing halt after one year. It was a bit much to feed all of these children every day, to provide all of the supplies for their schooling and to muster all of the emotional support involved in caring for the orphans. I had hoped the Lenawee County Orphanage would share some of their rations for our labor of love with the children. But they, too, were strapped and struggling to make ends meet. So, it became my goal to find good homes for each one of these nine children. I worked diligently to place each one of them in a loving home. This required yet a greater level of effort than teaching them all day. Yet, after this task was completed, I felt good about the future for all of these children, but I really missed our school.

Little did I know that a new adventure was about to surface on the Haviland horizon. At a family gathering we rejoiced with, one of my younger brothers, Sala, in his new venture to medical school at Oberlin College. As we stood in a circle around Mama's spacious dining room table, Papa gave a prayer of thanksgiving that I would never forget. "Father, we thank Thee for the many blessings and abundance of gifts Thou hast poured into our lives, for family, friends and time together. . . ." His big voice boomed across the room, which was completely silent except for Laura Jane's gurgles and coos, a constant joy for all of us. Life just couldn't get any better than this.

Mama allowed the older children to fill their plates and sit outside on the porch. The children loved being with their cousins. Their Uncle Daniel (Charles's brother) And aunt Phoebe (my sister) had two children, Joey, close to the boys age, and Sara, the same age as Anna. Then, of course, they always had to contend with beloved Uncle Samuel, who was now thirteen. They were laughing, playing games and pulling tricks on one another. Meanwhile, the men sat around the table. The women were constantly up and down, in and out of the kitchen, helping Mama, who had labored all day preparing for this wonderful family event.

I was pulling the biscuits from the oven when I heard Papa ask Harvey, "So, Harvey what's the news of the day from Oberlin?" I was so excited to get back into the dining room that I burned my finger as I slipped the biscuits from their pan into the bowl. Hardly noticing, I pushed my way through the door just in time to hear Harvey say, "The big event for this year is the Michigan State Anti-Slavery Convention in Ann Arbor. Our friends keep asking if Charles and Laura will attend."

As I wiped the moisture off my brow, I asked. "Well, why would they care about such a little thing as our attendance at this big, state-level gala?"

"My dear sister, Laura, thou hast developed quite a following for carrying on the work of Elizabeth Chandler. And, of course, as I have always wanted to be known for my prowess in business and farming, I now realize I am only truly known for being thy brother!" At this, peals of laughter rang out throughout the house. Harvey was always quick with his humor.

Mama commented, "Well, Charles and Laura have gained some notoriety right here in Raisin for taking in their beloved Hamilton family."

Love filled Mama and Papa's home along with the aroma of the savory meal that we heartily ate. Everyone ate until they were content. As we gathered the dishes from the table and began to heat the water for washing, Harvey approached me with words of encouragement. "Sis, I really believe that Charles and thee should attend this big meeting. Perhaps, I, too, could go."

Surprised, I asked, "Really, Harvey? Thee would want to go?"

"Well, why not? The date is after my planting season, and I can ask my nephews Harvey and Daniel, or even our brother Samuel, to help with the watering if need be."

"That's fine." I heard myself say. "What is the date?"

"It is the weekend of November 10-11. Many of the Underground Station Masters are willing to house those traveling from a distance. It will be a great way to network and connect with our Underground brothers and sisters from around the state," Harvey concluded.

As our Indian summer was coming to an end, fall with its beautiful burnt orange foliage was quickly passing, as well. The children were doing well with their studies, and Elsie's work continued to be appreciated. We occasionally were able to help a few other slaves as they passed by our way. Time seemed to fly. The sad realization dawned upon me that there was absolutely no way I could leave my six children to attend the anti-slavery conference. All of my relatives were busy with families of their own. With a determined spirit, I persuaded Charles into going with Harvey. "Someone from Raisin has to go. It is important for the Underground Railroad if it is to become more organized. We have to network, as Harvey says, with those from around the state." It was an exhilarating prospect to think that perhaps Raisin, Michigan, our little Lenawee County, might become a prominent stop along the Underground Railroad. I had shared this with the ladies in our Raisin Anti-Slavery Society, and they continued to encourage me in these efforts and thoughts. At times I thought I might be losing my mind. It had occurred to me that we might be risking the welfare and lives of our families, our children and our futures. Yet, what other choice did we have?

As I prepared to send two of my favorite men on their journey, I found myself tucking in warm clothes, blankets and staple food that would last beyond their day's journey. I found a Michigan State Map at Brother Hinshaw's Dry Goods Store that I was sending along with them. Not because they needed directions, but because I outlined the closeness of Adrian to Detroit and to Toledo, Ohio. I visited at length with the men about what a great decoy Adrian would be for the Underground Railroad. As a small, unassuming, peaceful, farming community with many rural farms, this would serve as a good place to secure fugitives from danger.

As I kissed Charles good-bye, he promised that he would present our cause during the Underground Railroad discussions. Harvey called out as Charles pulled away. "Now, don't thee worry thy little head, Laura, if he forgets, I'll remind him." As we waved our good-byes, I felt sure they would live up to their promises.

These four days seemed like forever to me! Yes, I had plenty to keep me busy. Laura Jane was sick, and before I knew it so were the rest of the children. I made a huge pot of chicken soup, seasoned with all of my best herbal cures. I fed them, sent them all to bed and found myself trying to do all of the boys' chores and run the household single-handedly. I sent Elsie home with Louisa. I certainly didn't want them coming down with this nasty ailment. Thank the good Lord for Willis, who came the last two days and took care of the animals and other chores. Fortunately, by the time Charles and Harvey returned the children were up and going strong. We had cleaned the house and prepared a great meal for the men.

We were all very excited to have them return and hear their news. Harvey and Charles talked non-stop about the people, places and the latest news for Michigan's Underground Railroad. It was difficult to follow their conversation. They were as hungry as they were talkative. When I asked about my request they both stopped mid-sentence. Harvey responded first, "Oh, yes, what were we supposed to ask them?" Before I could respond with a rebuke, both men had broken out into hearty laughter. Charles, the serious one, came to his senses first. "Oh, dear Laura, we did not forget, but it is not as thee might have expected."

"What does that mean?" I asked with an edge of disappointment in my voice.

"Well," Charles continued. "The discussion of the Railroad took place outside of the convention. This was done for privacy and security sake."

"Yes, and the organizers of the event spoke in code language, and we were not sure who we should share with for a while," Harvey added.

Charles continued, "Finally, a very distinguished man named Levi Coffin from Newport, Indiana, noticed our confusion and inquired regarding the nature of our concern. As we introduced ourselves to him, he asked about the welfare of the Hamiltons. We were surprised that he knew they were still staying on our land. Coffin directed us to another significant man, George DeBaptiste, who is the station conductor from Toledo to Detroit. He introduced us to DeBaptiste by saying, 'These men are the husband and brother of our Quaker sister, Laura Haviland, in Raisin, Michigan. They have a stop on the Railroad as we sent the Hamiltons, one of our couples, there seeking refuge. The Hamiltons have lived there now close to a year and are doing quite well. I think it might benefit our efforts to make

Adrian an official stop for those who need a decoy between Toledo and Detroit.' DeBaptiste agreed immediately and asked to meet with us following the evening's meetings. So, my dear wife, thy desire to make Lenawee County a regular stop on the Underground Railroad is about to become a reality."

Chapter Five

The Raisin Institute & the Underground Railroad

I couldn't contain myself, jumping from the table with joy! I kissed my husband, hugged my brother and ran into the kitchen to bring on the dessert. The children joined in with the festivities, though I was sure they did not completely grasp the meaning of this exciting new reality and what it might mean to their futures. But for tonight we rejoiced! When my feet finally hit the ground, Harvey said, "All right, Laura, now I want thee to pay attention to the true accomplishment of our journey."

"What!" I responded, "Could there be more?"

"Oh yes," Harvey continued. "The best is yet to come."

"Laura," Charles intervened. "I want thee to know this is completely Harvey's idea. I believe it to be a good one; and I'm sure thee will love it. Yet I think that we need to take time and pray about his proposition. Before we reach a decision, we must really think about the implications for Harvey and for all of us."

"Charles!" Harvey's impatience was noticeable in his voice.

"Of course, Harvey, sorry, it's thy proposition to share." Charles backed off.

"Proposition? Tell me!" I was growing impatient. They certainly had my undivided attention now.

Harvey thoughtfully shared his plan. "Laura, the new emphasis for sharing abolition principles is through education. Our main speaker, Rev. Smith Hobard is well-known for his work in transporting slaves in his double-bottomed wagon. He shared incredible stories, though names and places were protected. His stories mesmerized everyone at the convention. Rev. Hobard stressed we must educate the good-minded citizens of our state about the evils of slavery. It's not enough to educate those of our own race, but we must demonstrate that these fugitives of color are intelligent and able to learn. Through education we will win the battle against slavery!"

I think I must have gasped after Harvey shared this because I believed it to be so true. Urging him to go on, he said. "Well, I've thought about this long and hard. I want to sell my land and give Charles and thee the money to purchase buildings for a school."

"What?" I asked incredulously.

"Yes," Harvey continued. "If thou could afford to start thy own school, thou would do it in a heartbeat. Right?"

"Well, certainly." I stammered out of shock more than anything.

"The reason the school for the orphans closed was because there was a lack of funds. Correct?" Harvey was relentless.

Hesitatingly, I responded, "Correct."

"Money from my farm will eliminate that problem, and the school will be an important tool in serving the abolitionist cause!" Harvey emphatically declared.

"Uhhh," I continued to stammer with stars metaphorically dazzling in front of my eyes. Gaining my composure I replied, "I agree with Charles. This will take a great amount of thought and prayer."

I was still dazed after Harvey left. Actually I was in shock. Such a proposition would have never seriously crossed my mind. And to think that my dear brother was willing to make such a sacrifice to help us for such a beautiful cause.

Charles asked me as we were preparing for bed, "So, what dost thou think?"

"I'm just stunned," I answered.

"I knew thee would be," Charles replied. "It was all his idea. He became more and more excited with each of our sessions. He really has a vision for it, and he believes that we can succeed. He would be an outstanding teacher as well."

"Well, of course he would. But what dost thou think?" I asked.

"Well, I've given it a lot of thought. Since we are a free state, our risk would be minimal, except for those slave bounty hunters who would come around. Yet, I think that we could make a great statement for freedom and equality. . . ."

Interrupting, I asked, "What dost thou think about the safety and security of our family and all of the children that might be here?"

"I don't know, Laura. It seems to me that we have come this far. If we're in danger, we're in danger. But look about us. There is such strong anti-slavery sentiment. I was thinking about all of the women's names that thee has shared with me, those who have volunteered to participate in the railroad. If I visited with their husbands and could get several who would readily commit to our venture," Charles continued, "I believe we could develop a network of protection against anyone who might try to harm us. It seems the good Lord has been smiling down on our work, Dost thou think we should quit now?"

Of course, my dear husband already knew my answer to such a rhetorical question. I threw my arms around him, and the song of my heart and our time together could only cement the deep, deep happiness I felt within.

In 1837 Harvey sold his new farmland of 160 acres and used the funds to construct school buildings on our land. He arrived with his supplies on a beautiful wash day at our home. We were almost finished with the day's labor. The girls were taking the clothes off the line from behind the house. The boys had come in from the fields. As I looked out across the horizon, a bowl of dust mushroomed across the sky, and little Joseph cried out, "Mommy, Mommy, look it's Uncle Harvey's wagon!"

"It sure is. Joseph, run and tell thy Pa." I responded. As he ran around the corner to the barn, the other children gathered around. Harvey pulled up with a wagon filled with boards of all sizes. It was so loaded down that even the ties around the supplies looked as though they would split with just the slightest amount of extra tension. Harvey was covered with dust from head to toe from his long journey. He had purchased his supplies in Adrian which was a good ten miles from our home place. He was grinning from ear to ear like a Cheshire cat! It was quite obvious how proud he was of himself. The children surrounded him with hugs and kisses in spite of the dust. "Uncle Harvey, Uncle Harvey!" They bantered. He, in his characteristic style of being a dear uncle to my children, pulled out a bag of candy and said, "Who wants a piece?" They all jumped for joy as he tossed the candy into the air.

Anna questioned. "Uncle Harvey, what in the world dost thee have on thy wagon!" In his endearing manner, he responded in a big way with a big smile, "This, my children, is the beginning of the 'Raisin Institute!'" Daniel let out a soft whistle and said the words, "The Raisin Institute on the Raisin River," just to hear how the name sounded as it rolled off his tongue.

"Indeed, my son," was Harvey's response. As the older children ran down by the river to finish bringing in the animals from the pasture, Esther & Joseph clung to Harvey's side. We sat on the porch, and Laura Jane let out a little cry. Charles, walking around the corner, spoke with a smile creeping across his face. "Hey, what's all the excitement about?"

"Pa, Pa!" Joseph exclaimed. "Look at Uncle Harvey's wagon!"

Charles let out a long whistle. "Joseph, thanks to thy Uncle Harvey, we've got our work cut out for us. Come on, let's go inside and discuss our plan for these materials."

As the men went in to plan, I sat and watched the sun as it settled down over the horizon. The older boys came and moved the wagon into the shed, returning Harvey's horse to its post by the door.

What would the next few years bring? Could we do it? Would the neighbors truly support our school whose goal was to unite people, black and white? We were soon to find out.

Soon the farm was alive with activity, the hustle and bustle of strong muscle among our kinsmen and others now actively involved in the Logan Anti-Slavery Society. Meeting in our home, the men folk helped construct the school, and the women shared in the making of meals. These ladies included my mother, my dear sister Phoebe, three sisters-in-law, cousins and others from the Methodist Church and community. At meal time we also talked about our future plans for the school, as well as for our Underground Railroad System. It was exciting to have so many involved. We could not have been more blessed to have such supportive help from the folks of Raisin.

Each week there were many new accomplishments; one building after another was added onto our property. Charles and his crew began in the spring of 1837. By the middle of the summer, after several months of work, our farm had been recreated into the Raisin Institute. Thanks to Harvey and Daniel, we did name it "Raisin" after the "Raisin River," which ran behind our home. We knew that it would be a good, neutral name also identifying the location in Michigan.

Harvey had helped acquire the best, most knowledgeable teachers of Christian Spirit from Oberlin College to serve as administrators of the Raisin Institute, P.P.

and his wife, Anna, Roots. Harvey, an Oberlin Institute alumnus, along with the Roots had designed our new school on the "Oberlin Plan," opening the school for students of good moral character regardless of sex or color. In this day there was not a school in Michigan that would open its door to a colored person. Most of our recruited students were planning to teach. Although our abolition principles were very unpopular in this day, still the excellent and thorough discipline given in our studies began to draw the best intellect of young people from the northeastern section of our country.

On the first day of school, I sat trembling in my Quaker dress, thankful for the modest apparel to cover my knocking knees. The first day of school is usually a nervous time for parents and children, but on the day the Raisin Institute classes began, I was the nervous one as I helped register students into our brand new school. I was thrilled to see the children of our community walk through our doors. But I jumped for joy when children were brought in from far and wide to be educated in our humble school that could accommodate up to fifty students.

Sitting at the registration table welcoming our new students and their parents, I felt as though a miracle was taking place before my very eyes, and it was. Despite the knocking knees, I watched in awe as parents lined up at our doors. The Roots had done an excellent job advertising for the school. Families had come from Ohio, Indiana and Michigan because of their support for the Oberlin Institute's finest teachers. Some traveled from as far as fifty to hundred miles. Of course, our location was convenient, in Southern Michigan close to both the Indiana and Ohio state lines.

One such family was the James Martin family. They were enrolling young James Jr., thirteen years of age. His parents were free black citizens of our country. They had purchased their papers of freedom at a very high cost. They were determined that young James would have the best education and the best opportunities to live a life of freedom and equality. James was hiding behind his mother's skirt as James Sr. introduced him to me.

I held out my hand for him to shake, smiled, and said, "James, I am Laura Haviland. But thee may call me Aunt Laura."

I will never forget how he peeked around his mama's skirt and asked me, "Aunt Laura, why do you call me thee? You're talkin' strange!"

His Papa quickly reprimanded James Jr. by saying, "James, don't speak to Mrs. Haviland in that way!"

Smiling, I explained to him, "James Jr., I have been reared as a Quaker, and we speak just a little different from other folks. We believe that if we speak using such proper pronouns as 'thee' and 'thou' that we show a deep respect for all humans, and that is how God would want us to share one with another.

James suddenly piped up and asked, "What is a pronoun, Aunt Laura?"

Laughter broke out again. "Well, young man," I responded. "That is why thee is here." And with such an introduction, James Martin became an endearing, wonderful member of our family at the Raisin Institute. My son, Harvey, grabbed James by the arm and asked, "Hey, dost thee want to see thy room?"

James blurted out, "He speaks the same as you, Aunt Laura."

"Yes, he does. This is Harvey, my son. The two of thee will get along well."

"Come on, James." Harvey ran off with James following close behind to the boys' living quarters.

Another beautiful young student was Hannah Jackson. Her only living parent, her father, registered her. Timid and shy, my daughters Anna and Esther reached out to befriend Hannah. Hannah was twelve, several years older than my daughters, and she hesitated before slowly responding to their offer of friendship. My girls were mesmerized with Hannah's beauty and quiet way. The girls walked Hannah to her room. For Hannah it was most difficult telling her father good-bye.

She began crying and clung to him. Our hearts went out to her, knowing that he was her only earthly security. Mrs. Anna Roots and I worked hard to comfort her, but we just had no luck getting through to her. It was obvious she lacked a mother's love. But her tears would not subside. Anna and Esther both had tears streaming down their faces. They made it their aim to include Hannah in their daily lives.

Mr. Jackson reassured Hanna, "Honey, I will be back to get you in the spring. But it's important for you to complete your education. You need these women in your life as you continue to develop into a beautiful young woman yourself."

As we waved good-bye to the Martins, Mr. Jackson and several other parents whose children we would board for the semester, I felt a knot well up in my throat. God had given us a huge task and calling.

Life at the Raisin Institute was one of warmth, love and intellectual stimulation. However, we did have unexpected outbursts and unplanned controversies from the very beginning. Our family and staff prayed daily for these needs and concerns. We reminded one another that, being involved in a work of such a liberal social flavor, there would be those who simply did not understand. There were those who might create severe difficulties for the success of our school. Yet, we were deeply shocked when our first challenge at overcoming prejudice came from one in our midst.

It was our little Hannah. She was homesick, and to complicate her feelings of being in a new, strange world, she was distressed that our own James Martin had dark skin.

On the first day of school she pointed to him and cried out, "I can't sit next to this boy!" This took everyone by surprise. We were shocked and ill-prepared for such an outburst. We knew that all of our communications with parents and family members stated our principles quite clearly. Yet, Hannah's father either did not understand our ideals or simply did not think it important enough to share them with his daughter.

Hannah's outburst occurred at the beginning of algebra class. She ran out of the classroom to her room and slammed the door behind her. Quickly informed of the situation, I was on her trail, trying to catch her before she shut me out as well. But I was too late. She refused to come out, and all of the coaxing in the world would not persuade her. Anna and Esther pleaded with her. My sons, Daniel and Harvey, tried to do the same. It was Mrs. Root, calm and kind, who kept a vigil and continued to woo Hannah out of her shell with bribes of food and understanding. Hannah was concerned that she would be in trouble with our administration. Still she insisted that she must immediately send a telegram home to her father.

"I must go home! I simply cannot stay here any longer. My father does not know that there are black people in this school. He would not have sent me here had he known! Please send this letter to my father immediately." She insisted in a defiant voice.

This was the cause of our first emergency meeting of the staff and administration of the Raisin Institute. We agreed that we had expected the evils of prejudice to challenge our work, but no one dreamed that it would come from within our school. Hannah's outburst was considered inappropriate. Everyone on the staff recognized that. However, we decided as a team not to make an issue of the episode.

We talked to James who really needed our support. "James, did it bother thee that Miss Hannah pointed and said she would not sit with thee?" I asked.

James nodded that it did.

"I just want thee to know that I like sitting and eating with thee," I replied.

James looked up at me with his large, saucer brown eyes gripping my soul and asked, "Why doesn't Miss Hannah want to sit beside me in algebra or at the dinner table?"

"Well James, I have a feeling that thee actually knows the answer to that question; but it's the answer that is hard to understand! Some people do not value others who look different from them."

James nodded. So I continued.

"There are people in this world who believe that the color of our skin makes us different one from another."

"Oh, yes. I understand all of that, Aunt Laura. That's why there are slaves. But I am not a slave. My family is free." He spoke directly and to the point.

"Yes, that is true. Yet, there are those who won't listen to thy words or trust the official paper that makes thee a free man; rather, they will judge thee just by looking at the color of thy skin."

James shook his head vehemently and cried out, "Well, how could they be so ignorant?"

James's audacity and bright spirit surprised all of us. I started laughing and Harvey, my son who was close by, joined in as though we were sharing a good joke. After a moment of quiet reflection I gave him the most thoughtful response I could muster. "Thee is right, James Martin! They are the ignorant ones."

James had a wonderful perspective for his age. He had been raised by such a loving family, by a family that had dodged the impact of slavery from within, but like me, keenly felt the effect from without. Yet, there were greater negative implications to free black citizens, and that was just exactly what Hannah had highlighted by her actions. Most people judge by outward appearances.

James ran off with my boys who absolutely adored him. He told us how his parents had performed in several New York plays before they moved to Michigan.

They had trained him to play certain roles, and James loved to act. This was certainly foreign to my children, and made him the center of attention at the Raisin Institute.

At our evening meal, Hannah simply changed seats with my daughter Anna, who did not mind in the least. Anna was mesmerized with our James. She kept asking him questions about New York and the world of actors and playwrights. This discussion gave me cause to think about my early years in New York that seemed like a lifetime ago. Life in frontier Michigan did not include such types of entertainment and luxury. My children had to learn to make their own entertainment. Sharing our meals in the cafeteria with the children and our staff was the source of expanding horizons to the greater world around us.

During meals, our students received their mail and would often share messages from their loved ones back home. The Roots always shared the latest Oberlin news. I particularly loved hearing all of the Underground news from the Oberlin Institute, as well as any news from Sala, who was doing particularly well in his studies and was now considered a bonafide doctor. It was unbelievable to think of my little brother as a doctor!

The next morning, I sent Hannah's telegram from the Hinshaw's Dry Goods Store. I cringed at my purpose for sending this letter, but it had to be done. Mr. Hinshaw said it would take a few days before we should expect a response. He always enjoyed talking about modern technology and how the brand new telegraph system would change our country. Waiting on Mr. Hinshaw, I had eyed some gingham fabric. I could not help but overhear two ladies in conversation on the next aisle. Surely, they were aware that I could hear them. "Martha," one of them said. "Have you heard about the new school on the outskirts of Raisin? They accept niggers there!"

"No, you can't be serious! Rosalind, what should we do about such extreme-social folly? If it continues, it could ruin our economy!"

I stepped into their aisle addressing the prim and proper ladies. "Excuse me, I could not help but overhear thy prejudice. Dost thou not realize that Michigan is a free state?"

Mr. Hinshaw, watching this scenario play out, walked over and intervened. "Excuse me ladies, it doesn't look as though I have the color of yarn thee is looking for, Miss Martha. Perhaps thee and thy friend can find it in Adrian."

"Oh, well, yes! Thank you, Mr. Hinshaw," Martha said in a huff. "Come on, Roz. We need to head back to Adrian. The morning's getting away from us." Martha tugging on Roz's sleeve, the two ladies pranced excitedly out the door.

Rosalind followed behind lamenting immaturely, "Indeed!"

I watched from behind the shelving as they walked glibly away, pointing and talking, unaware that Mr. Hinshaw had moved directly behind me. As I turned I jumped, recognizing his gaze upon me. Looking smug, he replied curtly, "See for thyself, Mrs. Haviland. Continue on with this work and look at the hate that spews from these people's hearts!"

"Mr. Hinshaw, I thank thee for sending my telegram," I responded angrily with my voice inflection rising with each sentence. "I would also thank thee to realize that I have nothing to do with the hate that resides in these women's hearts! But reside there, it does!"

Not giving him a chance to respond I walked out the door and closed the door behind with a firm click. Walking out into the full sun, I realized how fatigued and exhausted I felt. My whole being seemed to wilt like a flower faded by the parched sun. It was absurd, the prejudice that people harbor! I was mad at Mr. Hinshaw though he was one who had rescued me from a war of words with the ladies.

Our school had experienced great success and excitement with its opening. We had also felt the favor of many neighbors and friends. But at this moment it seemed that the world was crashing around me. I can't remember a more deliberately slow wagon drive back to our place. Realizing I needed help from above, I stared out across the vast, wide Raisin River. There the words of the Psalmist rippled through my mind and quenched my weary soul. "There is a river whose streams make glad the city of God. Oh, Lord!" I cried out. "Let us be that river!"

Wiping the tears from my eyes, I pulled into our drive. Our home was now identified by the rock and plaque engraved upon it, "Raisin Institute, 1837." With a great sigh, I walked into the cafeteria. After chatting with several students, hugging my children and kissing my husband, I knew that God was in control.

My favorite days were Sabbath days and Wednesdays because of our special chapel services. Rev. Root, our school administrator, shared a great lesson from the Scriptures, and sometimes the children would give recitations from their studies. We still could not get Hannah to participate in her classes, though she was particularly astute and worked hard on her studies in her room. My girls kept chiding her to come to chapel and share her recitations. But she would not. Hannah would attend all of the classes for girls, as we had no black female students at the time. She asked for her meals in her room, but she was very respectful and would help in the kitchen in order to get this privilege. Yet, she still refused to go to algebra class. I knew we could force her to go, but believed that would defeat our overall purpose.

James grew more and more in his popularity in these early days. He was our first and only black student in the first year at Raisin. Each year we found ourselves with one to three black students! Still for those with minds poisoned by prejudice, it was "one to three" too many. Of course, we often had black refugees join in our classroom sessions. This proved most helpful for them on their flight to freedom.

At the end of our second week of school, we hosted a picnic down by the river. It was great fun for everyone, everyone except Hannah. She hung back, very frustrated by James's charm and overall likeability. She had not spoken a negative word against James since the initial incursion in algebra the first day of school.

Laughter pealed out across the hillside. Some of the children went fishing. Others played cricket on the flatland behind our house. The girls were chattering as they prepared their picnic baskets, and asked the boys to join them. If it were not for our little Hannah, we would have been one big, happy family.

Charles had been called to help a neighbor with a sick cow. While the children and our school staff were enjoying the picnic, I saw Charles ride in. Walking to the barn, I met him with a letter in hand.

"Well," he said handing the piece of mail to me. "Here's the news for which we've been waiting. It's addressed to us, as well as to Hannah."

"Is it good or bad?"

"I don't know, Laura, I did not have the heart to open it."

I opened the letter and read these words:

Dear Hannah and Leaders of Raisin School:

This is in response to my daughter's request. No, Hannah, I am not coming to bring you home. I've spent a significant amount of money to get you into this school with good teachers. I did not know that there would be niggers there, or I would not have sent you. But this will be a growing experience for you, my child. You'll be all right. I'll come for you in the spring. Father.

A smile crept across my face as I read the letter. Charles simply chuckled and said, "Upwards and onwards, my dear!" As Charles leaned over to kiss me, I felt as though heaven had opened its windows and poured down light from above, for the kiss and the message. Though I didn't like the prejudice that was apparent in Mr. Jackson's letter, we had been given an opportunity to win this child's heart.

I gave the letter to Esther to take to Hannah, saying, "Esther, stay with her and let her talk. She's going to need a good friend who will listen. Perhaps, thou can help her in this way. Maybe thee can also put in a good word for James."

Before she left I gave her a big hug, and she said, "Mother, why is thee so happy?"

And I said, "Can't I hug my lovely daughter?"

She laughed and ran off to find Hannah.

Hannah did not come back to the picnic that afternoon; neither did she go to the cafeteria for her meal that evening. Esther was mysteriously missing, as well, but we understood why.

The next morning Hannah came into the dining hall and sat at her place besides James at breakfast. Her face was as white as a sheet, and she never said a word. Thus was the life of our Hannah for quite some time. She was quiet. Thankfully she started attending algebra and all of her classes. She did her work and kept her mouth shut. Everyone did their best to be friendly with her. She perked up when asked questions about her goal of becoming a teacher.

So, it seemed that we fell into a routine, not necessarily a comfortable routine, but one that worked at the Raisin Institute. The enthusiasm of our students sustained us. The professionalism of our teachers was stellar. It was so exciting to be part of such a great endeavor.

As the semester rolled along, we had many firsts in our new buildings, our first classes, our first mid-term exam time, our first school picture and our first grading period. Our students groaned at times because of the difficult level of our classes, particularly those classes that were preparatory courses for prospective teachers, but they also rejoiced in the work that was accomplished. There were a dozen in our teacher education courses. They still had several years to complete their education. But these students learned to work together and learn from each other.

It was James Martin who was the head of this class. He was a great problem-solver. So it was to everyone's surprise that one day in algebra class, Hannah turned to James for help to solve one of the toughest algebra problems in the course. With great heart he walked through the problem with her step by step. She listened intently, clearly focusing on his problem-solving equation. As he completed his mathematical sentence, she responded in an "aha" moment, "Oh, I understand! How could have I missed that step? Thank you James," was her quick response. She immediately returned back to her own work.

The room was completely still and silent. No one wanted to breathe, just in case they had missed the moment. Life went on at Raisin Institute. Yet, it was obvious things were better, the tensions eased. James and Hannah began greeting one another each day in class. No one could believe they were actually speaking. Within two weeks Hannah, was laughing along with the rest of the class at James and his entertaining personality.

I cried for joy. "Where, oh where has her deep-rooted prejudice gone?" It was as if it had disappeared with the wind. Hannah and James were two of our best students, and they became friends, helping each other throughout the rest of their school years.

The spring day came too soon when parents arrived for their children at the end of our school year. My heart went out to Hannah. She had matured and grown so much in one year. Yet I noticed that her father never wrote like other parents did. As Mr. Jackson pulled in our drive, I wondered what her life was like at home with her father. He stormed through the campus in a hurry. He wanted to settle all Hannah's financial bills for the year as he said, "She will not be back."

Hannah was in the parlor visiting with James when she saw her father. Immediately, she came running to greet him.

"Papa, you're here! I'm so glad to see you. Come! Meet one of my new friends. Papa, this is my good friend, James Martin."

James held out his hand in courtesy and welcome.

Mr. Jackson's demeanor was distant. He turned away, ignoring James, and said to Hannah. "Come, let's get your things! You will not be returning next year!"

Hannah stopped in her tracks and said to him. "Papa, I'm not leaving this school. I am the class president. I'm doing well on my teaching track. If you tell me you're not going to let me return in the fall, then I will not go home with you."

With that, Hannah did what Hannah does. She stomped outside, went into the girls' living quarters and locked herself in her room. Of course, this was not at all funny to her father. I had to turn my face in order to hide the little smile that had spontaneously formed.

I offered Mr. Jackson a cup of coffee and asked Elsie to set another plate at the table expecting him to be with us for a while. My brother Harvey sat down with Mr. Jackson and they visited. Harvey took the time to share our abolitionist principles, questioning why the Jacksons had not been aware of this previously, as they were clearly outlined in all of our literature. Mr. Jackson admitted that he had not taken the time to read the literature, as he was just trying to find a boarding school for his daughter after his wife had passed away.

I joined the conversation, sharing with him the dramatic changes I had seen in his daughter. "Mr. Jackson, I find that many people are fearful of people with dark skin. They think that for some reason a different skin color indicates something wrong or suspicious about a human. Hannah has had the opportunity to get to know James, and she has discovered what everyone needs to know. It doesn't matter the color of our skin. It only matters that we were created by the same God and that we are here to serve together."

Mr. Jackson sputtered. He found my thoughts socially unacceptable, but he did finally say, "I personally have no problem with black people. Where I come from, blacks are slaves."

He stayed for supper, though I warned him that James would be seated around our table as usual. Mr. Jackson was quiet, and Anna had persuaded Hannah to come to dinner. She and James were laughing and talking about Mr. Root's trick question on the algebra final exam. Mr. Jackson just sat and watched his daughter in awe. He didn't know what to say, and he didn't know what to do. As he walked out of the dining hall, he asked to speak with me.

We walked away from the rest where we could privately talk, "Mrs. Haviland, could Hannah stay here this summer?" He asked, "I will pay you whatever you think is right."

"Mr. Jackson," I spoke out of alarm. "Thy daughter needs to spend time with thee while school is not in session."

He firmly responded, "Yes, but Mrs. Haviland, I have never seen her happy like this. If she comes home with me she will only have sad memories of her mother. I generally work twelve hours a day. I will be no companion for her. I promise I will come to see her on holidays. What do you say?"

Surprised by my own words, I replied. "I think thee is asking the wrong person. Thou will have to ask Hannah. If she wants to stay and help out on the farm this summer, she is welcome to do so."

Hearing a little squeal of delight from Hannah after her father had approached her, I knew her answer. I asked Daniel and Harvey to find a room for Mr. Jackson, as I was sure he would not be leaving until morning.

It is the melting of prejudice that gave us great satisfaction. As the fleeing fugitive found a resting place and cheer within our home, we richly earned the cognomen of 'nigger den.' Yet Heaven smiled and blessed our work. For all of the talk about our Raisin Institute and its opponents, we also found many sympathizing friends along the way. Some of these were from our Raisin Valley Society of Friends whom had deemed us too radical. We unwittingly began to feel even their care and support. This was just the beginning, a crack in the door that would one day open wide for unity.

Chapter Six
Joys – Underground, School, & Children

In the beginning of the Raisin Institute, we were glad to allow others in the community take a more prominent role in the Underground Railroad. Our home was only one of the 27 stations in Lenawee County. The importance of our network was that we could signal one another quickly. Given the Raisin Underground Map, we knew each station well. If someone traveled through looking suspicious or unfamiliar, we immediately sent a rider down the road to warn the others. Quickly, the word would get around to all of our stations.

The summer of 1838 was a particularly hot and tiring one. Just discovering I was expecting my seventh child—I was no "spring chicken," thirty years of age and still having babies! We had just experienced a wonderful first year in the Raisin Institute. The summer was filled with cleaning and preparing our buildings for another school year. Elsie was in the kitchen cooking, cleaning and keeping up with her two little girls and my Laura Jane. The men worked hard in the fields during the long summer days. Following our evening meal, the boys went down river to fish, the men talked shop, while the ladies and girls spent time quilting, mending clothes and sharing recipes. Later in the evening we would gather to sing and share stories. It was such a blessed time, full of great memories that would carry me one day, after they were long gone.

One morning I was coming in from the garden when I heard Elsie scream. The girls were washing clothes in the washtub out by the shed, the boys brushing down the horses and I came around the corner just in time to see Elsie grab her two little girls and run towards the house. She cried out to Clyde Webb, who was at our farm to purchase eggs. Webb turned around to see a strange man skulking off into the woods. Elsie ran inside the kitchen door leaving it open behind her.

As the children told the story, I learned they had noticed a strange man peeking over the fence of our front yard. Elsie begged the girls to keep quiet as she and her girls ran to hide in our attic. Anna promised she would let her know when it was safe to come out. The boys ran to get Charles, who immediately, investigated the situation. He had confirmed from one neighbor that a strange man was observed entering our property. Charles followed what he believed were the man's footprints. It looked as though the intruder had tethered his horse by the road and entered our road on foot where he could easily be hidden.

Willis came in from the field to comfort Elsie, but there was no comfort to be found. They had been discovered by the slave hunters. The Hamiltons decided to move on up the road, putting enough distance between them to hopefully distract the bounty hunters. That night John and Elsie pulled our wagon to the back of their home and packed all of their belongings. They spent their last evening with us, parking the wagon in our barn. We cried together as we bid them farewell, along with their two daughters. Late at night, my husband and Mr. Webb drove the wagon down the road, while the Hamilton family members were hiding underneath gunny sacks in the back. Traveling further north to the next Underground station, they remained there for several months. Then, once again "fleeing for their lives," the Hamilton family moved to Ypsilanti, where they stayed three years.

What a life, always on the move, always on the look-out! I missed my friends the Hamiltons, but all we could do was pray!

I missed Elsie's good work, and had to call on my dear sister Phoebe for support. She came to assist me during the remaining summer months. I knew that once school started we would be fine. We had so much wonderful help from the ladies in our anti-slavery society. I was thankful for their support and willing hands. I had never experienced such difficulty carrying any of my other children. My doctor, Brother Sala, had stopped by to see me on his way back to Oberlin. His words of advice were, "Stay off thy feet dear sister. Thee is not as young as thee used to be." So I stayed in bed, begging him to tell me about his adventures working as a physician in the Underground Railroad. He said, "Laura, thee really does not want to know just how awful our black brethren are treated. Many of them are beaten to death. Those who fall out of favor with their masters pray to die quickly. I just hear so many gruesome stories, and the injuries I treat testify to this truthfulness."

These words tugged at my heart. I cried out to my Maker for these poor souls. I encouraged Sala to stay on track—no pun intended—with the great work he was doing helping these poor disdained souls in the Underground Railroad. "God will bless thee and honor thee, Sala, for all of thy work on behalf of his poor children."

"Yes, dear sister. And God will honor thee for thy work at the Raisin Institute." Sala became more and more emphatic with each word. "But this school year, thee must stay in bed until this beautiful niece or nephew of mine is born. Dost thou understand?"

Though I loved him and hugged his neck, I also had the strange impulse to strangle him. It was worse than being expelled from school or being caught in a sin of omission (simply forgetting one's duty) for a Quaker. Staying in bed was worse than any other medical prescription I could have been given. My brother knew this about me, and he was prepared to carry out his wishes. He called in the whole family, and he shared with everyone his grave concerns and advisement for me to remain bedfast until the baby's birth. Everyone agreed with him, of course.

Thus, I found myself a prisoner in my own home. But I must say, the quality time that I had with each of my children, as well as my loving husband, made my prison stay bearable. Each day they would take turns telling me about the activities of the school and about all of their classes and friends. Little Laura Jane was my constant companion. She had grown so much since I had taken the time to stop and really look at her. I found that to be true with all of my children. I always had a special time of prayer with each one of them, and encouraged each one to think about what special gift God had given them.

Without a doctor on hand, Mrs. Anna Root, with the assistance of my very grown-up daughters Anna and Esther, delivered our new little bundle of joy on January 18, 1839. Her father and I named her Almira. She was another beautiful gift from God. What a sweet time we had together around my bed following Almira's birth. The girls were overwhelmed with the experience of childbirth. I thought they would never go to bed that night. They talked non-stop. I fell asleep listening to their chatter. The boys held their new little sister and kept looking at her in awe, while Charles sitting on the edge of my bed held my hand and kept watching me to make sure I was comfortable.

Finally on my feet again, with little Almira in a sling around my shoulder, I returned to teach my classes for the girls in our school: cooking, sewing, quilting, knitting and homemaking. My teaching methods required the girls to practice their skills, and thus fulfilling the needs of the school. Yes, the Raisin girls were divided into several classes, and they were a great help to me.

Not only was I working at school and in my home, but once again I became active in the anti-slavery movement. While I had been homebound, many visitors from our Underground Railroad group had asked me to create an organizational chart. Because I had been so involved with the work of the Raisin Institute, I really had not realized how active our local Underground Railroad had become. We had grown from a few fugitive families traveling into our stations to many fugitive families finding refuge here. I found that my services were needed in counseling and encouraging those in hiding. We also needed more supplies to be provided in these homes. I was back at the work I loved, traveling, speaking and serving the needs of our Underground Railroad Stations in the area.

With my passion for the abolitionist cause, I began to be known as an outspoken woman. I had never thought of myself as a speaker. Speaking to a group was always one of the most nerve-racking responsibilities to fulfill. I always tried to get my husband to speak on our behalf. But he would just say, "Laura, thou art the speaker in our family. I will stand beside thee and support thee, but I will not speak for thee." Yet, he was a calming influence for me. I always knew he was praying on my behalf. His support always carried me through the nerves and fears of standing before a crowd.

I was no stranger to the hurtful and unkind words of those against our cause. Yet, it always seemed like a double hurdle for women in these leading roles. It was the women from our group who took charge and spoke out against slavery in the beginning. There were many supportive men along the way, but it took a while to get the men in front of a crowd. And during that time, the opposition would whisper in our ears. Should a woman really be leading and speaking out? The Bible says that men are the spiritual leaders of their homes, the teachers of the Scripture. Why listen to a woman? Yet, when I looked into the eyes of my dear husband, Charles, nothing could stop the message that flowed from my heart. His support and love sustained me through the cruelty of many men who spoke out against me, our cause and other women leaders. I never doubted for one moment that Charles was the leader of our home and the impetus behind our work. So I answered the call to speak.

I spoke at a neighboring town, Blissfield, some thirty miles from Raisin. It was there that I had the opportunity to speak to the newly created Blissfield Anti-Slavery Society. They had just formed in 1838, and I was so impressed with the progress they had already made in their Underground activities. Charles and I enjoyed meeting those with common sensibilities as ours. We were able to support their society as they formed. It was here I met a formidable friend for the future, James G. Birney. When Henry Bliss introduced us to James Birney, we knew immediately that Mr. Birney would have a great influence in our government. But I had no idea what a special friend he would become to me years later. Birney was articulate, clear and very supportive of the abolitionist cause. In 1840 and 1844 James Birney ran for President on the new Liberty Party ticket. I knew he would be a great influence for abolitionism.

I would often listen to Charles and our brothers talk politics. I had no patience with the various political theories on the best way to end slavery in our country. I agreed with Elizabeth Chandler's friend, William Lloyd Garrison, who formed the Liberty Party to stop slavery. Garrison proclaimed slavery should end immediately. I wholeheartedly agreed. But then I would hear other positions that were more diplomatic and sophisticated. Many believed that change must come from within the Whig party. We must educate them, and over time they will see the abolitionist way is correct. My question was this. "Who cares about such theories?" There are people suffering simply because of the color of their skin, and the fact that they have been denigrated and disdained for such a long time is appalling! I had no time, nor patience, to talk politics. I wanted to do something, make a difference or provide a refuge for those innocent individuals.

In Blissfield we also met an astute young black man, Prior Foster, along with his parents and two younger brothers. Prior shared, wide-eyed with anticipation his burning passion to start his own school one day. We made arrangements for him to join our school in the fall. Charles and I both encouraged him to get his education at Raisin and follow his dream.

Beginning the third year at the Raisin Institute, life flowed into a steady routine. Prior Foster settled in well, with many friends and an intense desire to complete the teacher education program. As always, the majority of our students were white. Yet, they were gaining a perspective of the injustice and heartache experienced by their classmates with dark skin. These shared upfront and personal their heartaches through the cruelty and bigotry of slaveholders. I could not have asked for a better environment for my children to understand the atrocities of slavery. We were glad to provide a safe refuge for those minds that needed their intelligence and humanity nurtured and protected.

Charles and I were thankful that our children understood that their faith must be put into action. For those students who chose to live in our quarters and participate in our school, our goal was to fill them with the ammunition, a good faith education could provide. Our Underground community also grew in Spirit and truth as we labored together to free slaves from their shackles, hiding them in our homes, sending them safely on their journey with warm clothing, full stomachs and a kind word.

The years seemed to rush by. At the end of our eighth year in the Raisin Institute, I paused to wonder at how fast my little family had grown and how our school had prospered. I guess I should not call it a little family: Harvey, Daniel, Anna, Esther, Joseph, Laura Jane, Almira. . .and then that year, one final treasure – a gift from God, our little Lavina. Charles and I were blessed with eight beautiful children. Lavina was not one we planned or even expected, and yet, her presence in our lives was precious. The baby born in our later years stole our hearts and became a joy for the entire family!

Born in 1844 Lavina had siblings everywhere to "mother" her. My three oldest daughters loved to play with little Lavina, even Almira got in on the "big sister" act. My fondest memories were watching Almira, on tippy toes, feeding her baby sister. At the time we did not realize how important it was for us to cherish each moment; one never does. Thank goodness we had many beautiful memories of our times together as one big, happy family. Thankful for my older girls, who helped put meals on the table and helped provide care for the younger children, my life was not as overwhelming as it would have been without them. Yes, my life sometimes seemed like a dream, one beautiful dream that made me want to pinch myself, and just bask in this glory.

RAISIN INSTITUTE, 1840.

Chapter Seven

The Sorrows of my Heart

My beautiful dream life was to be short lived, and to be displaced by a horrible nightmare. The turbulent waves and tornadic winds of this nightmare obliterated my sweet, peaceful rhythm of life and changed it to a life set on edge, full of turbulent trauma and tragedy. No! Lord, please "NO!"

A nightmare was sent to prepare me for the severe ordeal so near at hand. In this dream I was standing in our front yard, looking eastward, when an angel sitting on a bay horse appeared in the place of the sun's rising. It was coming to earth on some mission, gliding over the tree tops toward our house, where my father, mother, sister Phoebe and Charles, holding little Lavina in his arms, were standing. I started to inform them that an angel was coming to earth on some errand, but his advance was so rapid I lost sight of him. I was speechless.

He stopped in our yard near me and said, "Follow thou me."

"I will," I responded, "as soon as I bid Charles and our family farewell."

The angel assumed a firmer tone, as he said, "Let the dead bury their dead, but follow thou me." At this command I responded, "I will," and followed him to the graveyard, where he left me.

I awoke with that image in my mind and his solemn, voice ringing in my ear. I related the dream, with its clear impression in my mind, to my husband, who replied, "That is a significant dream that I think indicates death. I think we shall be called to part with our infant daughter Lavina. Also, it is quite evident that consumption is fast overcoming Phoebe." Charles continued, "I think, Laura, it would be best to pursue a burying place for our little daughter. In case the Friends refuse us a plain marble slab with her name and date of birth and death in their burying ground, the corner of our orchard would a pleasant place." I silently assented with a nod to his suggestion. After spending a half hour in this conversation, he went out to his work. I prayed for my Savior's hand to lead me in whatever trial it was necessary for me to pass.

Little did I think of the heavier stroke which was first to fall. Charles was seized with a heavy cold, accompanied by a severe cough. He was able to be about the house and barn, giving directions as to outdoor work, and nothing appeared alarming.

I was aroused again by a startling dream of a coffin being brought into our front room by four men and I inquired who was dead.

The answer was, "A connection of yours."

"I want to see him, for that coffin appears to be for a small man."

"He is a small man," was the rejoinder, and "you shall see him." Upon this, the closed coffin was brought to me, and I arose and followed the pall-bearers to the graveyard. People were standing around the open grave to see the coffin lowered; I saw a little child standing on the very edge of the grave opposite to me. I exclaimed, "Do take that child away, for she will cave into the grave after her father!" At that instant the light sand under the child's feet gave way, and as it struck the coffin, the loud, hollow sound awoke me. Trembling, I had the strong impression that I was soon to part with my beloved companion and infant daughter, although both were sweetly sleeping by my side. With these chilling thoughts shaking my whole being to its core, I resorted to prayer for their restoration to health.

The clock struck four, and as I was leaving the bed to light the fire, my husband awoke. He said he had enjoyed the most refreshing sleep he had had since taking this cold, and felt so well he thought he soon should be rid of it. Whenever I spoke, the chattering of my teeth revealed my agitation, and he expressed fear lest I should be ill from a hard chill. Little did he understand the struggles of my troubled heart. Soon Charles's cough returned worse than before. This gave me the opportunity to send for a physician. At length he consented, as he said, to please me. While I went to awaken our son Harvey to go for the doctor, Charles began to experience severe pains in the region of his lungs, cutting every breath.

The doctor was soon with us, but he thought there were no serious symptoms apparent. I sent for Father Haviland, who agreed with the doctor that I was unreasonably troubled. Yet, during the following night Charles expressed doubts of recovery himself and requested his will to be written, which was done. As his fever increased, great effort was made to control our feelings in his presence. At one time when Charles awoke, he discovered my fast-falling tears and comforted me with the words of a poem. "Do not weep for me, my dear wife. *God moves in mysterious ways, His wonders to perform. Do not judge the Lord by feeble sense, but trust him for his grace; behind a frowning providence He hides his smiling face.*"

Charles continued. "Our separation will be short at the longest. Then we shall be reunited where there is no sorrow—no more dying in that glorious home." He called for the children. Looking upon us all, he said, "Oh, how dear thee all are to me!" Calling each by name, he gave advice and exhortations as none but a departing husband and father could leave with his family, a legacy more precious than all the golden treasures of earth. Then he added. "I want each of my children to promise me that thee will meet thy father in heaven. Will thee meet me there?" Taking our little babe in hands, he kissed her and said, "Dear little Lavina will soon be with her father." Struggling, he prayed, "O Lord, I commit my dear wife and children into Thy hands. Thou art the widow's God, and a loving Father to fatherless children."

He raised his hands and repeated, "O, Hallelujah to the Lamb!" His last words were, "Come, Lord Jesus, thy servant is ready," and in spite of the pain, he left us with a sweet smile and happy spirit on March 13, 1845.

Charles's disease was inflammatory erysipelas, at that time entirely new and not understood by our physicians. In the spring of 1845, this epidemic swept through our state. It proved fatal in most cases. My dear mother, who was with us during this week of sorrow, was taken home with the same disease, and in one week her happy spirit took its flight to God who gave it. She had not left us an hour before brother-in-law Daniel Haviland came for me to go to Phoebe, his dying wife, as she was calling for mother. He did not dare inform her that mother had died. I took my little emaciated babe upon a pillow, and went to my dear sister, who was soon to leave us as well. Her first query was, "How is our dear mother?"

"Mama is a happy spirit in heaven," was my reply, "and Phoebe, thee will soon meet her there."

She replied, "It is well, but I had hoped to meet her once more in this world, yet we'll soon meet to part no more." Within one week, Phoebe died in peace. Here was the third wave of sorrow rolling over us.

From this house of mourning, I was removed to my house with the same disease that had taken my husband and mother. My father and father-in-law thought me dangerously ill with chills and fever, with stricture of the lungs that made respiration painful. They were very anxious to have the best help that could be obtained at once. Papa said, "What is done for thee, must be done quickly." I told him that everyone who had been taken with this disease had died, as physicians of each school did not understand it.

But returning home as they suggested, I decided to use a water treatment. I would take a shower-bath every two hours over a twelve hour period of time. This was done, and every bath brought relief to my respiration, and my lungs became entirely free, though my neck and throat were still badly swollen and inflamed. Cold applications, frequently applied, soon overcame that difficulty, and in three days the disease seemed entirely conquered.

Unfortunately, I relapsed from catching a cold and was thrown into a stupor. Aroused by the words of a neighbor, I heard him say. "She is not conscious, and never will be, unless something is done. If she were a sister of mine, a doctor would be here as soon as I could bring him."

"I will see if I can get a response from her," said my brother Harvey, hovering over me.

"Mother, what can we do for thee!" cried my anxious son Harvey.

As I heard their remarks, a strong impression came over me that if I were placed in charge of a physician I should not live two days, but if I could tell them to shower my head and neck often I would recover. As I looked upon the anxious, fatherless children surrounding my bed, I made an effort to speak, but my parched and swollen tongue could not utter a word.

My brother took my hand and asked, "If thee wishes a physician press my hand, or if thee would prefer water treatment move your head on the pillow." I could not move my head in the least, and my only hope was to speak.

When asked if I wished a doctor, I prayed that my tongue might speak for the sake of my fatherless children. I barely squeaked out the word, "No."

Harvey, my brother continued. "Does thee want cold compresses, or shall we gently shower thee with a thin cloth on the swollen and inflamed portion of thy neck and head?"

"Shower," I eeked out.

"Cold or tepid?" Harvey asked.

"Well."

"If thee meant well-water, how much?"

"Big pitcher."

"How often?"

"Twenty minutes." My words were barely audible to my family.

My son Harvey responded, "It shall be done. I will sit by her every minute tonight."

I felt a positive impression that my Heavenly Father had answered my prayer, directly granting a token of assurance for my recovery. I praised the Lord for his loving kindness.

I fell back into a dreamy consciousness while my wishes were faithfully fulfilled by my son and brother. At twelve o'clock I awakened, and inquired where all the people were who had filled the room earlier. I was surprised to learn the hour of night. They said as my breathing became more natural, the neighbors left and the children went to bed. I could speak easily, and the purple appearance of my skin had disappeared. In the morning the pain was entirely gone, but the soreness still severe. With frequent compresses during the day, the swelling subsided.

I wondered why Papa did not come, as he had not been to see me since Phoebe's funeral. My brother informed me that he had taken a chill during the funeral and had not been able to leave home. As he had experienced a few spells of the ague some weeks previously, I supposed he would improve. The day following, Sala returned home and in reply to my inquiry after Papa said he was no better. Papa had sent a request for me to be very careful, and he hoped I would soon recover.

"Sala, tell me more about Papa," I begged.

"Laura, Father has thy same disease and he specifically requested that thee stay home for the sake of thy children.

But I could not be satisfied without going to see my dear Papa once more. Though the pleading of my dear children was overwhelming, I had to go. "If I am rolled in quilts and laid on a bed in the wagon, I am confident I can be taken to Papa's house safely," I assured them. In this way, I was taken to my dying father, though unable to walk across the room without assistance. As soon as he learned of my coming, he directed my sons to place me on a bed until I was rested. A few minutes later they led me to Papa's bedside. Placing his cold purple fingers over my pulse, Papa said.

> "I am glad to see thee, but I fear it is too much for thee to bear. There is a little fever about thee yet. I am more concerned for thee than for the rest of my children, on account of thy large family that will so need their mother's counsel and care. Laura, look to the widow's God for guidance, for wisdom from him is so much needed with the heavy responsibilities now resting upon thee. Do not allow thy bereavements to crush thy feeble frame. I have feared they have already seriously affected thy health."

With other advice, Papa became weary, and said, "Now take her back to the other room and lay her on the bed until she is rested." During the next few hours he frequently sent for me to talk a few minutes at a time. With six of his children present he gave a farewell blessing, leaving bright evidence that all was well with his soul.

Papa said, "In me there is no merit. I am fully trusting in the merit of my crucified Savior, who shed his precious blood for my redemption. I can say with Job, 'I know that my Redeemer lives,' and because he lives, I shall live also." With his last breath, he said, "Here she comes."

With this he left the tabernacle of his body for the building not made with hands, eternal in the heavens. Papa and Mama were lovely in their lives, as well as in their death, only two weeks apart. It seemed that the last of my earthly props were gone. Three weeks later, my baby Lavina followed her father, aunt and grandparents into eternity. Within six weeks, five of my nearest and dearest were taken from me.

Within two miles of our home, not one family was left without having lost at least one or two loved ones from this horrible disease. Such despair and death had not rested upon the community of Raisin before or again during my lifetime as that of the Erysipelas Epidemic of 1845. As the world reeled around me, friends, family members and loved ones from far and near came to offer their condolences, their support and love. We were thankful for Brother Patchin, who completed his teaching assignment that traumatic year even with the overwhelming sadness of losing his wife to the disease.

Our family took hope and courage when our community met us with an ever-increasing desire to support our abolition principles. The Raisin Institute had a strong influence on the consciousness of our community, as well as on the students who were benefitting from our exceptional teachers and education. This gave me cause to praise God in the midst of all of my sorrows. God was my source of comfort and strength during this terrible time of sorrow. I had to rely upon God's support for the double-load of responsibilities and indebtedness that became my lot.

Still reeling from my sweet baby Lavina's death and my slow recuperation from illness, I sat down with pen on paper and calculated all the expenses for our farm and home needs and their coinciding due dates. My mind reeled when I realized our income was only half of what was needed by the coming fall. As my heart sank, I methodically began to do the only thing I knew to do. I made visits calling on each of our creditors, sharing with them my situation. Then, an extraordinary miracle took place. None of these creditors were concerned or wanted the money I could not supply. I was exhausted, but incredibly thrilled by God's provision and the burden He had taken from my shoulders through dear friends and business leaders.

Yet, there were some tough times as well. As I visited with Mr. Davies, a grain salesman, he bluntly asked, "You're not seriously considering continuing on with your husband's business, are you, Mrs. Haviland?"

"I thought of doing the best I can with it," I calmly replied.

"Well, I'm sorry, Mrs. Haviland. You will be sadly mistaken if you try to assume this venture alone. You need to appoint a trusted man who can handle your business transactions on your behalf."

"Mr. Davies, I have seven children at home and seven hundred dollars of debt. How could I ever afford to hire an agent to work on my behalf? Good Day."

Marching out of the grain operations office, my hands were trembling. I knew deep within that Mr. Davies was probably right. I had no idea how to operate my husband's farm. I had no knowledge of dealing with my husband's business. Mr. Davies had not meant to be unkind, but I felt my overwhelming sadness return, only to be compounded by a deeply broken heart.

One lone creditor remained to be appeased, Mr. J.B. Lane from Palmyra. I had written to him stating that I could pay half of what was owed him, forty dollars. He made a call on me a few days later, saying he had received my letter and that my terms were completely unacceptable. Though I explained my situation over and over, Mr. J.B. Lane responded. "Sorry, Mrs. Haviland, it shan't be any other way. I have a debt that must be paid at the same time yours is due. I have no choice but to either accept full payment or come and reclaim my equipment."

I could see there was no use in continuing to plea or make different arrangements. Once again my inability to negotiate in a man's world of business dashed my hopes. I had no idea where to turn for these problems. Everyone I knew, family and friends, were trying to survive these hard times. I wanted to do the proper thing, yet I felt completely overcome and overwhelmed by the enormity of my situation.

As I fell asleep that night, doubt loomed over my spirit, and the heaviness of my burdened heart ached within my bones. But I resolved to pray to the widow's God. I had searched the Scriptures in my time of devotion and had found such a precious promise in Isaiah 54.

> Fear not; for thou shalt not be ashamed: neither be thou confounded; for thou shalt not be put to shame: for thou shalt forget the shame of thy youth, and shalt not remember the reproach of thy widowhood any more. For thy Maker is thine husband; the LORD of hosts is his name; and thy Redeemer the Holy One of Israel; The God of the whole earth shall he be called.For the LORD hath called thee as a woman forsaken and grieved in spirit, and a wife of youth, when thou wast refused, saith thy God. For a small moment have I forsaken thee; but with great mercies will I gather thee (Isaiah 54:4-7)

Clutching to a strand of hope in this promise, my heart ached as I drifted to sleep. It was there in the middle of the night that once again God spoke to me in one of those dreams that I had come to dread. Yet, this time my dream was surprisingly peaceful. I experienced comfort from God's angels, and when I awakened, I felt only bliss and joy.

Several days following this peaceful experience, Mr. J.B. Lane visited my home once again. My first thought was dreadful. Then I quietly remembered the Savior's care.

After our greeting and sharing of niceties, I initiated, "Mr. Lane, I suppose thee is here about the claim thee has against me."

"Yes, that's right," Lane countered. "I have come to inform you that your debt has been postponed!"

"Postponed?" I replied in complete astonishment.

"Yes," Mr. Lane said. "I will not need any money from you this fall, and perhaps I will only need half of your debt the following year."

"But- but. . ." I stammered and stuttered, "How can this be?"

"Well, Ma'am, you see, I have just received one hundred dollars that I had supposed was lost and gone forever. So, as I have been blessed, I wanted to return the favor to you. As I was within a few miles of your home, I wanted to stop and let you know."

Thanking him repeatedly for his kindness, I also thanked the One who alone can melt mountains of impossibilities. While this might seem a small matter to some, I greatly rejoiced at the unexpected turn of affairs. As the sole provider for a large family and the Raisin Institute, I sold 40 acres of my 160 acres of land. This met most of our pressing demands. Often I would reflect on the admonition of Mr. Davies when my burdens were heavy and, at times, crushing. Just when I thought I might falter, the Great Provider would intercede.

The greatest tug on my heart was for my children. I prayed they would be guided along the right path in life, in the midst of the many slippery paths that all youth have to face. My children never ceased to surprise me as one by one they traveled the road of discipleship following our Savior. Once again the passage of Isaiah 54 provided precious promises for me, "All your children shall be taught by the Lord, and great will be thy children shall be taught by the Lord, and great will be they children's peace," (Isaiah 54:13).

June 1846, brought great occasions for celebration, the marriage of my oldest son, Harvey, and the marriage of my daughter, Esther, in a beautiful double wedding. Through tears of joy, my greatest hope was that these children of mine had found great happiness through marriage, the doubling of joys and the dividing of sorrows.

In spite of our great sadness, fugitive slaves continued to find their way into our home and community. One such fugitive refugee, George Taylor, worked for us through the 1846 seasons of harvest and hay-making. His presence kept my heart and attention on the plight of runaway slaves. George, an honest Christian man, made his escape from his Southern master, who was preparing to sell him farther down the river. He had made an attempt at freedom once before but had been unsuccessful. When caught he was shackled in iron chains that pressed deep sores around his ankles. Acting badly crippled, George played the role of a submissive slave who was unable to move quickly. Before long he was considered to be safe. I sat mesmerized as George shared his story. "I'se rubbed this asafetida gel on my ankles to keep the bloodhouns away, and I's made my big break. . .followin' the Northern star, until I'se reached yer home, Missus Haviland."

George's story was so astounding because his ankles were still unhealed. . . .but while hiding in the woods the first two days of his escape, he had succeeded in breaking his irons with a stone. While nursing his ankles, I began to consider a change of roles in my anti-slavery work. George's plight touched me deeply, and appealed to my heart so completely, that I resolved to assertively assist slaves in their flight to freedom.

Chapter Eight

Life Goes On – At Gunpoint!

Just as quietly and unobtrusively as our friends the Hamiltons left our farm, so they returned to their ten acres and old log house built several years earlier. They returned a few short months following Charles's death to lend me a helping hand. Thankful for their support, little did I know that I would be the one to lend them a helping hand. Nothing prepared us for the adventure that was soon to enter our lives.

After the Hamiltons many travels through the Underground, a friend wrote a letter on their behalf to their old friend Deacon Bayliss (Willis's ex-master who had freed him) making inquiry of their two daughters still in slavery. The Hamiltons had ached for years to find them. They received a prompt reply from Bayliss. He was thrilled to hear from them and wanted to know everything about them. Being wisely advised, they kept their whereabouts secret. Willis asked Bayliss to use his return address, and it would be forwarded to them as they were on the move.

Shortly after they arrived back at our home, another letter arrived from Deacon Bayliss. Willis and Elsie urged me to reply. I refused. Their pleas grew stronger and their desire to make this connection seemed unbearable. Several weeks had passed since they first asked for help. Once again they returned with their same persistent pleas for me to write a letter on their behalf to Deacon Bayliss. I remained unflinching. I lovingly reminded them of a slave family who had lived twenty years in freedom and had recently been recaptured and returned into a miserable, hopeless bondage. I adamantly refused to write to anyone who lived in slave state. I advised that they needed to find a safer means of information regarding their daughters.

Realizing that I was not going to change my mind, they turned to our good friend, J.F. Dolbeare, an esteemed trustee of the Raisin Institute. Dolbeare, not realizing the grave danger, wrote the letter on their behalf, sharing their past history, desires and plans for the future. They kept this a secret from me for some time, until Elsie heard of my dream.

Yes, another strange dream, this one was about three poisonous green viper snakes which had popped out near a fire. I poked them so close to the fire that their sacks burned to a crisp and all of the poison ran out. Though they seemed powerless, I could still hear their hissing and see their threatening heads pop out at me. Elsie, after hearing of my dream, feared greatly that these three snakes might be three slaveholders!

Elsie forced Willis to tell me about the letter. He finally confessed that he had wanted to tell me sooner. Instantly I was concerned and felt grave about their imminent danger. I knew their actions could generate severe repercussions. I chose not to chastise or criticize them. Instead, I simply said, "We will just hope and pray for the best!"

A few days later a stranger appeared at our gate with an inquiry regarding a stray horse that had gotten away at Tecumseh. Finding no help at our place, he traveled on to the Hamiltons's with the same inquiry. The stranger asked for a glass of water and for directions. "Auntie," he asked sipping his water. "Where does this road lead that crosses the river east?" Trying to veil her fear and fright at being called 'Auntie' in the Southern style, Elsie responded "to Palmyra." Quickly she retreated into her home.

Three days later, Willis Hamilton received an urgent note from his old friend, the deacon John Bayliss. The note informed Willis that he had come to Ohio on business and had taken seriously ill. He begged Willis, Elsie and the little girls to come and care for him at the Toledo Hotel during his critical illness. His occasional visits from the doctor gave him little hope of recovery. In closing, Bayliss penned these words with a shaky hand.

> Whether I get better or die, I am resigned and can say the Lord's will be done. I shall have every train watched until you come. God bless you. Respectfully yours, JOHN BAYLISS.

Comparing this letter to the handwriting of the first, it was immediately evident to me that both letters had been written by the same hand. I gave Willis a stern lecture for the utmost caution in this matter. Then I exclaimed, "I smell a rat!"

Willis made an immediate plea on behalf of his old boss: "Oh! I know the old boss too well, he's true as steel. He won't have nothing to do with trap business. I've got my free papers and I'm not afraid to go, but I won't take Elsie or the kids." Elsie, unlike Willis who had been freed, was the escaped slave of John P. Chester. Chester still held the two older Hamilton daughters in his grip.

I immediately opposed his idea of making the trip to Toledo. My son, Daniel and I were just leaving for a trip to Adrian, and Willis had almost talked me out of my rational concerns, when Joseph Gibbons, our neighbor, joined the conversation and reinforced my fears, persuading Willis to stay home. Instead, he suggested that our James Martin (now a young man), who was about Willis's color and size, go in his place.

After all parties agreed to the plan, Willis gave me the three dollars sent for the fare, and James, Daniel and I left in our wagon for Adrian. We barely made it in time to catch the train. Once settled on the train I began to realize the absurdity of this. My heart cried out to God for wisdom. I desperately needed Him. I prayed for God's guiding hand to direct and protect us if we found ourselves within the enemy's camp, face to face with the traffickers of human souls and bodies!

Arriving in Toledo, James was immediately flagged down and addressed by the porter of the Toledo Hotel. "Is your name Willis Hamilton? Is your wife with you?"

"No, sir," said James.

"Perhaps I am mistaken. But. . ." the porter's voice trailed off.

"Who do you wish to see?" asked James.

"Willis Hamilton. His friend John Bayliss, who is dying at the hotel, is expecting him."

"Where is this Mr. Bayliss from?" asked James.

"Tennessee, I believe."

"Very well, if there is such a man here, I want to see him."

"Come with me, and I'll take you to his room," said the porter.

Daniel and I were close behind as we entered the hotel, but we tried to appear oblivious of them. Our plan was for Daniel to keep a close watch on James and to report to me immediately any news. As expected, I was shown into the parlor, while the men went up a flight of stairs to the bar-room. Daniel was following when the porter suddenly turned and said, "The bar-room for gentlemen is below. I am taking this man to see a friend who is very sick. No strangers are allowed." The porter closed the doors abruptly behind them, leaving my son alone in the upstairs hallway.

James was taken from room to room through the dimly lit hotel hallway in search of the "sick deacon." As each door opened, there was no sick patient only a dark, empty room

At one stop the porter commanded James to enter. James countered, "Sir, there's no one in this room. I'm not going in." By this time Martin completely distrusted his guide. He thought about making his escape down the stairway and into the parlor where we were waiting, but he decided he should at least discover as much as he could about this suspicious crew.

At the moment he wanted to bolt down the stairs, three other men suddenly appeared. The porter disappeared while the three surrounded him, and each butted a revolver into his side cursing and threatening him. One of these was John Chester, Elsie's master, who threatened. "If you stir, speak or even breathe one word, we will kill you. Get into this room or you're a dead man!" In this deadly light, they pushed him in the room and locked the door. "Now, Hamilton, damn you, we've got you!"

"James Martin is my name, not Hamilton," our young James's asserted confidently, shaking in his boots.

"Damn you," rejoined Chester, "I know you. You were once a slave in Tennessee."

"No sir, I never was a slave, nor was I ever in a slave state. I was born and brought up in the state of New York."

Grabbing James and turning him around by the nape of the neck, he pointed the gun at his head. Chester swore, "Then you're a damned spy, and I've got a great mind to shoot you this minute."

Hearing his heart palpitations throb louder than the voice of his captor, James donned dramatic survival skills and retorted back. "If you call me a spy because I came here to see Mr. John Bayliss for Mr. Hamilton, then you can do so, for this is why I am here. I came with no intention of harming anyone, I am entirely unarmed. I have not so much as a penknife with which to defend myself, but I tell you, gentlemen, I have friends here in this house."

At this two of them dropped their weapons as though they had been shot. Chester exclaimed, "You shan't be hurt! You shan't be hurt!" Then he yelled at his son, "Tom, put up your pistol!"

"No," said Tom. "I'm going to search him for weapons."

"No, you shan't do it. I reckon it's as he says."

James recognized that these slaveholders were thoroughly intimidated, which gave him a minute to catch his breath. The Southerners, of course, did not know but that a posse of armed men were waiting outside for him instead of one little woman and a lad of seventeen.

John Chester addressed James in a subdued tone and manner, asking him to sit down. He said, "I'll tell you all about it. Mr. John Bayliss is here and he is very sick. He is not expected to live. But I am Elsie's master. My name is John P. Chester. I bought her out of pure benevolence to save her from going down the river with a drove. Willis was going from house to house begging for someone to buy his wife, crying like he was nearly crazy. I felt sorry for him, and told him if he would help me buy her by paying three hundred dollars in work for me, I could do it. He entered into a written agreement with me that I would feed and clothe him the same as my other servants and give him a good price for his work. Before he had been with me a year, he took my property and ran away with it. I want it back."

"Why don't you go and get it, then?" asked James.

"Oh, there's such a set of damned abolitionists there, I can't do it," said Chester. "Hamilton wrote to me that he put in ten acres of wheat this fall on shares of a widow lady's farm, and that he owned a yoke of oxen, two cows, pigs and chickens."

"Yes," said James, "that is all true."

"Well," said John Chester, "you can have all he has there, besides whatever amount of money you name, if you will assist me in getting Hamilton and his family here. Will you do it?"

James replied, very recklessly, "Well, I don't know? How much money are we talking about? I might help you for enough."

"You see," said Chester, "if I can get them here, I can find my way through Ohio, and when I strike Kentucky I'll be all right." Two hours were consumed in planning and making arrangements for this great heist when the porter of the hotel burst into the room with the immediate demand for James Martin to report to his people in the hotel.

Meanwhile, Daniel and I waited those two agonizing hours in the parlor. It seemed an interminable amount of time. Daniel requested the presence of James Martin twice. Finally, the porter said, "Yes, yes, of course, you shall see him soon." But thereafter he kept out of our sight.

Finally, my son stood up to his full height and said to a hotel worker. "If our young friend is not forthcoming at once, a writ of habeas corpus will be served on him. We must see him immediately! We also insist that you inform Mr. Woodward, the proprietor, that my mother has a message for Mr. John Bayliss, whom we understand is here and desperately ill!"

Mr. Woodward summoned the porter and minced no words. "Bring this young colored man here now. Otherwise, there is trouble ahead! Tell them to send him down at once." Who knows what would have happened had we not sent that writ of habeas corpus?

In less than a minute, the porter, three men and James appeared in the Victorian hallway. The haggard appearance of the three in such an elegant hotel was unbecoming. This stark contrast was even more noticeable when the voices of twenty chattering, half-drunken Irishmen suddenly were silenced. One could have heard a pin drop at the sight of this black man visiting with the other men, free and unfettered. The slaveholders had earlier devised a plan that Willis Hamilton was to be in chains in the hallway, when all of these Irishmen were to surround and force him into a closed carriage. Willis was to have been sent away. The sight of this motley crew of drunken Irishmen called into question the intelligence of the plan and those assigned to carry it out.

Yet it was James Martin, our actor, taking the situation into his own hands. He gave my son a pinch and said, "Mr. Haviland, let's go into the dining room and call for supper." This gave him the air of freedom and independence while at the same time gave the drunken riff raff time to retreat from the bar. As they walked into the dining room, the porter asked me if I still wished to meet with Mr. Bayliss.

"Absolutely!" I replied.

"Well, he is too sick to be disturbed, but his doctor is here and I think he could speak with you if that would prove helpful to you." The porter continued.

"It would," I said.

A tall gentleman entered the room and addressed me. "Madam, are you the lady who wishes to see me?

"Yes, I am. I presume thee is the physician of John Bayliss of Tennessee?"

Bowing politely, the tall man said, "I am."

After a few pleasantries and parleys, I asked him. "How long has Deacon Bayliss been so ill?"

The doctor replied, "Almost seven days, madam."

"What is his prognosis, Dr. Taylor?"

"It's hard to say, Mrs. Haviland. At first it was just a violent attack of stomach flu with a high fever. But for the last three days, I fear it has taken the form of typhus."

"Well, Dr. Taylor, Willis and Elsie Hamilton are both very concerned for their old friend. They asked me to personally come and give their reasons for not appearing themselves."

Dr. Taylor replied, "It seems rough to think the dying request of a poor old man cannot be granted. He seems to consider this family almost next to his own. He's so disappointed they did not come."

"Yes, I'm sure," I sympathized.

Dr. Taylor continued. "Mrs. Haviland, do you think that you could persuade the Hamiltons to come and visit him? He possibly has three days at best."

"Thee has spoken like a candid man, so allow me to return the candor. I cannot unless thee allows me to see him."

At this, my tender-hearted Aesculapius sighed deeply and said, "Well, I am so very sorry that anyone would entertain such distrust. Bayliss may not survive longer than three days, and he may not survive twenty-four hours."

I replied, "Well, of course, we are not aware of any specific plan to recapture the Hamiltons, but one cannot be too careful with this slippery issue. We were just thinking about possibilities. It is quite an important cause to me."

I began to wax eloquently regarding the death grip of slavery:

> I would not for one second want to be instrumental in returning one escaped slave into bondage. I believe firmly in the Golden Rule and in our Declaration of Independence that all men are created equal and free. Therefore, no human on the face of the earth has a right to own or make merchandise of another perhaps born in humbler beginnings. It is even worse in my opinion to treat humans on the same level as stock animals. Why should one human sell another, knocking them off the auction block to the highest bidder; and in the

process separating families in an offense to the purest and most tender feelings that God has given. These wicked actions of men go against the laws of eternal rights given by our God and our Lord and Savior Jesus Christ, who made of one blood all nations who dwell on earth. Christ's work done on the earth stands in stark contrast to the atrocities of slavery. He left the glory above to bring blessings to all. Part of that mission is to loosen the heavy burdens and let the oppressed go free. There, there I go! Now, I've gone to preaching.

"No, no. That's all right. . .I respect your feelings," Doctor Taylor remarked.

Slavery is the greatest curse in our otherwise happy country. But Mrs. Haviland, I assure you there is no cause for your fear. There is NO conspiracy here to recapture or cause harm to your colored friends. I do hope that for the sake of their dear friend Deacon Bayliss, they will rethink their decision and come visit him, satisfying his one dying request. Allow me to consult with his son. Perhaps if you promise to remain quiet and not disturb Bayliss, he will allow it. But of course, he is under the influence of strong opiates, in a heavy stupor and certainly is in no condition to talk with anyone tonight. Mrs. Haviland, would that work for you?

"Well, it makes no difference to me. But I think it might satisfy the Hamilton family," I replied as my voice dropped off.

In a few minutes the good doctor returned saying that an agreement had been reached, as long as no loud word or sound of footfall was heard in the room. To this I agreed, and Dr. Taylor tried to prepare me for the sight I was to see. He said, "You won't be able to see the poor man. The Deacon's face is covered with wet vinegar cloths to draw out the fever," Taylor commented, "He is in such a deep doze and I do not want to disturb him." Dr. Taylor described the nervous, spastic behavior suffered by this patient. It had taken four men to hold him down while a small service was held earlier, eulogizing Deacon Bayliss for his Christian patience and fortitude.

Leading me into the room the doctor halted, but I stepped on into the center of the room, as if I had forgotten that I was merely to enter. There across the empty-looking hotel room lie the dying Deacon Bayliss.

Dr. Taylor stepped to my side and said, "That is he on the bed yonder."

Taking a mental inventory for a moment I recognized immediately that this Deacon Bayliss was a good six feet tall and slender, not at all the description I had been given by Willis of a short, heavyset John Bayliss, two hundred pounds. Smirking inwardly, I recalled many a sick person who had lost weight during illness, yet never known a soul whose illness created a growth spurt. As the wet cloth covered his face, I could not see it directly, but passing my hand over his face, I found it to have long and thin features.

I whispered to the doctor, "I'd like to take his pulse."

He whispered back, "Use the jugular vein." I did so and found the skin of the fever-stricken man to be quite normal.

"Dr. Taylor," I continued to whisper, "I'm used to taking the pulse on the wrist." After some resistance from the dying man, I found his wrist and my suspicions proved to be fact. The man's pulse was a full, strong, regular pulse of a well man. In that second I had no doubt in my mind that I was alone at the midnight hour, far from home, in a room with the three snakes from my dream, alas—three slaveholders.

Sketch by Marlene Lofgren

Stepping away from the bed, the doctor asked me if I was satisfied. In that moment, I meekly replied, "Yes, I am."

Suddenly, the son stepped in, rubbing his eyes, and asked, "Doctor, do you think father is any better?"

"Son, I cannot conscientiously give you any hope." the doctor sympathized.

Whining, the son continued, "Oh dear! What shall I do? I'm almost sick myself from caring for father night and day. If I had only known that day, near Tecumseh, that the Hamiltons were near, perhaps I could have seen them and invited them myself. I had so hoped that father would have been better when I returned, instead he is so much worse."

Gazing through the darkness of the hotel into this man's eyes, I stepped forward and asked the son, "Art thou the gentleman who was inquiring for a horse in our neighborhood a few days ago?"

"Why, yes," he replied.

I gushed. "Thee was at the Hamiltons's home, and Elsie gave thee a drink of water."

"What?" the younger man responded. "Do you mean the place where that black woman brought me a drink?"

"Yes," I bantered back. "That was Elsie, Hamilton's wife."

"Really? Can that be possible?" He incredulously asked. "Do you mean that little log house where the pumpkins were piled up in the yard?"

"Yes, that's it." I remarked smugly.

"Oh, if I had only known it, they could be here right now helping us! What bad luck we have had. I reckon father will die, and I shall have to go home alone. God knows what an awful trip this has been," the son moaned.

Dr. Taylor ushered us out of the room for fear we would disturb his patient. But first he pointed to a white bowl of black bilious vomit. Peering into the bowl it appeared to be the contents of a coffee pot with a bottle of black ink poured in and a few spittles floating on top for good measure. Once outside the room, he said. "Now, Madam Haviland, as I can see you are fully satisfied, isn't there something you can do to get the Hamilton family here?"

"Certainly, I am willing to do anything in my power to help. What more can I do?" I emphatically queried. "I will inform them of these state of affairs when I return to Adrian on the morning train."

"Ah yes, but perhaps you could write a letter to the Hamiltons to come immediately. These were the son's wishes. What do you say?" Dr. Taylor suggested.

The two had hired the porter to deliver the letter for ten dollars, and the son would send another ten dollars for Willis to come with his family.

"Dr. Taylor," I resisted. "I think my plan best, as the road through the cottonwood swamp to Raisin is most likely impassable."

But they were not to be budged. The son paced the floor, sighing, groaning and bemoaning his dire calamity, and suddenly he selfishly demanded, "Father wishes the letter to be written."

The doctor went in search of writing utensils and the door was closed behind me.

Suddenly Daniel burst into the room excitedly, whispering, "Don't write, mother, there is no sick man here. That tall man is Elsie's master, and they held James at gunpoint all of that time we were waiting for him." Daniel was concerned that since I knew nothing of James's experience that somehow the slaveholders had won my affections.

"Shhh, Daniel!" I hushed him. "I know there is no sick man here, but they do not think I dream of a plot. It is now midnight, and it is unwise to let them think that we don't trust them. Sit down and talk with me as though nothing is wrong."

Soon Dr. Taylor returned with the writing utensils needed. I sat down to write while he visited with Daniel about the weather, farming and the economy. Knowing they were watching my every move, I cheerfully wrote each word dictated, not omitting a single fact. I handed the letter to Dr. Taylor and Bayliss's son to read. After sensing their satisfaction, I added, "Oh, I need to add just a few lines of my own. Elsie will not be prepared with sufficient clothing for such a long trip, and I can easily loan her the needed garments."

"Indeed, ma'am. That is very kind of you. They can get ready much more quickly," Bayliss's son replied.

So, I added at the bottom of the page: "Elsie, take my black alpaca dress in the south bedroom, and the two pink gingham aprons and striped flannel dresses in the bureau in the west room for the little girls. To come to Adrian, take the double team and farm wagon. Affectionately, Laura." I handed the letter to the delighted son.

After an exhausting time at the Toledo Hotel, we were escorted by candle light to the Indiana House. Before James had finished his story, the night watchman reported that three men were pacing around our hotel who he suspected to be thieves. We spent a few hours trying to sleep in spite of all the excitement of the night. Yet, the morning light would reveal that these suspected thieves were actually our three Southern slaveholders.

A few minutes before we left our hotel for the morning train, an abolitionist man of color approached James. Quite excitedly he said, "We have just heard there is a colored man here having trouble with slaveholders. If it's true, there are enough here to take care of the trouble makers. We'll do whatever is necessary."

Stepping forward and taking him aside, I replied. "There is trouble." Giving him a brief sketch of James's experience, I told him I felt we would be safe during daylight, yet we would appreciate any support possible at the depot.

He said, "We will be watching very carefully at the depot. Whatever you need from us, madam, we will do it."

In the morning light I immediately recognized my pious doctor friend, his son; and then the other, a tall, slender young man of twenty-two, was, no doubt, the sick and suffering deacon. Their object in guarding the house was to see that we sent no messenger to defeat the letter I had so kindly written for them.

Our three Southerners were at the depot as we expected. Poor James felt sick and decided not to take the train, as it looked as though they intended to go with us.

I dissented, "James, thee must go with us. There is no other train until late tonight. There's no telling what they might do under the cover of darkness."

As Daniel and I boarded the train, trouble surrounded us on all sides. The three jumped aboard and were determined to sit with us. The young ailing deacon was right by my side. Following Daniel and I from coach to coach, I caught view of his snake eyes and I jumped off the train to find James, whom I was sure had not yet boarded.

Daniel called out to me, "Mother, where art thou going? This is our car."

"Yes," I replied, "but I see a lady up in the next car that I wish to sit beside."

At this the young Southerner exclaimed, "I'll be damned if I don't get to that seat first."

Daniel frantically raced his way to the car ahead and breathlessly reached the seat first. In the process he noticed the loaded gun from inside the pocket of the young snake-eyed Southerner flash his direction. Thankfully, there were so many trying to board this particular rail car that our young adversary was pushed aside. The sick deacon limped away, cursing and yelling behind him. "We're not through with you yet, Mrs. Haviland!"

During all of this excitement I suddenly remembered that our newly found Toledo friends were watching our every move from a distance and standing by to protect us. So I beckoned the man who had called on us at the hotel and asked him to summon James to our railcar immediately. Thanking him, I also asked him to share our sincere thanks with his group of abolitionist friends as well.

James jumped onto our car as the train began to move. When inside he excitedly spoke, "I'm afraid we've got trouble." At that moment the conductor passed by, and I asked him, "Sir, will we be perfectly safe here, should we have trouble on our way to Adrian?"

"Most certainly!" the conductor responded. "I will vouch for the protection and safety of every person on board this train."

Ten miles down the road at our first stop near Sylvania, the train halted to sand the track, and to our consternation, once again our Southern slaveholders boarded and stood in front of us. The elder Chester, pointing to James, growled out. "We'll see you alone sometime," and turning to my son, "You, too, young man!" Then, directing his anger towards me, he roared out: "You nigger stealer, you've got my property; I'll show you, you nigger thief!"

Drawing his revolver from his pocket, with his son doing the same, two revolvers were pointed towards my face. "Do you see these sophisticated tools? We have more of 'em here," holding up a traveling bag, "and we know how to use them. We'll be here for about three weeks. Before we leave, we will have our property that you have in your possession! You DAMNED NIGGER STEALER!"

Perhaps it was the element of surprise or because of the prayer on my lips, but I was simply stunned by my own quiet, calm resolved reply.

"Man, I fear neither thy weapons nor thy threats. They are powerless! Thou are not at home in Tennessee. And as for thy property, I have none of it about me or on my premises."

Pale and trembling with rage, they still shook their pistols in my face, and Chester, in a choked voice, stuttered, "I-I'll-I won't say much more to you—you're a woman—but that young black man of yours, I'll give him five hundred dollars if he'll go to Kentucky with me."

The conductor appeared, to our relief, and called out. "What are you doing here, you villainous scoundrels? Stop! You are under arrest! Just give me a minute to flag down our law man."

At this the three Southerners fled the train car, disappearing into the woods, and the last we saw of these scoundrels from the land of chivalry were the heels of their feet receding into the thicket like snakes.

I and my two male companions became instant celebrities. We answered innumerable questions all the way to Adrian. Though we were terribly fatigued from our escapades to Toledo and back, we told the story over and over.

Among the people of Sylvania, the news spread like wildfire, and it was reported that over forty men were at the depot with hand-spikes and iron bars, ready to tear up the track in case the Hamilton family had been captured on the train.

Thank goodness we finally arrived at Adrian. My son Harvey and Willis were there to meet us.

Daniel spoke first. "Willis, thy old friend, Deacon Bayliss was not present!"

"No?" Willis questioned wide-eyed.

"No!" Daniel exclaimed. "Less than an hour ago, Elsie's taskmaster and his posse held us, including our dear Mother, at gunpoint!"

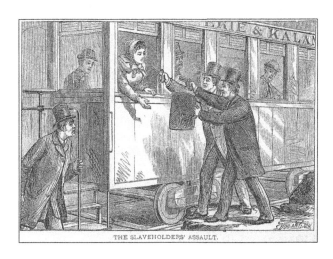

THE SLAVEHOLDERS' ASSAULT.

James exclaimed with animated gestures, "Yes, they pointed their pistols at our heads and threatened our lives!"

I had to interject. "Poor James was the victim of their brutality twice in one trip."

I wished everyone could have seen Willis's face at that moment. Willis could hardly speak from disbelief and sadness. "Oh, Missus Haviland, I'se so sorry we put ye all in this danger."

People who heard the news began to press around us. Harvey tried to guide us away from the crowd.

Harvey filled us in on the happenings while we were gone. He said my letter arrived before sunrise, but that no one believed I had anything to do with it. However, as the porter swore he saw me write it, Professor Patchin and J. F. Dolbeare were called. They also distrusted its validity and truthfulness.

Elsie had no faith in it at all. "If," said she, "the old man is so very sick, as he hasn't seen us for years, they could bring him any black man and woman, and call them Willis and Elsie, and he'd never know the difference. As for the letter, Mrs. Haviland never saw it. I believe the slave-holders wrote it themselves. They thought as she was a widow she'd have a black dress, and you know she hasn't got one in the house. And where's the pink aprons and green striped dresses? And there's no south bedroom in this house. It's all humbug! I shan't stir a step until I see Mrs. Haviland."

I had to chuckle to myself, as I knew Elsie would respond in just that manner. My confidence that the letter would fail to fulfill the mission the three slaveholders desired had been fulfilled.

The porter, seeing he could not get the family to respond, offered Willis ten dollars if he would go to Palmyra with him, but he refused. He then offered it to Harvey if he would take Willis to Palmyra.

"No Sir! I shall take him nowhere but to Adrian to meet Mother!" was Harvey's reply. What an annoyance the porter had become, following Harvey and Willis to the Adrian depot. He again offered the ten dollars, while Lawyer Perkins and those close by advised Harvey to just take it and give it to Willis.

When I came on the scene the porter was still looming around, listening to every word. He heard me say, "Don't touch the money that has been offered!" I continued to explain the letter's code, at which everyone in earshot erupted in laughter. The porter heard the threatening remarks of the people, who declared anyone attempting to harm the Hamilton family would have trouble on their hands. Finally realizing that he was not welcome, the porter left us.

We went home thanking God that public sentiment had made it too difficult to allow unprincipled and avaricious men to cast our persecuted neighbors back into the seething cauldron of American slavery. Our home swarmed with neighbors and visitors eager to hear the story that was spreading like wildfire throughout the community. At midnight I finally had to send friends home saying, "I am thoroughly exhausted—never have I been so fatigued from talking—but tomorrow on the Sabbath evening, I will share the whole story in the Raisin Valley Schoolhouse (It was the largest gathering place for our community in that day).

The following evening found the Raisin Valley Schoolhouse with standing room only and people listening at the windows. One onlooker reported that a spy for the slaveholders was listening just outside one of the windows. I shared the whole story, not leaving out a single detail. Elijah Brownell, one of Raisin Valley's best anti-slavery lecturers, gave a few spirited comments at the end. He suggested that a collection be taken in order to defray our roundtrip expenses of the Toledo trip. By the end of the night, fourteen dollars were placed in my hands.

We later discovered through a mailman from Toledo, a friend of our letter-carrier, that the slaveholders had planned to capture, gag and bind the Hamilton family, traveling through the night and hiding them from one point to the next until they reached Kentucky. These were the same plans they had shared with James Martin. We also learned that the Chesters discovered the Hamiltons were in Michigan because John Chester was the postmaster at Jonesborough, Tennessee. In that role he intercepted the letter that Willis had mailed to John Bayliss, just as I had feared. Chester suspected that it might contain information about his former slaves, and thus the whole plot of assuming the character of John Bayliss was born. We thanked God that none of these plans were successful!

The citizens of Adrian continued to meet on a regular basis to take measures that would secure the safety of the Hamiltons and other such families from the grasp of slaveholders. They had me return and retell our story. It was incredulous that the Chesters's plans were so deeply laid, and that they were audacious enough to come after not only Elsie and her children, but Willis, who was a well-known free man. Their concern to take precautions for the safety of the Hamiltons warmed my heart.

One cannot help but shiver in fear at the iron grasp of the oppressor whose strength and power serve the cause of evil. The public excitement was so great that our chivalrous, slaveholding trio from the South found our Northern climate a little too warm for their liking. They fled to the milder climate of Tennessee with as great speed as Elsie and Willis fled from there fifteen years earlier.

Over the next few years, I received threatening letters from John and Thomas Chester. I have chosen to share a few extracts from one of these written by Thomas Chester.

> It is unpleasant for me speak abuses to a woman. I would not do it now, if I did not feel in perfect conscience that it is my right and duty in the matter. You are a thief, a robber of man's just rights recognized by the glorious Constitution of our Union. Why would I engage in a contest with you? A damnable thief, a Negro thief, a criminal in the sight of all honest men. . .the mother of a son who is a pussy, who permitted me to curse and damn you to your face at the train in Ohio. I would rather be caught with another man's sheep on my back than to engage in such a subject and with such a damned nigger-steal as old Laura Haviland.
>
> Tell Elsie that since our return my father bought her eldest daughter. She is now his property, and the mother of a likely boy that I call Daniel Haviland after your pretty son. She has plenty to eat and shoes to wear in the winter, an article Willis's children had not when I was there, although it was cold enough to freeze the horns off of a cow. . .What do you think your portion will be at the great day of judgment? I think it will be the inner temple of hell!

In my letter dated March 16, 1847 to Thomas Chester, I informed him that he and his father's putrid words outmatched even the black, bilious great disease that he and his father shared with me in the sick room of the Toledo Hotel. I also stated, "We thank thee for the namesake. May Daniel possess the wisdom of Daniel of old, although his lot will be cast in the lion's den. May he, like Moses, be instrumental in leading his people away from a worse bondage than that of Egypt."

I must admit that I pitied the young man, whose intense, bitter hatred had made him incorrigible. He was a "chip off the old block," blinded by the brutal lie that enslaving another human being could somehow be a just cause. I tried to give him some good advice, although it is obvious that I yielded a bit to the temptation of irony and sarcasm.

A correspondence came from Thomas Chester while I was out of town; but as it was addressed to Esq. Laura Haviland or Daniel, Daniel opened it and found it to be so full of foul and abusive language that he passed it to our school administrator. Rev. Patchin was so indignant that he took it upon himself and sent a reply on my behalf. It started like this:

> Sir, As John Quincy Adams and Henry Clay were seated in Congress, they saw passing on the street a drove of jackasses. Said Henry Clay, 'There, Sir, Adams, is a company of your constituents as they come from the North.' Adams quick reply was. 'All right, they are going South to teach yours.' I personally think one of those long-eared animals has strayed down your way. Mr. Chester, had your ma sent you to his school, even for a short time of instruction, your epistolary correspondences with Mrs. Haviland would have been vastly improved.

Upon my return home, Daniel shared Patchin's response with me. Patchin said, "that rabid fire-eater has been treated in a manner too mild. He needs a dose of his own medicine." What we did not know until later was that Rev. Patchin had sent another acrimonious letter. We were told in Chester's next correspondence that Laura Jane was said to have written the letter as I dictated it.

Shortly thereafter, I received just a few short lines from Thomas Chester, informing me that he had copied my last letter and circulated it in a number of Southern States. Neither I nor Laura Jane ever saw the letter that we had supposedly signed. We learned later from many reliable sources that a reward for $3,000 was attached to the circular. Rev. Patchin, who wanted to end the unpleasant correspondence once and for all, had no idea that he was creating a greater controversy. For years I continued to travel throughout the Southern states with the status of a "wanted" woman, a wild abolitionist with a $3,000 bounty on my head! Never in my peace-loving Quaker days would I have ever dreamed that such a status be given to me, a meek and mild woman of the faith.

Chapter Nine

Cincinnati Underground – John & Jane White

At age 38, widowed with seven beautiful children who could care for one another, I began to seek God's guidance for my future. There was no need or time to feel sorry for myself. Like Job of old, I was blessed by God. I am also told that I have become somewhat of a local celebrity. Why should doing the right thing make anyone a celebrity? Yet one sad reality haunted me. My children had simple human privileges that those of black slave children couldn't even imagine. A still small voice whispered in my heart, "Thy children are not in danger of being beaten and demoralized and sold away from thee." I asked, "Lord, what can I, one lone woman, do to help these in terrible need?"

In the fall of 1847, Mr. J.L. Smith, who claimed to be an Ohio schoolteacher, arrived on my doorstep. "Hello, Ma'am. I'm J.L. Smith. Are you Laura Haviland?"

"Yes," I replied.

"I've heard about your delightful school. Would you have a few minutes to give me a tour?" he continued.

Distrusting his cultured appearance, I replied. "Sorry, Mr. Smith, I don't have much time today; I'm on my way to care for my neighbor's infant baby."

Continuing on I said, "If thee needs a boarding house, there's one two miles south of here."

"I see," he smirked with an air of arrogance. "Well, Mrs. Haviland, I also work for *The National Era*."

"That is a reputable and well-respected periodical," I replied with no emotion.

"Yes, and you run a reputable and well-respected school here. I was hoping that perhaps you could give me a tour. For such a favor, I could give you a great deal on a subscription to my paper," Smith pitched.

"No, Thank thee. I already have a subscription to a good abolitionist paper," I said, trying to avoid the sales pitch.

"Yes," he responded, looking at a periodical on my buffet. "I can see you are a *New Nation* kind of subscriber. Mrs. Haviland, your reputation as an abolitionist with the Underground Railroad is well known." Smith smoozed. Flaunting the names of stations and agents, he intimated that he knew that the Indiana and Ohio Underground routes were being detoured through Michigan. He spoke of five slaveholders lying wait in Toledo, Ohio, to recapture their escaped slaves.

He had my attention now. I decided I must discover the motives of this so-called Mr. Smith, deciding that these five slaveholders might be part of his group. So, I calmly replied. "Perhaps I could give thee a short tour of our school before running to my neighbor's home."

"Thank you for your kindness, Mrs. Haviland. Could I beg of you a bowl of bread and milk as well? I had no time for breakfast this fine morning," My guest asked, taking control of my time.

While eating, he began to probe me about the refugees that traveled through our station. I shared with him our acclaimed story of the Tennessee slaveholders and the Hamiltons, as well as the wonderful community support that protected our refugees and assisted many to Canada. I watched his face astutely.

He began to argue. "Mrs. Haviland, the law is on the slaveholder's side. The honorable Judge Ross Wilkins will issue papers to force those of you hiding slaves to return their property to the judge in Detroit, and a trial date will follow."

I laughed aloud at this absurdity, "That will never happen in this community. Before a posse can arrive, the refugees will be safely moving to freedom's shore!"

Suddenly, it dawned on me. The scheme of our Mr. Smith must be to capture one of our freed men! The only one it could possibly be was John White from Kentucky.

Mr. Smith's short tour had taken more than an hour's time, and the Raisin school administrators, Professor Patchin and J.F. Dolbeare, became concerned and wanted to send Mr. Smith on his way. But thinking better of it, I allowed him to visit classes in Latin and Geometry, as Mr. Smith said his favorite class was mathematics. During this time, one of our Raisin students set our Underground warning system into action, riding into Jackson County to inform Mr. Watkins and warn John White of the impending danger.

Mr. Smith quickly organized his posse after leaving the Raisin Institute. White's slave owner, George Brazier, had hired Smith and several other lowlife gunmen from a local saloon to recapture White. Smith was tipped off by a boy along the road that John White was working for Mr. Watkins in Jackson County.

By the next morning Smith's posse drew up to Mr. Watkins property. There was no John White. Enraged, they accosted Mr. Watkins outside of his home with their foul language and surly questioning of White's whereabouts.

Mr. Watkins calmly responded, "I suppose he is in Canada, as I took him and his trunk to the depot yesterday for that country."

George Brazier cursed, "That damned old abolitionist, Laura Haviland!"

Mr. Watkins informed the men, "Mrs. Haviland has not been here. There are many other individuals who gladly took a stand to support Mr. White's freedom. He is greatly esteemed in our community."

The Kentucky posse continued to curse my name and make personal threats of bodily harm, so much that Mr. Watkins warned the men, "There is a law to arrest and take care of men who make such threats. I'd be mighty careful if I were you!"

The Kentucky gang left for Tecumseh, four miles from Adrian, where they caroused at Snell's Hotel, displaying their table pistols, dirks and bowie-knives. Brazier pointed to them and boasted, "We'll have the life of that damned abolitionist, Mrs. Haviland, before we leave Michigan."

The five men jumped a stage to Adrian. Receiving word through a note delivered from Judge Stacy of Tecumseh regarding these men's evil intent, I asked the messenger to keep it quiet. I did not want to worry my children or anyone at the school.

In spite of this, the word spread quickly. Four young male students were placed outside my home to keep watch. I was ordered to keep my windows closed. Others encouraged me to take a trip to Canada. "No," I said, "I will not run or change course from my original plans." Not to say that my knees didn't knock now and then listening for strange sounds at my window, but I would drop to my knees knowing the great Protector was by my side.

I learned that the posse had finally left the area after several inquiries had been made by Mr. Smith regarding my land and property. When Smith was satisfied I was the sole owner, he had made arrangements to serve a warrant for my arrest in the following fall if Mr. Brazier had not recovered his slave, John White.

I decided that I needed to see the atrocities of slavery firsthand, rather than hearing of it second handed through my work in the Underground. I wanted to travel into Kentucky, posing as a berry picker, to find the whereabouts of John

White's wife and family. I heard that John White was growing more anxious about finding his wife and children. Many, including John himself, had raised money for my journey. Before heading into Kentucky on this dangerous expedition, I was encouraged to stop in Cincinnati and meet with dear friends and leaders of the Underground Railroad Movement, Levi and Catherine Coffin.

At our meeting in Mr. Coffin's private parlor, the plan was conceived to travel to Rising Sun and meet with Jane White, John's wife. Working with mutual friends, the Berkshires and Edgertons, I would make the connection. Jane White was owned by Benjamin Stevens, and another one of Steven's slaves, Solomon, crossed the river every Saturday on his master's business. The plan was to slip a note to Jane through Solomon.

Unfortunately, Solomon didn't cross the river on that designated Saturday. Our plan failed. We were disappointed, but not daunted. We moved to our next plan. Mary Edgerton and I would travel to the Stevens's vineyard to buy some plums. Mary had white skin; though partly African, it was not obvious to the naked eye. I played the role of an aunt who everyone knew was planning to visit. I looked so much like Mary's mother; it was easy to pass as her aunt.

When we pulled into the Stevens family plantation, Mary introduced me to Jane White as Aunt Smith. They ushered us into the basement, which served as the kitchen for the Stevens house. Benjamin Stevens was considered a very kind master. Surrounding planters boasted that the "Stevens's niggers believed they were white." Creating a mental picture in my mind, this was the first slave dining area I had encountered, and I wanted to soak in every detail.

> There on the bare table, made of two long, rough boards on crossed legs, was a large pitcher with a broken top. It was filled with as much sour milk as the cracked pitcher would allow. There were

corn dodgers spread out at convenient distances across the table, a saucer of greens and a small piece of pork cut in thin slices. These were all divided among the twelve men and women slaves who sat on broken chairs. Everyone sat on the edge of their seat. All of their utensils and earthen vessels, dishes and plates were broken. Not one whole plate or dish was in sight. Yet the crew ate with zest, and as there were not enough utensils, each shared a fork or knife without any thought of disdain or disgust.

Nan, one of the house slaves informed us, "Sorry, there are no plums for sale today."

"Oh!" Mary quickly regrouped and replied, "We would be willing to buy blackberries instead if they are available."

Nan ran quickly to ask Miss Agnes, the lady of the house, if she and Jane might show us the way to the blackberry patch. Returning, she said, "Jane, why don't you go? I need to make another batch of jam for supper. But Miss Agnes says we must first serve these ladies dinner."

A tablecloth was placed over one end of the table, and the sister slaves brought wheat bread and butter, honey and a cream-pitcher of sweet milk. None of the nine little children asked for a taste of our food, and all that was left was taken upstairs.

We were invited to call upon Miss Agnes Stevens, who welcomed us cordially. She had to show us that she was teaching Jane's seven-year-old daughter how to sew. After these pleasantries, we left to gather blackberries.

When alone, I disclosed to Jane. "I am the one who wrote you a letter from your husband."

Jane confided, "I never received it. It was snatched away. But I was given a lock of John's hair tied with a blue ribbon that had been enclosed in the letter. My master told me John has remarried and is happily riding around smiling with his new wife." She suddenly burst into a flood of tears.

Comforting her, I said. "I assure thee just the opposite is true. John wants thee to come with the children. Thee can accompany his friend William Allen, who also plans to make an escape with his family."

Jane stopped crying and even forced a smile to her face. She admitted, "I would gladly work day and night, until my fingers and toes are without a nail, and willingly see my children work in the same way, if we could only be with John."

She paused for a while and then said, "Mrs. Haviland, ask John to wait two months and come when all of the children will be back together. Right now the two oldest are working in the home of Stevens's son."

"Of course I will relay your message," I promised. Jane was completely shaken and her face red from the tears. I was afraid her mistress, Miss Agnes, would be upset at our length of absence. Hastily we worked together to pick the blackberries.

My heart was distraught and disturbed over the lot of this poor woman and her children. It was appalling to think this cruel taskmaster Benjamin Stevens was considered one of the best slaveholders! I gave Jane a little memento from her beloved John, and found it difficult to leave this poor, heartbroken, crushed spirit. Here was a woman and sister whose widowhood was more desolate than even death had made my own, and her poor children were worse than fatherless.

The journey home to my anxious children and friends passed quickly. Sharing my findings and the fate of these poor slaves was eye opening for all of us. John was encouraged, and confident that William Allen would make the great escape if he only knew how many warm, kind friends there are in the North to assist him. He begged me to return. After a short three month stay at home, I headed back to Rising Sun. There I waited a short while for William Allen to find me.

Not making the connection with Allen, I decided to make a call at his master's home. Taking a boat I sailed four miles below on the Kentucky side and called at the house of his master under the ruse of waiting for another boat going up the river. As I had been ushered into the parlor and left to read the paper, I intermittently conversed with the woman of the house. Not realizing that there had been great excitement over counterfeiter abolitionists such as myself, she had called the sheriff and deputy to discreetly study my demeanor. I overheard their whispers in the hallway.

"That lady is no counterfeiter, I tell you," one claimed. That was the defining moment I realized I truly was the object of their concern and conversation. Shortly thereafter, the sheriff entered and we shared pleasantries.

"Good afternoon, Madam." The sheriff bowed, courteously removing his hat.

"Good afternoon," I replied politely.

The sheriff declared, "It's certainly a great day to travel."

"It certainly is, sheriff. Yet I'm hoping I will not have to wait long for the next boat." I confided.

"I hope it goes well for you, Madam. Good-day," He concluded.

"Good-day," I replied and continued reading the paper.

I heard the sheriff confirm, "There's no reason to suspect this woman. She's all right."

Concluding I probably would not see William Allen, I excused myself and headed to the boat. The hostess insisted, however, that I stay for dinner, as I would have plenty of time to meet my evening boat. She pointed out a path across a pasture that would shorten my half-mile walk. Acquiescing, I left after dinner following their path. Just as I stepped out of view from the house, there he was, William Allen, his wife and ten-year-old daughter. I recognized them instantly. They were exactly as John had described.

Delivering John's message, they were thrilled to hear from their old friend. William requested, "Sister Haviland, continue on to Berkshires and in two weeks I will bring a plan of escape for Jane. Right now any travel is difficult because of the counterfeit scare."

I replied, "Friend, it is not safe to talk longer." I gave them a parting handshake, sharing with them that the sincere prayers of many Christian people in the North were daily lifted up for their safety and deliverance.

William responded, "May God grant the answer!"

As the weeks passed, I received distressing news from my home. Harvey, my eldest son, was extremely ill. Before I could board a boat to go home, I received a second letter informing me of my dear son, Harvey's death. Reeling from this devastating news, I wanted to immediately return home. But I had acquired a suspicious cough and had been advised to wait for milder weather. I waited in agony for weeks, during which I had found solace in a dream. Harvey appeared to me and said, "Mother, I'm home here in heaven. Do not worry. Keep up thy good work!" His words brought me great comfort. I was also thankful for the kind words and support of dear friends through this time of great distress and grief.

Having waited as long as I could, I made the sad trip home to Michigan to finally gain some closure over my son's death. Harvey had been the one to urge me take this trip. When my other children worried about my welfare because of my fragile state, Harvey insisted that I would be safe because my presence was so inconspicuous. Daniel, my second born, said, "Mother is a stranger to fear though she might be in great danger." Harvey calmly replied, "That seems to me to secure her safety."

We had lived through so much death, and not so long ago. Now, to lose my firstborn son Harvey brought such great sadness. I was relieved to find that Harvey had left me great spiritual assurances and had simply slipped asleep into the arms of Jesus. I spent time with all of my children, embracing them and catching up with all of the important things happening in their lives while home.

The opportunity had not been ripe for William Allen to cross over to give Jane the message, and sadly I had to "let go" of my assistance in reuniting John and Jane White. Unfortunately, John decided to take matters in own hands. John, himself, made the trip with a friend to rescue his beloved wife and children. The White's had a passionate, wonderful reunion. If only it could have lasted, but alas, it was short-lived.

John, Jane and the children made their break on the Indiana side of Rising Sun just a few short miles away from Stevens Kentucky plantation. They hid in the woods during the days. With the aid of Solomon, they built a raft in which they could cross a creek to reach their team on the opposite side. Suddenly, out of nowhere, six armed men pounced on them, capturing John's family and Solomon. From a distance White's friend held him fast in the thicket in order to save John's life against an impossible struggle. Finally, John fell into his arms in despair, having risked life and limb for a losing battle.

John cried bitterly in despair after his loved ones were recaptured. Later, John learned that his master, George Brazier, swore he would chop him into pieces if he ever had the opportunity to do so. He offered a $600 reward for John, dead or alive. Sadly, Benjamin Stevens had made a similar cruel offer of $600 for his own slave daughter Jane White and his five grandchildren and Solomon. Yes, Jane was Steven's daughter! Later, Stevens sold all of his grandchildren for the price of $1,000, with the provision that they were not to be separated. But poor Jane did not live long enough to grieve over her disappointed hopes. She died of cholera shortly after being captured.

Heartbroken beyond belief, John White headed north. Thinking that he had entered into a fugitive-friendly territory, he headed to the home of a Quaker family who lived forty miles from his old home in Kentucky. John settled in under the assumed name of James Armstrong. His plans were awry again as the famous bounty hunter, Ray Wright, and posse captured him, mounted him on a horse and pulled him across fields and back roads. Crossing the Ohio River he was dumped in the Woodford jail, a short distance from the river, directly across from Madison, Indiana.

Wright dug through White's papers and found the want ad of an escaped slave, Henry Armstrong, belonging to the widow Armstrong of Maysville, Kentucky. Wright immediately scheduled an interview with the widow hoping to obtain his reward. She was completely uninterested, as Armstrong would be willed free at her death, and as he had been gone so long she believed he would be of little use.

Not wanting to lose his investment in the captured slave, Wright approached John and asked him if he might have friends in Michigan who would aid him with $400 to ensure his release. Thus, it happened that a scratch letter containing the scrawl of John White made it to our place. He had sent it to the son-in-law of Mr. Watkins, one of our neighbors, so as not to implicate any of us who had assisted him in the past.

Once again because of the anti-slavery efforts in Adrian, I found myself in Levi Coffin's parlor in Cincinnati, consulting his counsel on the best way to assist our imprisoned friend John White. Coffin's nephew, Micah White, agreed to be our advocate for John, and Dr. Judkins was our beneficiary for the money. We had instructed Micah to negotiate a lesser amount if possible. I urged Micah to do his business and get on the first boat for Madison to ensure John White's safety. Whatever was done must be done quickly. Ray was willing to accept $350. The money was placed in the hands of the boat clerk until White was delivered to his friends in Cincinnati. Micah White was our witness to the payoff for Mr. Ray. The day after John's release, George Brazier showed up at the Woodford jail to claim his property, as he had been told White was there, only to be informed White had been released less than twenty-four hours earlier. Just a few months later, Brazier traveled to Baton Rouge, LA, with a group of slaves for sale. He, too, died thereafter from cholera, thus my homestead was safe from George Brazier.

Three weeks later I returned home with John White by my side. "Time stands still for no one," as the old adage goes. John married a young woman in Canada where they settled for several years having children. Later, they moved to Ann Arbor, Michigan, where he educated his children and was joyously reunited with some of his freed slave children by Jane. I was excited to hear that the eldest daughter married Solomon, after both had been freed. Brighter days were beginning to dawn. Thanks be to God!

Chapter Ten

George & Eliza Harris

Levi and Katherine Coffin became dear friends and invited me to Cincinnati to serve alongside them in the Underground Railroad there. Living in their home I worked at nursing in order to pay my bills. We were too busy to keep track of the number of slaves aided or assisted into Canada. The numbers never mattered. Our goal was to snatch up as many persecuted souls as possible from the snares of slavery and move them to freedom.

George and Eliza Harris, a couple I had the privilege of assisting, became household names in Harriet Beecher Stowe's *Uncle Tom's Cabin.* I first met George and another runaway slave, James, in the basement of the Zion Baptist Church where I had taken their measurements to find suitable clothing. After securing a summer suit for both of the men, I quickly moved them to a safe hiding place, where they remained until our Underground team could move them on to a Quaker settlement eighty miles north of Cincinnati. James moved as quickly as possible into Canada, but George stayed in the country for several months unbeknownst to us all.

After earning eighty dollars over the course of a year, George began to create a secretly devised scheme. Traveling back to Kentucky in the darkness of night,

George revealed himself and his plan to his slave wife, Eliza. He gave her the full story of all the kind friends who had paid him good wages for his hard work. He told her of the promise of freedom and the opportunities that were available to them if they would faithfully follow his plan. Eliza agreed, and the two of them lived out this incredibly well-constructed drama in front of their masters and the entire community.

This is how it is to play out, George told Eliza.

> I will go back to my master, give him the money, tell him I's sick of my freedom and beg him to take me back. Then I'll say, 'Eliza mus' be mighty mad,' he went on, 'case I come back; and say, 'If he's a mind to make sich a fool of his self, as to be so julus, case I talked leetle while wid Jake, long time ago, as to run off an' leave. He needn't think I'll take 'im back. I won't have nothin' to say to 'im, never!' And I'll quarrel 'bout you too, an'when all ov 'em is done fussin' 'bout me comin' back, I'll steal to you in a dark night, an' lay a plan to meet on Lickin' River; an' we'll take a skiff an' muffle oars till we get to the Ohio, an' I knows jus' whar to go in any dark night, an' we'll be free together. I didn't tell Jim I's gwine to make massa b'leve all my lies to get you; for I tell you Liz, I ain't got whole freedom without you.

And that's exactly how it happened. George's master believed him. He spoke with pride to his neighbors about his Tom coming home, returning the money he had earned. But George's neighbors were not convinced. The surrounding neighbors wanted nothing to do with George. They warned George's master and said they didn't want him near their slaves or on their property. But George's master was completely persuaded, and he totally believed in his honesty.

His master boasted, "George came back perfectly disgusted with abolitionists. He said they will work a fellow half to death for low wages. And I have found the reason why he left. He and Liz had a quarrel, and now he don't care a fig about her. I heard yesterday that her master says she'll shoot him if he dares to come on his plantation. But he needn't worry, for you couldn't hire George to go near Liz."

So George's master confided in him that all of the area planters did not trust him. They believed George would make a liar out of him yet.

"I'll stay at home, then, and won't even go out to meetin's, till all ov 'em will see I means what I says," George emphasized.

"That's right, Tom. They don't know you like I do. But I told them t'would do all the niggers good just to hear your story about the meanness of abolitionists. Wasn't that just what I told you? They pretend to be your friends, but they are your worst enemies."

"Yes, massa, I al'us bleved you, and if Liz hadn't cut up the way she did I never'd tried 'em."

The plan was going smoothly. George became a model slave. His master constantly praised him for his diligent and faithful performance. George always put his master's interests above his own, and after three months of this outstanding behavior even his neighbors began to allow him on their premises to attend gatherings with their own slaves. But George carefully waited for his master's prompting and suggestions before taking on these events. He was never gone for more than a day. He visited with the neighboring white folks about his trip up North, and he always told the same story that he had given his master.

Before long George's stories had been told far and wide among both blacks and whites. He had quite a reputation, a pet missionary, so to speak. Lizzie's master finally believed George's conversion to be true and sent the hound home that had been kept on hand to drive George away.

There was a good eight miles between their homes, and George and Lizzie hardly ever saw each other. They did have a special dispatch through whom they sent messages.

One day Lizzie found a bundle of George's clothing that included a Sunday suit, which he had left in her cabin before he ran away to the North. Lizzie, carrying the bundle of clothes into the parlor to her mistress sitting by the master and asked,

"Missus, what'll I do wid dese ole close Tom lef, when he get mad an' run'd off to spite me. Now, I' burn 'em up or giv' 'em to de pigs for nes', I ain's gwine to hav' 'em in my way no longer."

"Oh, don't burn them. Can't you send him word to come and get them?" Her mistress asked.

"I sends 'im no word, if he never gets 'em, I'd heap better giv' 'em to de hogs."

Her mistress turned to another servant and asked, "Will you tell Page's Jim to have George come and take his trunk away, unless he wants Liz to pitch his clothes in the fire!"

George was in no hurry. He shrugged off the message and said, "One Saturday evenin' I went to have my las' quarrel with Lizzie. I called her bad names, an' she flung back mean names, an' twitted me with runnin' away to make her feel bad, when she didn't care a picayune for me; and' I tole her I never wanted to see her face agin, an' we almos' cum to blows."

Months later George got permission to visit his aunt six miles in the other direction from Lizzies' home, and Lizzie got permission to visit her friends five miles in the opposite direction of George's house. This was the plan. Both George and Lizzie would travel in the direction each had told their masters' they were going, and then both would head for Licking River.

Lizzie went up the river, while George travelled down the river until they met. George grabbed the first skiff with oars he could find, and they beat it down to the Ohio River. They made great time as they traveled during the night. When dawn broke they had to hide their skiff and oars in separate places, a distance one from the other, in case one or the other was taken. They hid deeper into the woods in a place where they could watch their craft through the thicket. To their dismay a group of boys found their skiff, and while not finding the oars, made due with makeshift poles. Lizzie and George held their breath and prayed not to be discovered while the boys were hunting for the oars, breathing a sigh of relief when the boys pushed out of sight. After nightfall, when all was still, the two surfaced and searched for two hours before finding a smaller, harder to manage skiff. Still, they reached the Ohio River at sunrise.

On the opposite side of the Licking River two men called out, "Where are you going?"

"To market, sir," George replied.

"What have you got?"

"Butter an' eggs, sir"

George saw the two pushing a skiff in their direction. Seized by fear he was terrified they would be overtaken. George rowed with all of his might and would not look back until he crossed the middle of the river. He saw that the men had given up their pursuit and had almost returned to their starting point. George told us later, "Lizzie wuz tremblin' so hard her overcoat shook." Lizzie replied, "I reckon you shook just as hard as I did when you was pullin' for life. I specs you sent fear clear down into them paddles you's sweatin' over."

This called for a round of laughter, as freedom was close at hand.

George had no fear once he made it into the basement of Zion Baptist Church, his old hiding place. I was told that a couple had just arrived. Walking through the basement I didn't see a soul. Newcomers were often so shy and fearful.

Then I heard a voice from the next room say, "Come right on in, Mrs. Haviland, we are not afraid of you." As the fugitive clasped my hand in both of his, I exclaimed, "Where hast thee seen me to know my name?"

"Don't you 'member Jim and George? You giv' us full suits of clothing las' summer. You giv' me the linen pants an' blue checked gingham coat and straw hat, an' you giv' Jim thin pants and coat and palm-leaf hat. Don't you remember we went out in a market-wagon to a Quaker settlement?"

"Yes, but why is thee here again?"

"It was for this little woman I came back."

Our vigilance committee decided that George and Eliza, along with another slave, Sara, and her little boy, should go to my Michigan home with me. Sarah, a woman of Christian character and intelligence, was a beautiful octoroon, and an excellent house servant. She received good wages, living with a quiet Christian family. In spite of this, she found that she was to be sold away from her little boy. Because she was considered a "fancy girl," attractive in appearance and worth more because of it, her Christian owner would sell her out. Brokenhearted and knowing the fate that would await her upon such a sale, she made a "run for it." Never looking back, she did not stop or risk her liberty until she had travelled over one hundred miles from her old home.

We received a few more refugees on this journey. It always amazed me how runaway slaves could find us. From a Virginia southbound steamer, we received another mulatto woman and her teenage daughter. The owner/captain of our boat sent a young man, Lloyd, our way. In order to avoid suspicion, we received all of these individuals at different points throughout the journey. Levi Coffin caught up with us before we reached the third bridge with a young man, William, who was a future Underground Operator.

The instructions I gave everyone was to be discreet as follows: "Don't tell a soul of going further than Toledo, Ohio, and say nothing further back than Cincinnati. Do nothing to stand out in the crowd." However, my instructions were not always heeded. Here are a few examples in point.

George, pointing to the telegraph wire, explained to Eliza what it was. Jumping frantically as though she had just seen her master, we were very fortunate that there were no strangers in sight as her movement could have betrayed us. George continued to explain to her that these wires were harmless and that operators at each end transmitted messages and information over them. Yet, she was not to be consoled until George asked me to confirm his explanation. Poor Eliza!

Then the day before we were to reach Toledo, one of our ship's crew left and the captain employed our boy William. Before I realized it, he was steering our craft and taken in as a crew member. Unfortunately, he began to speak freely answering personal questions. He disclosed that he was from Vicksburg, Mississippi, and continued wagging his tongue to the point of sharing his master's name. Our party became quite frightened as the crew had practically adopted the boy, and none in our party were able to get a message to him. The next afternoon a shower burst drenched William while he was steering the craft. The crew came to his rescue and even gave him clothing with the ship's insignia. I could not find a way to get a message to William without being very obvious. I, like Eliza whom we had teased earlier, began to fear the power of those telegraph wires!

Thank goodness William came to his senses and recognized the error of his ways. On the guise of running an errand, he came searching for me and found me sitting on the deck alone. "Oh, Mrs. Haviland," he lamented. "I have failed our mission. I have told these men everything about myself. Now, what shall I do?"

"William, I have a plan." But even I wasn't sure what it was until it rolled off of my tongue. "We will arrive in Toledo within three hours. This is what thee needs to do. Stay behind on the boat with Lloyd. When I leave with our party, the ladies and George, I will leave my shawl on deck. Once they are in a safe place I will return for the two of thee on the pretense of retrieving my shawl. Thee both must stay on the boat and out of sight." William nodded in agreement and ran off concerned that he might get caught talking with me.

The plan worked. As I returned for the shawl, I kept circling so that the boys could spot me and keep me in sight. As the crew was relaxing, laughing and slapping one another on the back, I boarded the boat to get my shawl. Staying on the boat until the crew had gone on shore and entered a saloon across from the dock, I signaled for William and Lloyd. They followed me at a safe distance.

Thankful for abolitionist friends in Toledo we were safe. I had enough funds for the six fares to Detroit, but needed to secure the remaining funds for the fares to Canada. Leaving two from our party in Toledo, I sent the rest of our party on ahead to the boat. Due to the generosity of friends, I arrived at our boat with the needed funds and five minutes to spare before our morning sail time.

Still concerned that William could be in danger, I began to relax a little when we made it to the middle of the river. There was always that chance that yesterday's crew could have sent a telegram to William's master, and that we could be stopped by officers in Detroit. Once we could see the other side of the river, I said to Eliza, "There it is, the place thee has been hoping to reach – Canada!"

"No!" Eliza cried out. "It isn't, is it?" with a trace of hope and awe trailing off in her voice.

"It is certainly. It is a place where no slave-owner can claim a slave!"

Eliza ran shouting the good news to George. He didn't believe her, nor did any of the others in our traveling party!

Running up to me one by one, each asked, "That ain't Canada, is it?"

"Yes, my friends, this is the land of freedom for each one of thee," I said with a smile.

Silence reigned and tears of joy began to fall as they gazed upon the shore of what would be their new home, a "place of refuge." The final minutes passed quickly, and as they stepped out onto "free" ground, they began to jump and leap for joy. This truly was all I needed to see. It was a rich payment and the only reward I needed for my efforts and care. Though Jake and George carried guns just in case there was an attempt to capture them, they need not have been concerned. I left this happy party in their new-found freedom, handing each one fifty cents.

Chapter Eleven

Maria's Free!

Maria's dramatic flight to freedom while I was serving with Levi and Katherine Coffin in Cincinnati happened something like this.

For two years, the Champlins, a New Orleans plantation owner and his family, had been planning a summer trip to Cincinnati. The Champlins always traveled with their slave nurse Maria. Her job was the care of the children, night and day.

Maria and her husband realized that this could be their great break for freedom to Canada. They had been saving all of their silver pieces and had accumulated $100, which would provide for Maria's boat fare into Canada. Her husband would sneak onto a boat and meet her there. He wanted her to keep the money, as she would need it, and he could get by on little. The money was wrapped securely, tied in a little rag and hidden in Maria's clothes in the trunk along with the children's clothes. Maria had no fear for her money as her mistress never so much as peeked into this trunk.

In Louisville Mr. Champlin was warned they would lose their slave girl if they stayed in Cincinnati, as the word was the "city is cursed with free Negroes and abolitionists." So instead the Champlins stayed in Covington, KY, just across the river. This put a damper on Maria's plans and she was greatly disappointed. Even worse, as she was setting up the children's wardrobes, she discovered that her mistress had gone through her trunk and stolen her treasured $100! Obviously, the warning had caused Mrs. Champlin to examine the trunks, and finding the money, she kept it. Maria was devastated. She put on a brave face pretending nothing was wrong, all the while heartbroken that her only hope for freedom had just been snatched away from her.

After a few days, Maria said to her mistress, "Mrs. Champlin, ma'am, you will not believe how much cheaper shoes are here than back home. Look at these shoes of mine, they're coming apart at the seams, I was wondering if you might give me fifty cents in order to purchase a new pair."

"Do you need new shoes? Yes, Maria, I guess you're right. Why don't you allow me to pick up a pair of shoes for you? If I forget, I'll give you money in a few days."

When neither shoes nor money arrived after three weeks, Maria again dared to venture her request.

Rudely Mrs. Champlin replied, "Maria, I think your shoes are good enough for a while yet."

One of Maria's favorite tasks was to walk the children to the river. There they played, picked up pebbles and watched the boats while their parents were gone. Maria would tearfully and longingly gaze across the river thinking her own sad thoughts. Unbeknownst to her, she had been noticed by a white man, who one day stopped and asked her if she wanted to cross the river.

Hesitatingly she responded, "O, tank ye, but it don't mate' e'en if I did, I hav' no mony to pay far a far'."

During their short conversation she shared her plight telling him that her master was from New Orleans.

Sympathizing with her sad situation, he said, "Ma'am if you promise to never tell a soul, that I'm the one who helped you, I'll take you across tonight without a penny. But if anyone should find out I would be ruined." Maria exuberantly promised, and while the three children were off at a distance the two made their plans.

He told her, "Hide under this large root on the bank. You must wait until you hear a low whistle, then come out and step into my skiff. Don't say a word. I will muffle the oars so they won't be heard."

"O tank ye," Maria whispered, breathless at the plan. "But where wil' I go whin we git acros?"

"I know a very nice colored family on the other side. They will keep you safe, and then send you on your way to Canada."

"O that's wonderf'l! I promis' I wan't til a soul." Maria thanked him ecstatically. "But how can I go' on, whin I's got no mon'y?" She kept thinking of questions.

"They know of a way to send such people as you without money. You'll be connected to those who will see you safe to Canada. Never fear!"

Maria shared this account with me after we met.

I never can tell you how strange I felt about sich good news as this, and wondered if it could be true. I jus' trimbled like a popple leaf all the evenin'. Master and missus was over in the city to a lecture on Fernology, and didn't get back till twelve o' clock. I ke'p the chillen awake later'n common, so they'd sleep sounder. Then I tied my clothes up in a tight bundle, an' had my shoes an' hat whar I'd lay han's on 'em, an' put out the light. I was snoring', when missus looked in an' said, 'All's asleep-all right;' an' I waited till the clock struck one, an' all still. I cre' sof'ly out on the street, and down to the root, an' waited for a whistle. The clock struck two. O, how long! Will that man come? Chillen may cry, an' missus fin' me gone. Had I better wait till it's three o'clock? May be he can't come. He said, if anything happen he couldn't come to-night, I mus' go back, an' try another night. Jus' as I began to think I better go back there come the whistle. I stepped in, an' we went over, but the clock struck three before we got half across, an' he was mighty fear'd he couldn't get back afore daybreak.

The news reached our Cincinnati Underground that a woman had crossed the river early in the morning, and she was too close to the river to be safe. Once it was dark and the night could shield us from Champlin and his slave hunters, the lot fell to me to lead her to a place of safety.

Grabbing a black Quaker bonnet, a plain dress-skirt and a drab shawl, I met Maria in a dark room, where I dressed her in my disguise. She was worried about her lack of funds and told me the story of her $100 loss. I took her by the arm and said,

"Hush, child. Thee won't need any money while thee is with us. Now make haste. Hang on to me and limp. Thee must limp all the way. There are plenty of Kentuckian slave-bounty hunters along our path. We've got a long walk."

Disguised under all my Quaker wraps, we walked taking short corners to dismiss suspicion. We had travelled almost half a mile up Central Avenue to Longworth when we passed through a throng of men, one of whom said,

"I'm going to line my pockets to-night. Thar's a $500 reward out."

Another said, in a low tone, "When did she cross?"

"Last night some time, they say."

I could feel Maria's limping body trembling by my side, and with good cause, after passing so closely by her pursuers. My Quaker sister was still trembling when I left her with the kind Burgess family on Longworth Street.

I felt confident that I had left her in a good spot with true friends until Levi Coffin said "Ruffian, the most greatly feared slave-hunter in the city, just moved next door to the Burgess family."

Instantly, I began to tremble and my fear was almost equal to Maria's.

"Laura, thou hast left thy fugitive with a good family, but in a poor place," said my venerable friend.

"Wait until to-morrow evening, when thee can move her to a safer place."

The next evening before the trip I decided Maria needed to look more "white" through her veil, given the lighted streets. So, with a saucer of flour in hand, I powdered Maria's face thoroughly. She happened to look up into the large mirror, caught a glimpse of herself and laughed aloud. I instinctively put my hand over her mouth and gave her a little shake.

"Don't laugh aloud, for pity's sake, or better yet for thy liberty's sake. Remember the next door neighbor will get his $1,000 reward from Champlin if he finds thee here."

"I won't look at that glass ag'in, but I looks so qua'nt," Maria whispered.

"Hush child!" I chided lovingly. "Now stay in time with me."

Maria and I walked back to Central Avenue, meeting Levi and another friend of ours, Hughes. They walked a half block ahead of us and turned on Ninth St. to Hughes's house. There his sister Catherine hung a white cloth on the second story balcony. We took the outside steps to the fourth floor leading to the attic.

Maria had to remain there for two weeks, not daring a move while the bloodhounds and slave hunters of the New Orlean's plantation owner were everywhere throughout the city. The search for and plight of Maria was the talk of the town. By this time Champlin was ranting with rage and had again doubled the reward money for Maria to $2,000. He was determined to find her if he had to "step one foot in hell after her." One could almost imagine him foaming at the mouth, all the while cursing profusely.

Adding to this unusual level of excitement was a short note in the *Cincinnati Commercial,* the city's newspaper. It stated that Maria's mistress had stolen $100 from her prior to their arrival in Covington.

This note brought an outraged Champlin into the *Commercial's* office the following day. Pointing to his pistols, he said, "I will have $3,000 or the life of the one—be it you or anyone else—who would vilify my wife. I will take nothing short of my demand! You, Mr. Editor, have until mid-morning to give me the name of your source." Champlin then stomped out of the room, slamming the door behind him.

The editor made a call at the Coffin's home as I was the informant. Catherine Coffin, Levi's wife, called for me, explaining the situation. "Laura, we need thee to help straighten out the tangle with the New Orleans slaveholder." Entering the parlor Levi introduced me and immediately said, "This young man has invested his livelihood in this firm, and Champlin will probably ruin his business if he fails to give his source for Maria's tip. As we gave him the facts, Champlin will next come after us. It is obvious he is determined to get revenge."

It took me a moment to gather my wits and think through the situation. Maria had shared her story with me. I owned no property in the state of Ohio, and the small amount that I owned in Michigan had already been arranged to stay out of the hands of slave owners. So I responded, "I will stand in the gap. Use my name. I certainly do not want anyone to lose life or limb over this."

"But Laura," Levi continued. "This could terminate in a serious affair. Champlin could send thee to prison. He is so disposed, and thee and thy children in Michigan would suffer greatly."

"Levi," I replied. "I am not afraid that anyone is going to put me in prison for long. I believe that the law would not allow it, but in any case give them my name if need be."

Astonished, the young editor thanked me and left, saying that if he could manage that exasperating man, "no name" would be given the next day. We were all on "pins and needles" waiting to hear the potentially fateful result of this meeting at the *Courier's* headquarters.

Champlin strode into the office right on time with his stern query. "Are you ready, sir, to give me your source, or abide by the consequences?"

"I am ready sir. The colored family where she first stopped informed us."

"Do you take a nigger's testimony seriously?"

"Certainly, I do. They are respectable and honest, though poor."

After cursing and staging a temper tantrum, he said. "I wouldn't stoop so low as to notice what a nigger would say, for they are all a pack of liars!" He stomped out of the office, much to everyone's relief. Immediately the editor called on us with the great news that Champlin's pistols full of powder had flashed in a pan.

With Champlin's bounty hunters still thick as fleas, we disguised poor Maria yet once again for another walk to a family's home on Fourteenth Street. I wrote a letter to Mr. Champlin in Maria's name, dated it ahead, enclosed it in another envelope and then sent it to a friend of mine in Windsor, Canada West. She then mailed the enclosed letter to Champlin at the address and on the date requested. The letter read as follows:

Dr. Master Champlin, Canada is a beautiful country. I have grown very fond of it, as well as the freedoms I have found here. It's not nearly as cold and barren as you had always told me. Here, they raise bountiful crops of beans, corn, peas and potatoes, everything I've ever seen in Kentucky. Also, I have made so many wonderful friends since I made my departure. Please give the mistress and your children my love. Maria

It took less than two weeks before Kitty Darun's niece came into the Coffin's shop in great haste to inform us that "Champlin had caught poor Maria, and Aunt Kitty is nearly crying her eyes out over this sad news that a colored man brought over last night."

"That is all a mistake," I said.

"Oh, no, it's no mistake, for that colored man worked near White Hall yesterday, and he said the report was just flying."

I gently whispered, "Hush! I can take thee to Maria in ten minutes. I know just where she is."

"Are you sure, and may I go tell Aunt Kitty?"

"Go and whisper it, for there are but few friends who know she is in the city, the search is too close to home."

Kitty came in with a new story the next day much relieved. "Champlin didn't get Maria, but got a letter from her in Canada."

I smiled and said, "I had heard that, too, and would tell her all within a few weeks."

The letter certainly worked its intended effect, as all of Champlin's hired hunters were withdrawn. Three days later we received two young slave men who had escaped during their free time privilege. They rowed across the river, ten miles further from their home, feeling sure that they would not be missed until the morning.

Cazy, one of our vigilance members, arrived before sunrise to inform us of our young men visitors. Catherine Coffin called me from my bedroom: "Come, Laura, here are more runaways. Cazy is here and they want thee."

We had an impromptu meeting within five minutes to decide on a plan of passage for these two and for Maria.

"What shall we do? Our funds are out, we haven't a dime in our treasury," Cazy moaned.

"We must find the funds to take the two young men and Maria as far as the Stubbs settlement tonight," I replied. "All is quiet now over Maria, and by to-morrow the city will fill up again with slave hunters."

"That is exactly what I told Cazy before thee came in, but he says he has a job on his hands he cannot leave," Levi explained.

"Where is Hughes?" I asked.

"I don't believe I could get him to leave his work to see to it, but maybe he'll do it for you, Laura," wiled Cazy.

"I'll try." Throwing on my shawl and bonnet, I searched and found Hughes, and told him, "Thee must go tonight and take Maria and the two young men who have just arrived this morning."

"But what can we do without money?" He countered.

"I'll get it today. How much do we need?" I asked.

"It will take eight dollars to hire a closed carriage and team to go thirty miles to-night, and I must be back to work by eight tomorrow morning," Hughes insisted.

"We can do it. We must go tonight!" I replied.

Conceding he said, "All right, I'll call at Uncle Levi's by noon to see whether you have the money. Then I will call the livery stable to secure the carriage and team for seven-thirty this evening."

Hughes checked on my progress at noon. I already had four dollars in my pocket plus a traveling suit for Maria. I told him, "I'll be ready Hughes. I know just where I can get the rest of that money. Now, thy job is to manage the men, and I will take care of Maria."

"Fine," said Hughes. "But there are two toll-gates that are closely watched for colored people, and I want you to go with us past those gates. Two white persons in front will pass the load; not seeing any colored people, they will make no inquiries."

"No problem," I agreed.

The plan was for William Beckley to follow at a distance until we made it past the toll gates, then I would return with him. I needed to return for the night, as Catherine Coffin was ill and needed my assistance.

Our crew of stowaways travelled up Central Avenue as far as the orphanage. There they met Maria and me. This was quite an elaborate plan. As Hughes passed by our street, he pulled out a white handkerchief and wiped his face. William Fuller, Maria's host, signaled us as he turned toward the house. We were to walk down the street for one half-block where Hughes was waiting for us.

It wasn't quite that simple. I found it necessary to implement one of my old rules. That is the rule of being "carelessly careful." Word had gotten back to us that Kentuckians were now renting the homes on both side of the Fullers and someone had overheard them saying they believed there were "niggers hiding at the Fullers, for the blinds in the second story hadn't been opened in two weeks."

Several factors emerged that called for greater scrutiny on our part: warm weather, a full moon rising and the neighbors sitting outside on their front porches. All combined placed our little runaway in full view.

Just as we were on the lookout to start, Maria bundled up her clothes to carry. I said, "Maria, no, we cannot create suspicion. Thee can send for them later.

"But they's all I got, an' I will never see 'em ag'in," Maria lamented.

"But thy liberty is of more value than a cart load of clothes."

"I knows it. But can't I have a change of clothes?"

"Hand them to me," I quickly wrapped them into the shape of a six month old baby and rolled it into a shawl. "I'll carry the baby myself."

The watchful wife said, "William is turning back, and I will walk to the corner with you." On reaching the gate, with neighbors in full view, the little Fuller girl called out, "Mamma, I want to see the baby. I didn't know that woman had a baby." The excited mother hushed her child in a smothered voice, and I feared it could betray her fear and excitement. "Let her go with us, mother," I replied. "But auntie hasn't time now to let little sis see the baby. Wait till next time we call, because we are late, and our folks will be looking for us." We leisurely made our walk with Mrs. Fuller calling out an invitation to come again soon.

Sister Fuller and her girl left us after we turned the corner and we picked up the pace to our carriage in waiting. Our decoy caught Hughes by surprise as he stood by the hitching post. He did not recognize us at first because he knew there was no baby on this flight. He looked a little wild with excitement until I tossed my baby into the carriage and he recognized my voice. "Take care of my baby, Hughes!"

"Is this is one of your tricks, Mrs. Haviland?" Hughes laughed. "I should have known."

We clipped at a quick pace, passing the two feared gates without as much as a sharp look by either gate keeper.

Shortly beyond, I said, "It's time for me to return."

Hughes, knowing the terrain better than I, said, "There is a short piece of woods ahead. Once we pass that, the coast will be clear the rest of the journey." He wanted me to stay with them until we made it through the wooded area. Just before we entered the grove, we heard loud voices, singing, laughing and talking. Hearing this rather wild company of a dozen men or so in front of us, Hughes asked the two men in the back. "Are your pistols ready?"

"Yes, sir," said each, pulling out a pistol.

"Boys, if those men attempt to take our horses by the bits, and I say, 'Fire' Will you do it?"

"Yes, sir," They responded.

Trying to calm everyone, I said. "Hughes, be careful, be very careful. Thy excitement will betray us if thee is not very careful."

"We don't know what rabble we are going to meet, and I propose to be ready fur 'em," Hughes insisted.

"Calm down, I believe we are safe." I continued.

"I don't know it, and if they make the first move to stop us, be ready, boys. Are you ready?" He repeated.

"All ready," They chanted back.

Shuddering, I realized to my own dismay that I feared the two six-shooters behind me and the one in Hughes's hand more than all the slaveholders in Kentucky.

Then suddenly we heard one in their crowd say. "It was good we stopped that beam from falling, or 'twould have killed Smith as dead as a hammer." Relieved, we realized that they had been "raising a building" and more than half in their crowd were drunk.

It was not until a mile or two down the road that the excitement subsided. It was then safe for me to leave their company. I charged each one to remain quiet so as not to arouse any suspicion. I made it back to the Coffins's by midnight. I learned the next morning that our "valuable freight" had made it safely to the next Quaker Underground stop, and they were now on their way to Canada!

Chapter Twelve

The Fugitive Slave Law of 1850

LAURA S. HAVILAND WANTED

DEAD OR ALIVE—$3,000 REWARD

It was common knowledge in the Adrian community that my picture was plastered across the South in handbills thanks to the snake-eyed Chesters. My family always worried for me as I continued to carry this bounty on my head. But I continued to believe that my small, Quaker appearance was one that protected me along the way. One would never suspect a little middle-aged woman, like me, to be involved in rogue, abolitionist endeavors.

Following the 1850 Fugitive Bill, slave hunters could come and claim their slaves in free states, as well as slave states. Following this Michigan was no longer a safe haven for runaway slaves. However, by the time bounty slave hunters poured into the state, our Underground Railroad System was such a well-oiled machine, we never feared the new law.

The number of fugitive slaves we were able to assist with the Underground Railroad was significant. Daily, fugitives came to our headquarters in the Zion Baptist Church in Cincinnati. Under the leadership of Levi Coffin we would create a plan for their escape and pray daily for their protection, as we knew our work was ordained and blessed by our great Creator. Yet we were always very cautious in our activity. We took every precaution for safety.

One of our abolitionist friends, Calvin Fairbanks, alarmed us with his careless activities in securing freedom for fugitives. One wintry December day, Fairbanks made a call at Levi Coffin's home. He had just completed a three-year sentence in the Kentucky penitentiary for aiding the escape of slaves. Fairbanks confided in me a plan of rescue that he wanted to conduct. He had received a letter that a slave woman in Louisville would cross the river if a friend would meet her on the Jeffersonville, Indiana side and take her to a place of safety. I cautioned him, "Calvin, stay as far away from Kentucky as possible. Thee is well-known in that state." As Levi was not available at the time of his call, I told him to speak with Dr. Brisbane, one of our other Underground leaders.

"I knew that you would oppose my plan," Fairbanks reacted abruptly walking out the door. Later, I shared my conversation with him to the rest of our team only to discover he had not confided in any of the others.

Shortly thereafter, I was called away to nurse for three weeks in College Hill, Cincinnati. On my return Levi called me into his store, saying. "We have a letter for thee to read. Somebody is in trouble. Samuel Lewis, Dr. Brisbane and I have been trying to figure out who it is. The signature is of stars that he says is the number of letters in his name, but we can make nothing of it." Handing me the letter with a return Louisville jail address, I knew immediately. After counting the six stars in the first name, I said, "Levi, it is Calvin Fairbanks." As we counted out the last line of stars, my hunch proved to be correct. Sure enough, *Fairbanks* fit the number of stars.

Dr. Brisbane sympathized, "Poor man, how he will suffer when they discover who he is. People are so very bitter against him in Kentucky. I fear he will die there, for they will have no mercy on him."

"He sends an appeal for help, but I see no way we can render him assistance," replied Levi.

Several weeks later, a colored man came to us from the Louisville jail. He said he had been released after they realized he had been mistaken for a slave. He shared with us stories of the suffering the prisoners had to endure. Instead of beds, the prisoners had to sleep on filthy piles of straw in their cells. He had met Calvin, who requested that he come beg us for a quilt, some flannel underclothing and a little bit of cash. Fairbank's messenger reported that he was afraid he would die if he did not receive help with these small essential items.

Yet, it was not safe to travel. One abolitionist named Conklin had failed an attempted rescue of a slave woman and her four children late one night. The woman and her children were returned to their owner. Conklin was bound and gagged by ropes and thrown into the river where his body was found a few days later. Another abolitionist, Williams, was lynched attempting to return two mulatto girls to their free-born parents near Baltimore, Maryland. These two murders caused fear to grip the hearts of those in the abolitionist camp of the North. Calvin Fairbanks's case was continuing to stir up trouble with the exasperated South.

Yet a brother was suffering in prison; after much prayer I determined to go help Calvin. I expected the Coffins to oppose my plan. To my surprise they did not; instead, they supported it. Catherine Coffin filled a trunk of bed clothes and flannel underwear to provide for Calvin's needs. We shared Fairbanks's plight with friends. Levi was able to raise fourteen dollars for Calvin and enough money to cover my traveling expenses. Levi had secured passage for me to Louisville on the Ben Franklin No. 2 with a friend of his, Captain Barker.

Dr. Brisbane, just returning from a trip, adamantly opposed it! He referred to Conklin's fate and was quite concerned the same would happen to me. He had so discouraged Levi that he said to me, "Perhaps we have been too quick in giving thee words of encouragement for this trip."

I replied, "I find no geographical lines drawn by our Savior in visiting the sick and in prison." By that time I felt God had given me a clear answer. Fairbanks was a suffering brother who had fallen among thieves. It was my duty to go.

Before leaving, Melancthon Henry, known as the freed slave son of Patrick Henry who had emancipated him, said to me, "You are going into the lion's den, and my prayer is that you may be as wise as a serpent and harmless as a dove. I know the venom of the serpent is there in power, but God will give his children the wisdom without the poison." With that he pressed three silver dollars in my hand for Brother Fairbanks.

I replied, "Amen, and thank thee for thy prayer."

Soon we were sailing south on Captain Barker's ship. The captain was most helpful in securing my safety by sending a letter of introduction to Colonel Buckner, the Louisville jail keeper. Barker was a friend to Buckner, and the good captain told me to make sure and mention this connection.

I arrived in Louisville at dawn and took a hack to Colonel Buckner's home next to the prison. Buckner, the Louisville jailor, lived in a big, bright yellow, colonial home graced with a wrap-around porch. Marveling at the spacious yard and home, I had the driver place my trunk on the porch at the front door. In response to the doorbell, a woman I presumed to be the colonel's wife answered.

"Good afternoon," I said. "My name is Laura Haviland, and I'm here to see Colonel Buckner, ma'am."

Stepping back into the house, I heard her call for her husband. Then I heard a male's voice ask in a low tone, "Who is it?"

"I don't know," she replied. "She is genteelly dressed and came in the hack from the direction of the river."

Colonel Buckner stepped out to meet me. I gave him Captain Barker's letter of introduction. The colonel politely introduced me to his wife and daughter, as well as to his wife's sister and daughter from Boston, making a quite lively social picture.

I immediately said, "Sir, I don't want to interfere with thy family festivities. I have just come to deliver this trunk to Calvin Fairbanks."

Colonel Buckner responded, "Of course, madam. I must first thoroughly examine the trunk. I'm sure that you do realize this is my duty as the keeper of the jail. Not that I believe I will find anything improper in your trunk. It is just a routine part of my job to ensure the safety of our prisoners, their visitors and, of course, our staff."

"Yes. Sir, I completely understand. However, I would like to make it back on the same boat to Cincinnati on which I have arrived. It departs at four o'clock this afternoon."

"Why so soon?" he raised an eyebrow curiously.

"My errand here is accomplished when I see these things delivered to Calvin Fairbanks. I also have a little pocket change sent by his friends in Cincinnati. I would like to see Calvin, as I shall write his mother upon my return home," I concluded confidently.

Buckner responded. "I will see if the sheriff thinks it best. There was great excitement in the city when Fairbanks was arrested and brought here. Shotwell, the injured man who lost his servant Tamor and her child, was very enraged. As Shotwell is a man of great wealth and influence here, I dare not take you in to see Fairbanks on my own. I'll ask the sheriff, and if he thinks it is all right, we'll go."

Colonel Buckner took the trunk and a little note to Calvin and brought back a response with his handwriting. He questioned, "I suppose you recognize his handwriting?"

I said, "Well, I've seen his handwriting though I'm not familiarly acquainted with it. But I am perfectly satisfied with this response."

Buckner continued, "I went into see our sheriff only to find that he has left town and will not return for a couple of days. So, I think you had better wait to see him. You are welcome to stay at my home. It shall not cost you a cent."

"Oh no," I responded, "Thank thee. But my friends in Cincinnati will be waiting for me at the wharf in the morning. I really have nothing further to accomplish here. I'm satisfied that Mr. Fairbanks has received the needed articles. So I will return today."

Colonel Buckner urged still harder. "It will be unfortunate for you to return without seeing him, as you are the only friend that has called on him since he has been here. I know he wants to see you. He asked if you were coming to visit. I told him we are waiting on the sheriff's permission. I think, Mrs. Haviland, you had better wait for another boat, as your stay here is as free as air. We would like you to stay. Then I reckon the sheriff will not object to your going in to see Fairbanks. But I dare not take you in without his approval."

Finally I consented. The Buckner's provided great hospitality. They were very polite, and I slept as sweetly as if I were at home. The following day, the Colonel and I had quite a lengthy conversation. He wanted to share with me his own thoughts on the false ideas of slavery in the North. He spoke freely of Elizabeth Margaret Chandler's poetry on slavery that I had spied on their parlor table. He said his wife's friends from Boston sent Chandler's work to her, but "it was nothing but a pack of lies."

"Colonel Buckner, Elizabeth Chandler was a dear friend and neighbor. She lived and died next to me and was nothing if not a noble woman," I emphasized.

"But she never lived in the South. She had no right to judge our condition without the knowledge of it," whined Buckner.

We were interrupted by a young man who had been falsely accused, imprisoned and now released. After introductions this young man slipped a secret message for me from Fairbanks. Written on a small piece of paper was the request, "Forward Tamor's trunk of valuable clothing to this secure place." The man claimed to be Fairbank's confidant, saying there was a mark on the trunk and pointed to the address on the paper where it was to be sent.

I responded in complete surprise. "I have no idea of Tamor's whereabouts. Wasn't she arrested alongside Fairbanks?"

"Oh, No, She was not." Buckner and his new man both piped up immediately.

"Well," I said. "I have no business here except for delivering the few articles of clothing that I hope will bring some relief for Mr. Fairbanks."

Presently both men took their absence from me. After a short time, the newly freed man returned with another note that he claimed was from Fairbanks. It contained a list of names and inquired whether I knew any of the persons listed. I said, "I do not, and thee can tell Calvin so."

He urged me to send Fairbanks a note. He would ensure that neither the colonel nor anyone else would know of it.

I simply said, "There's no need, my good friend." I had become quite satisfied that this man was an informant for the colonel rather than a friend to Fairbanks. Later, I found this to be true. This man had been released in the hopes of discovering additional information from me with which to convict Calvin, and perhaps, even myself.

Later in the evening while visiting in the parlor, I made the acquaintance of yet another male friend of the family. We sent two hours in conversation. After leaving Louisville I discovered this man was spying on me, to see if my true identity was that of Delia Webster, a woman my new acquaintance claimed to know. The Colonel had read in the Louisville Courier that Delia Webster from Cincinnati was quartered for a few days in the city. This little notice in the papers had created such a sensation among the folks that Buckner was trying to positively identify whether I might be Delia. As the caller left for the evening, he assured Buckner that I was not Delia Webster and that he believed there was nothing to fear in me, a little Cincinnati lady. He also said he would set the editors straight on this matter.

I knew nothing of this excitement, as it had been carefully concealed from me. Buckner claimed he had enough to convict Fairbanks with a 25 to 30 year sentence. But he kept me in his home as long as h could in order to gain further evidence. The next day both Louisville papers printed the following correction:

It is not Delia Webster, but Mrs. Haviland, from Cincinnati; and as abolitionists generally travel in pairs, she had better keep a lookout, or she, too, would find an apartment in Colonel Buckner's castle.

I discovered that Delia Webster was an abolitionist who had been arrested close to the same time as Calvin Fairbanks's first arrest, and supposedly for the same offense. She was sentenced to serve time in the same prison. In six weeks she was pardoned and released.

My time with Colonel Bucker was never boring. He had only one topic of discussion, the faulty ways of abolition principles. I found his discussion quite enlightening, particularly as he was not only the jailor, but also a Methodist Sunday School class teacher.

Said Buckner, "I want to convince you that abolitionists are all wrong, especially when they go against colonization; black people are needed to serve as slaves in this system. You can't deny it, Mrs. Haviland. If there was ever a heaven-born institution it is colonization."

I replied, "Oh, no! We just belong to a different race." I said, "Whatever privilege thee claims for thyself, or I claim for myself, I claim for every other human being in the universe, of whatever nation or color. If the colored people choose to go to Africa, I have no word to say against their going. It is their right and their privilege. And if they wish to go to any other part of our world they have the same right."

"Aha!" Buckner gleefully corrected. "That is a defect in your thinking. It is your idea of slavery that troubles you. As I said about Miss Chandler, it is the same with you. Because you have never lived in a slave state you know nothing of their contented and happy condition. They have no cares; if they are sick, the doctor is sent for, and they are tenderly cared for as our own children. Their doctor's bills are paid. I know if you would live here a few months you'd see these things very differently. You would see our slaves marching out to their work, singing their songs and hymns as merrily as if they'd never had a troubled thought in their heads. Take my wife for example, she was born and raised in Massachusetts, and now she thinks as much of our institution of slavery as any of us who have been raised here."

"Well," I interjected. "If thy slaves are so happy and contented, why do they make thee so much trouble in their efforts to reach Canada?"

"There are those free niggers who are stirring up the devil in their heads, but their notions are not fit to mingle with our servants. And then there's some good in the colonization of these free Negroes. I know of one man who freed two of his slaves to have them go to Africa as missionaries. There's the design of Providence in bringing those heathen Negroes here to learn the Gospel plan by Christ, to save the dark and benighted heathen of their own country. We have reports from these two Negro missionaries. Their master sent them off to school a year or more to fit them for their work," Buckner proclaimed.

I chimed in, "Why not give them all an opportunity of education, to enable them to read the Bible and books and papers? That would improve the race at home. Instead of sending them off to other countries, they could be preachers here among their people."

"Hmmm," He said, thinking aloud. "I tell you that wouldn't amount to anything, as there are but few who can learn anything but work, and that's what they are made for. Their thick skulls show that they can't learn books. If you knew as much about them as I do, you'd see it, too. You are such an abolitionist you won't see it."

My Quaker indignation being aroused, I admonished Colonel Bucker, "I have seen many colored people in the North who are well educated and intelligent."

"Oh yes, there are a few who can learn, but I speak of the race. They are different from us, you know. Not only their skin is black and hair curled and noses flat, but they stink so," Buckner boasted.

I retorted, "Colonel Buckner here is thy house-servant Mary, preparing thy meals, setting in order thy parlor and private rooms, and waiting on thy wife and daughter. Her hair is as short, skin as black, and nose as flat as any thee will find. Yet a disagreeable smell only troubles you in connection with the principle of freedom and liberty!"

"Mrs. Haviland, there's no doing anything with you. You are such a disagreeable abolitionist!" Buckner rebuffed, and left the room.

Buckner returned quickly saying: "And, there's another thing I want to talk with you about, and that is amalgamation. If you carry out your principles, your children would intermarry with Negroes. How would you feel to see your daughter marry a great black, buck nigger?"

I tried not to sound as disgusted as I felt. "Colonel Buckner, this is the least of my troubles in this lower world. As far as amalgamation is concerned, thee has twenty cases of amalgamation in the South to one in the North. I say this fearless of contradiction. Amalgamation is a fruitful product of slavery. There are hundreds of slaves held as property by their own fathers. It is found wherever slavery exists, even right here in thy own city of Louisville."

With a shrug of the shoulders, he conceded, "I will acknowledge this is a sorrowful fact that cannot be denied."

Following a lovely evening meal, we were enjoying conversation before a blazing fire in the dining room. I thought perhaps this would be the end of our discussion on the subject of slavery. I knew from where I sat near the kitchen door, which was ajar, that all of my responses to Colonel Buckner had been within the hearing of the family slaves. I had been careful to avoid answering some of his questions in their presence.

Suddenly as out of nowhere, the colonel asked. "I would like to know, Mrs. Haviland, where you abolitionists get your principles of equal rights."

I held nothing back and gave this square reply:

> Colonel Buckner, we find them between the covers of the Bible. God created man in his own image, in his own likeness. From a single pair sprang all the inhabitants of the whole earth. God created of one blood all the nations that dwell upon the earth. When the Savior left his abode with the Father, to dwell for a season upon our earthly ball, he suffered and died the ignominious death of the cross. He shed his precious blood for the whole human family, irrespective of nation or color. We believe all human beings are objects of redeeming love. Our Heavenly Father gave the power of choice to humans He created for his own glory, and this power to choose good or evil is a truth co-existent with man's creation. This, at least, is my conviction.

An awkward silence filled the room, but no reply was given. Then Colonel Buckner suggested, "Why don't we retire to the parlor? There the topic of conversation changed to more pleasant topics, and there were no further references about slavery.

Mrs. Buckner and I visited during the day in Colonel Buckner's absence. It was not unusual for us to talk for an hour or more. She, too, seemed to have only one topic for discussion and that was slavery. She told me that she had never purchased or sold a slave, except upon the request of that slave. Mrs. Buckner explained:

> Our black Mary was one of the most pitiful objects you ever saw. She was treated shamefully, and was put here in jail, where she lay three months, and was so sick and thin. Nobody would buy her. I felt so sorry for her. I used to take her something she could eat, and I had her clothes changed and washed or I reckon she would have died. She begged me to buy her, and I told Mr. Buckner that if she was treated half decent I believed she would get well. So I bought her and paid only $400; and now you can see how she looks hale and hearty. I wouldn't take double for that now.

Mrs. Buckner continued.

> In contrast there is poor black Sally; just four weeks ago today she was sold down the river in a gang, and I never saw any poor thing so near crazy as she was. She was sold away from her seven children. As I heard her screams, I grabbed my bonnet and shawl and followed her to the river. She threw herself down on her face

and poured out her whole soul to God to relieve her great distress and save her poor children. Oh, how she cried and prayed! I tell you hearts made of stone could witness that scene and melt. Many shed tears over poor Sally's prayer. A man standing by went to the trader and bought her, and told her that he lived only eight miles away. He bought her, and told Sally she should go and see her children occasionally. She thanked him as he helped her stand up for she was weak. But in just two weeks from that day she died. When the doctors examined her, they said she had died of a broken heart. There was no disease about her, but she seemed to sink from that day, growing weaker and weaker until she died.

Mrs. Buckner's eyes filled with tears as she told this sad story. Yet she quickly recovered and said, "Mrs. Haviland, come with me into the kitchen." Mary was preparing dinner with her fat, laughing baby, bolstered up in a cradle made of rough boards next to her. "There, isn't, he a fine boy? He's worth $100. I could get that to-day for him, and he's only eight months old. Isn't he bright?" Mrs. Buckner asked.

"Yes." I smiled and sighed, "He is certainly a bright little fellow."

Mary looked downcast. She was ebony black, though her child was a light mulatto. I couldn't help but notice the heavy-hearted sigh that escaped from Mary as she listened to her mistress set a price on the baby's head. Poor Mary, what choice did she have, either to submit to her owners or rot in a jail cell?

On the Sabbath morning, Ben Franklin No. 2 arrived, and I made preparations to meet the boat, even the though the sheriff had not yet returned home.

Colonel Bucker said, "I don't like to have you leave without seeing Fairbanks, as you are the only friend who has called on him. I have a mind to assume the responsibility of just taking you into the jail a few minutes before you go."

"I would thank thee very kindly," I replied, "if thee think it prudent, but if not, I shall not urge thee in the least."

"I reckon there can be no harm done. Come on, we'll go." So after my several days wait, I followed Buckner into the jail without the sheriff's permission.

My meeting with Calvin Fairbanks was deeply sad for me, knowing that such bitter prejudice was the true charge of his crime, and that there would not likely be any justice in the case. Besides Fairbanks, there were forty other persons in that jail who had not committed a crime. They were there for safe-keeping, Colonel Buckner had told me. They were kept here by a slave trader who would prepare them for the slave market. They would be sold in different venues within the market. None of it made sense to me. As I looked at these slave men, they were all shades of color, from the darkest ebony black to those of fair skin and hair with blue eyes. Some hardly had a tint of African appearance or descent. I could not help myself. The tears flowed freely.

Calvin's eyes were filled with tears as well. He took both of my hands and said, "Let us keep good courage. I think I shall be released after my trial. I want you to see my lawyer, Mr. Thruston. He says he will take my case for $600."

I exclaimed, "Calvin, I have no power to hire an attorney on thy behalf."

"But," he said. "Perhaps Dr. Fields, a well-known abolitionist, would help you. Call him. He may be able to influence Mr. Thruston to lower his attorney fee some $200 or even $300. Don't leave without seeing him."

"But Calvin, I cannot imagine what good it would do for me to see a lawyer or contact Dr. Fields, as neither I, nor our vigilance committee in Cincinnati, have the means to pay any such figures," I countered.

"Perhaps he might reduce his fees if you see him?" Calvin pleaded.

After hearing this encounter, tears misted from everyone's eyes, including Colonel Buckner's.

"I think it is your duty to comply with Fairbanks's request and see his lawyer as well as Dr. Fields. You can continue to stay with us and be welcome," Buckner insisted.

We had already been with Calvin twice as long as the jailer had suggested. So I said, "We have overstayed our time. Calvin, God be with thee, my friend."

Colonel Buckner pointed to a few men standing behind the cell bars just a few feet away from Fairbanks and asked, "Do you know these men?"

I knew them well, though I would never intimate that to Colonel Bucker. All were fugitives who had found themselves recaptured, thanks—or perhaps it should be said, "no thanks"—to the 1850 Fugitive Slave Law. There was Baker, whom I knew well. One would never even dream he was a slave, as his hair was straight and his skin fairer than many Anglo-Saxons. The four men were grateful that I was there, nodding and smiling through their tears. I wanted to encourage them, to give them a word of hope. Yet, I dared not. I understood clearly that one misinterpreted word could make their plight even worse than it was now. Each of them had sampled a taste of freedom, but now had been cast headlong back into the dark world of bondage and bitterness. The only correct thing to do was to give a slight "bow" to them as I walked away.

There were four officers who had kept guard in front of the iron gates while Fairbanks and I conversed. As we turned to leave, they summoned Colonel Buckner. As the colonel opened the outer gate, he asked, "Would you mind passing through the prison yard back to our home alone?"

"Certainly, that will be fine." I responded.

Turning to me, he said, "Those officers have beckoned to speak to me for a moment."

I withdrew my arm from his, as he had politely escorted me through the prison. Walking through the yard, I met the official prison slave caregiver. He asked me in a low tone, "Did you see Fairbanks?"

"I did," I said in a similar tone.

"Glory!" he cried, barely above a whisper, but I heard him.

As I entered the colonel's residence, Mary met me by the door, and she likewise whispered, "Did you see him?"

I merely nodded my assent.

She lifted her hands and clapped for joy. "Wonderful!" she whispered holding her voice down.

Colonel Buckner returned with his face as "white as a ghost."

He exclaimed excitedly, trembling as he spoke. "Mrs. Haviland, those officers are boiling over with excitement! They wanted to know if I noticed how the sight of you was like a current sweeping through the crowd of slaves. One of the other officers said, 'Didn't you see those four runaways cry at the sight of her?' I told them my attention was on Fairbanks, not the others."

I looked at him, annoyed, but without a response.

He proceeded. "They say it is very evident that you are dangerous and deserve to be in this jail just as much as Fairbanks. They wish to have you arrested at once. Mrs. Haviland, if they pursue you, I can't say that I will be able to protect you. There have been threats in the papers every day since you've been here. Shotwell has had his posse hunting in every hotel for you, but we have kept it carefully concealed from the public that you were with me. Yet, now these officers are determined to arrest you."

Looking him straight in the eyes, I said, "Colonel Bucker, should thy officers come this moment I have nothing to fear. The God of Daniel is here. Should I be arrested, thou wouldn't keep me in thy jail three days. I have no more fear than if I were in my own room in Cincinnati."

My calm demeanor must have soothed him considerably as the trembling in his voice had vanished.

"Well, it is a glorious thing to feel like you do; but I reckon you'd better go over the river to Dr. Fields, and when Mr. Thruston comes into the city I'll send him over to see you. I advise you not to set foot on the Kentucky shore again, as I know it will not be safe. I've been told by my officers there is great excitement in town over you. Wait, I'll go to the river with you."

We started towards the door when he suddenly stopped. "No, I don't think I had better go, as the officers may come out and make trouble. I reckon you'd be safer alone."

"Very well, I have no hesitancy whatever in going alone. Good-bye Colonel Buckner."

Walking along the sidewalk down to the wharf, I passed one of Louisville's nicest hotels. Standing out front was a group of fifteen to twenty men. There did seem to be a buzz of excitement hovering around them. My first thought was to cross the street to the other side. Then a phrase from the Good Book came to mind. "I will neither turn to the right nor to the left, but pass through their midst." It was just the thing to do I supposed. The men were so occupied in the buzz topic of the hour that they hardly saw me, but I did overhear just a bit of the conversation.

One said, "Great excitement in town today."

Another chirped, "Yes, Sir! You can see a group of men at every street corner."

I almost laughed aloud, but managed to simply smile and chuckle at the thought. "They had no idea that I was the little old lady causing the town's excitement."

Thank goodness, I soon made it across the river to Jeffersonville, Indiana. Inquiring of Dr. Fields's residence, I was pointed to the house directly across the street. There on the front porch was a cluster of people watching me. Walking through the gate, I inquired of them if I had found Dr. Fields's home.

"I am Jason Fields." a tall, likeable gentleman stepped forward. "Are you, Mrs. Haviland?

"That I am in the flesh." I responded.

"Oh Mrs. Haviland, we are so glad to see you. We have been anxiously looking for you, most concerned for your welfare since the day you arrived in Louisville."

This was an unexpected show of kindness and I felt as though I was at home, immediately clasping hands and meeting new friends.

"How dost thee know anything of me?" I quipped.

"Come in, make yourself at home. We'll show you all of the newspapers from the past week," Mrs. Fields gestured.

Jason seated me at the parlor table and began to share each of the articles from the Louisville Courier. He spoke out of great curiosity. "Mrs. Haviland, you can't tell me you haven't seen any of these articles?"

"No, Dr. Fields. I have not, though I have heard about a few of them."

"Please call me Jason."

"Jason, thank thee," I responded. "The jailer, Colonel Buckner, had told me about a few of these articles and threats.

As I began to pour over the scurrilous articles, there was no doubt the intention of the editor was to inflame an already very excited public. I was dumbfounded, as was Dr. Fields, that I had not been discovered as I was almost too close to miss. I hoped that my Cincinnati friends had not been privy to these papers, as I knew they would be deeply concerned. I had sent them a note the same day that I had arrived in Louisville with my reason for delay. I hoped they had received it.

The next day I sent word to Lawyer Thruston's office. Soon I received this note.

> Mrs. Haviland, I am sorry that I missed you. I have been ill for these past two weeks. I am back and I would like for you to come see me as soon as possible. I will protect you should any harm come your way. Sincerely, Adam Thurston

Dr. Fields informed me that Thruston was a lawyer of considerable influence, and could help Fairbanks. There was the small matter of crossing back over the river and repeating the trip through Louisville past Colonel Buckner's prison. Because it was snowing, Dr. Fields gave me a huge umbrella and pointed out its resourcefulness. He said, "Mrs. Haviland, this will keep the snow off of you, but can also be used a blinder screening your sight from that detestable prison." I laughed and thanked him, as I started my journey.

I found Lawyer Thruston a very kind gentleman, who was quite easy and pleasant to discuss my concerns regarding Calvin Fairbanks. Thruston said he would do the best he could for Fairbanks, not to worry. We might pay him as we found it possible. What a surprise blessing!

Most thankful to see the return of the Ben Franklin No.2 Ship, I had one piece of unfinished business to complete before I boarded. I sent a little article for the "Correction" section of the *Louisville Courier.*

> Notwithstanding the pretended laudability of Mrs. Haviland's errand to our city, we are still satisfied it was out of no good motive, as birds of a feather will flock together.

My trip home was quite enjoyable. I made the pleasant acquaintance of several individuals. One of our topics for discussion, a jovial Louisville physician discussed the value of hygiene and hydropathy. We laughed at his animated intellect over what the rest of us simply called cleanliness and bathing. Laughter ringing out from our ranks, I couldn't resist changing topics and remarking about the excitement identified in the Louisville papers during the past week. It all seemed to have something to do with an old lady who took a few garments of underclothes and a couple of quilts to the imprisoned Calvin Fairbanks.

"Oh, yes! Were you in the city?" The physician asked.

"I was," I replied, "and I was quite surprised at the excitement produced by her presence."

"Well, yes," he responded. "I suppose Shotwell did make a great stir over the loss of the house servant that Fairbanks had helped escape. I understand he spent $300 in his effort to find that woman, as he thought this little lady knew where his slave was. I have forgotten her name."

"Mrs. Haviland, from Cincinnati, was the one threatened in thy dailies," I replied.

"Oh, yes, that was the name. I heard. You are going to Cincinnati; do you know anything of that lady?" The physician asked.

"I do. I have been acquainted with her from childhood."

"You have! What sort of lady is she?" he quizzed.

"Well, if thee should see her, thee would not think it worthwhile to raise such a breeze over her, or anything she could do. She is a little, insignificant looking woman, yet I think she is conscientious in what she does," I replied.

The physician replied in all seriousness. "There wouldn't have been such a stir, if it had not been for Mr. Shotwell, who felt himself wronged in the loss of his house servant."

"But he is considered one of thy most influential citizens, I am told."

"Yes, madam; I reckon we'll have to excuse him, for he is quite nervous and angry over Fairbanks," the doctor sympathized.

After this conversation, a lady friend, to whom I had relayed a portion of my Louisville experience, had to share my joke on the Louisville doctor and called me by name.

At this the astonished doctor asked, "I reckon this is not Mrs. Haviland, is it?"

"That is the name by which I am called," I said, smiling.

"Is this indeed the lady we've been talking about, and of whose appearance you gave such a brilliant description?" The doctor laughingly replied, "Well, well, Mrs. Haviland, don't judge our city by this little flurry of excitement. I hope you'll visit our city again sometime, and you'll find a different class of men who would rally to your aid. Your errand was perfectly proper, and the more sensible people of our city would honor it."

Arriving in Cincinnati, my dear friends were very concerned about me. They had not received either of my letters. And yes, they had read all of the threatening ads in the *Cincinnati Courier* and were quite anxious concerning my welfare. Our abolitionist leaders were extremely discouraged over the mistreatment of Fairbanks, his illegal capture in Indiana and hauling him into a Kentucky prison. There were also lynchings and other violent treatment towards other abolitionist leaders. Dr. Brisbane was just sure that I, too, had been locked up in the Louisville prison. My dear friend, James G. Birney, was sick at heart and expressed deep regret that I had traveled during such a volatile time with all of this excitement between the North and the South.

It was with great joy that I returned unharmed with good news regarding help for Calvin Fairbanks. I knew that God had answered my prayer for safety, a prayer I had lifted up before the journey began and never doubted along the way. What an opportunity I had been given inside Colonel Buckner's home to share a better way of life with them. I never heard from them again. Buckner was such a contradiction in soul and spirit.

"Will the day of slavery ever end?"

Chapter Thirteen

Beaten Slaves, Backdoor Spies, and Bloodhounds

Following my Kentucky trip I was glad to return to my Michigan home. Having the opportunity to reconnect with my children, our school and hear of the local happenings with the Underground Railroad was a needed change of pace for me.

One morning I noticed a mulatto man passing by my gate. Walking outside, I found him on my porch swing waiting for me. Handing me his Underground Railroad ticket he said, "Ma'am, there'll be six in my group."

"Six?" I asked. "Where are the rest?"

"My brothers are back a-ways," he said, "cause we feared it wasn't the right place."

From our visit I learned they were a family who had run away from their Kentucky home on their flight to freedom. They were missing a young wife who had been sold three years earlier. She had escaped at that time.

After my new friend felt confident that our place was safe he returned with the others. They explained they had left their mother and two grandchildren in Carthaginia on the promise when they found a safe home, they would return for them. So, there were really only three young men. They weren't sure if they should move on to Canada or perhaps search out Michigan, as that was where they had heard from the young wife last. As they investigated our fair city, the town folks said, "If anyone knows of her whereabouts it will be Laura Haviland."

I gave each of the brothers a new name for their protection, the family name of Koss and the given names Benjamin, Richard and Daniel. While doing this I noticed, Benjamin, the one I first met, had a sad countenance and sighed frequently. Thinking he was concerned over the welfare of his mother, I told him that the Carthaginia Friends were fine people, and I knew they would take good care of her and the little girls. Yet, nothing I said seemed to lessen his level of anxiety. I decided he must be concerned about other friends left behind. Finally hours later, Benjamin hesitatingly asked in a trembling voice,

"Do you know anything of a colored girl by the name of Mary Todd?"

"Certainly I do," I replied. "And do you know her?"

"Yes, ma'am," was his reply.

"Do you know whether her husband was sold? She worried a great deal about him." I questioned.

"No, they talked of selling him lately." Then after a pause, he asked. "She isn't married again, is she?"

"No, why dost thee ask? She is a very steady, nice young woman. Everyone in the area likes her. Perhaps thee is acquainted with her husband. Do you know why he doesn't come? He promised to follow her as soon as he could."

His demeanor lit up instantly, and he exclaimed, "I am the man. I am her husband!"

"Why didn't thee tell me that before?"

"I was 'fraid of bad news," he continued.

"Afraid she had married again?" I asked.

"Well, it's been mighty nigh three years, an' I culdn't get off the plantation for a long time after she left."

I told him that Mary lived twelve miles from our school. I sent one of my children to tell Brother Canfield, our Methodist pastor, that the older brother of our new Koss family was Mary Todd's husband.

"Is it possible?" Brother Canfield exclaimed after hearing the news. "Mary's husband has come at last!"

The good news buzzed around our neighborhood, Mary Todd's husband had come for her. Early the next morning Brother Canfield orchestrated their happy reunion buggy side. Mary Todd introduced her husband to his young son he had not met. It was a great celebration, rejoicing as Brother Canfield officially remarried the lovebirds. He said, "We forgot the black skin when we saw these two fly into each other's arms. Skin colors may differ, but affection dwells in black and white the same." Soon a home was prepared for the mother and granddaughters and there was another joyful reunion for their family.

Another fugitive slave came our way that I shall never forget. Traveling five weeks on foot, he had slept only one night of those five weeks. Moving at night he would bury himself in the hay to avoid freezing to death and being caught. His wife and child had been sold from him six years earlier. After a season of bitter tears, he made the resolve to "go for" his freedom and made the flight. Unfortunately, he was captured in Illinois after a severe struggle and had battle scars to prove it. He showed us two large scars that had originally been bowie knife gashes, and he had four pistol-ball holes in his arm. His master saw an ad in the paper and came to claim him. He whipped him so severely that the flesh on his back was badly torn. He had to sleep on his stomach for a month, unable to turn his body due to the raw flesh.

After his recovery, his master, a proprietor, placed him as an engineer with iron works.

> If I hadn't been one of his engineers, he would have sold me instead of giving me that awful whipping that he thought had conquered me. He was mightily mistaken, for it only imbedded in my heart a more bitter hate than ever. I appeared content and performed my work well. After a few months, he said, 'I've made you a good boy, Jim, and now I'll let you go to the big city with me.' I was obedient, but little did he know of my determination to escape as soon as I could make sure work of it. I wouldn't even talk with white people till I found Michigan, for we have heard that people in this state are friendly to us, and that it is next to Canada.

This determined man who remained nameless to us would stay only a few days. During his time at the school he made quite an impression upon our students. Still ill at ease and wanting to reach Victoria's dominion of freedom, he left. We made sure he had comfortable clothes and pocket change on his way to the next station and into Canada.

During the semester break from Raisin Institute, I returned to Cincinnati to attend an anti-slavery convention. There I met a white slave man, Charles McCain, from Little Rock, Arkansas, who had left his home in the middle of the night. In the morning light, McCain jumped on a street car as any free white man would do. It seemed strange to me that such a man could be enslaved without a visible mark of African descent. Reaching Cincinnati he found friends in our vigilance group. Levi Coffin advised him to accompany me to Michigan. Charles attended our school and learned much from the children, as well as from a colored minister who taught him in the evenings.

Charles could often be seen in tears as he was very anxious about the welfare of his sister. He said she was as white as he, and had perfect Caucasian features, straight, auburn hair and blue eyes. Charles wanted someone to get the word to his sister explaining how easy it had been for him to escape and that she, too, could escape and find freedom. My heart went out to him, and a number of our friends offered to support his cause. One pressed thirty dollars into my hand and said, "Sister Laura, couldn't thee travel to Little Rock and find his sister?" I wrote to his minister in Little Rock, who returned a note celebrating Charles's success. There was also word that Ann, his sister, was anxious to come see him. Charles wrote her, saying he would send the necessary means and instructions for her to come to Michigan. I decided I would be the one to deliver Charles's help for Ann.

Many in the North insisted that our abolition workers exaggerated the dire straits and suffering that slaves endured. So, in order to answer them honestly and directly, once again, I went undercover as a spy. Was it just a few slaveholders, unprincipled in character, by which we were judging the entire system of slavery?

I completed a thorough study of a map of Little Rock's streets and houses before leaving home. Giving myself a new identity, I once again assumed my maiden name of Smith, Mrs. Laura Smith. With that, I left my dear family and school again, with the prayer and conviction that the God of Daniel would continue to keep me safe.

Stopping over with my friends Levi and Catherine Coffin, I unfortunately missed my boat. It had left an hour earlier than planned. Levi said "Perhaps thou will find it's all for the best." On the second day of my journey, we passed the vessel I was supposed to be on, burned along the shore. There had been a great loss of property and life. There was burned furniture floating on the surface of the water and other items from the boat that had already been hauled to the bank while the rest had sunk. I bowed my head, thankful to God for my disappointment.

At a Napoleon Hotel I waited to catch another boat heading up the Arkansas River. There I observed a group of Southerners also waiting for a boat. Among them were several with whom I became acquainted. There was a young Dr. Jackson, a very gregarious, talkative man who enjoyed the ladies. He gave a twirl of his cane and bowed before the four young ladies on the couch in front of him, asking,

"How did you rest last night, ladies?"

"Quite well, Thank you," one answered.

Dr. Jackson boasted,

> "Indeed, I am happy you did, for I did not. I dreamt all night of a shooting and could not sleep. I suppose it was because when I was here last, I witnessed a nigger fight, or rather a fight over a nigger. He started to run away, fought like a tiger and armed himself with a six-shooter. I tell you he made the bullets fly lively. The nigger had shot one man dead and wounded two or three others. Then they shot the nigger, and I was called to extract a ball from the shoulder of one man."

Feeling self-conscious and out of place, it seemed the folks around me were from a foreign country, not my United States of America. I spent time writing letters home, and I was relieved that our small boat, the "Rough and Ready." had docked and would be ready to set sail in two hours. Then I found there were two boats, and I could choose between them. The other was large and would leave in the morning. The larger one looked more like a slave vessel than a civilized craft.

Though I had made my decision, two women next to me were vying to be my traveling companion.

The older one who wanted me to take the larger vessel said, "Now, Mrs. Smith, I'll make a bargain with you. There is a rich widower on this big boat, and he's got lots of niggers and money. I'll let you have him if you'll go on that boat with me. I tell you, he's as rich as Croesus."

Smiling I said, "Oh, my, no! I wouldn't think of being that selfish and take him from thee. But thank thee." I had to pretend to enjoy such familiarities.

Thus it was settled I boarded the "Rough and Ready" with Miss Springer, the younger woman. The next evening after sunset we landed in Little Rock, so I stayed at the Anthony House close to the dock. Before sunrise I gathered with the minister and other abolitionist friends, making a plan to wait for a message from Ann, Charles McCain's sister. It would be delivered on a boat passing through Little Rock. I needed to find a boarding house, and my friends suggested the "Shears House." As I knew this was where Miss Springer from the boat was boarding, I set out to investigate. I called upon my young traveling companion and her mother. They immediately invited me to stay with them. They thought that Mrs. Shears might have a room, but if not, I could easily stay with them in their room. Mrs. Shears did indeed have a room, but, I still spent much time in the Springer's room sewing with them.

Mrs. Springer and her daughter took in sewing from her son-in-law who owned a tailor's shop. I told them I'd be glad to help out while I was there. Mrs. Springer asked me to make a "shally" dress for her. When it was completed she ranted and raved that she couldn't have made it as well herself. She urged me to think about opening a dress shop with her and her daughter. Mrs. Shears, hearing of my work, asked me to do some sewing for her as well. She would come in to Mrs. Springer's room often and talked frequently about the trials of training her little slaves.

The somberness of my stay here overshadowed any possible joy. Mrs. Shears was a very cruel slave mistress. She complained often about little Jack's insolence. Jack was her 12 year old slave boy.

"Don't you know, after I paid $800 in gold for that nigger, I haven't got him fairly broke in. . .It just happened I was ready to leave the auction when a nigger-drover brought a few slaves he had left and said he'd sell cheap, as it was the last he had on hand. He wanted $900, but I told him I'd give him $800, when at last he conceded." Mrs. Shears continued to lament. "I set Jack to shell a barrel of corn, and he spent all that day doing nothing. Well, I don't s'pose he shelled a dozen ears after I was gone. Can you believe it, that nigger spent all that day bawling after his mother, a great booby 12 years old! He might have some sense in his head. I gave him one beating to begin with, for he's got to know who his master is. I've had him six weeks, and he isn't broke in yet."

Unfortunately, I could not reveal any of my thoughts or show any signs of concern or sympathy. My job was to listen and act indifferent. It was my most difficult task yet. My heart was broken for little Jack. Poor motherless child! I ached for little Jack's mother and her separation from her son.

One evening Mrs. Shears told me she had more company than usual and asked if I would take her daughter's bed just for that night. As it made no difference to me, I acquiesced. The next morning at gray dawn, the two little slave boys, Jack and Jim, came in from the kitchen with fire for the kindling. Rolling out of her cozy bed, the mistress angrily responded by dealing blows on the poor boys' heads.

"How come you niggers wait till this time o' day in here to build fires?" she screamed.

"Aunt Winnie didn't wake us," The boys cried.

"I'll wake you up. Here it's almost daylight, and there's not a fire built, when these four fires ought to have been built an hour ago. And didn't wake up, Ha? I'll teach you to wake up!"

She continued with heavy blows, chasing them around the room, all the while the boys were crying, "We're sorry. We will get up early, missus. We will get up early." In my mind this seemed an unreasonable punishment.

Joe Shears, her son walked in just as the boys had gone to light the other two fireplaces. Hearing the commotion and staring at the two fires brightly burning he asked. "What are those niggers about, that these fires were not all going long ago?"

Mrs. Shears replied. "Oh, they couldn't get up this morning. They said Aunt Winnie didn't wake 'em."

"I'll wake the young devils! We'll see whether they sleep till broad daylight," and out the door he went.

Jim and Jack were usually kept busy in various tasks during the day. Not only did they build fires, but Jack was also a wood-chopper and his little brother Jim was our waiter at meals. Soon after this sad mishap, the boys were both mysteriously missing from all of their chores. I carried an uneasy feeling that they were suffering wherever they were. As I looked out from the rear porch into the barn, I could see the little boys, as I had supposed, hanging by their wrists on a pole over the bay.

Joe Shears, who sat by a nice warm fire sipping his brandy and playing cards, whipped the boys mercilessly alternating from one to the other. By noon little Jim had been let down. He returned to his post with eyes red and swollen and his voice hoarse from crying. I could see by the way he walked that he was suffering greatly. Jack was not back to his wood chopping. Soon the strike of the lashes and the hoarse cries could be heard once again.

By four o'clock, I was so distressed that I excused myself from the sewing room with the need for some exercise and fresh air. In reality, it was such a relief to walk up and down the streets and allow my tears to fall freely. As I returned, I heard the barely recognizable hoarse cries of Jack as the beatings still continued. I had no glimpse of poor little Jack until the next day.

That evening I was sitting by a warm, cozy fire with the Springer ladies and Joseph Brink, Mrs. Springer's son-in-law.

Mrs. Springer said, "We don't feel half thankful enough for this fire. Just think, Joe Shears has been whipping those two little boys all this blessed day, and I should think that they must be half dead tonight."

"What have they done?" asked Joseph.

"I don't know, do you, Mrs. Smith?" Mrs. Springer queried.

"Yes, I slept in Mrs. Shears's room last night, and the boys came in at nearly daylight with their pan of fire and kindling. The mistress wanted to know why their fires were not built earlier. They said Aunt Winnie didn't wake them. Joe Shears came in and swore at them, and said he would wake them. She whipped them with her shoe quite a while," I replied.

"And that was it? Just think!" cried out Mrs. Springer; "You know Aunt Winnie was sick yesterday. And just because they hadn't built these fires before daylight they've had them tied up in the barn all day. Joe used that cowhide Mrs. Shears keeps hung on her door-knob to beat those two little niggers. I tell you, people this cruel, make dealing with the devil look almost tolerable."

Joseph moaned under his breath. "Be careful. Don't talk so loud, or you will make a fuss here."

"Well, I don't care, I am mad. I tell you, Joseph, Hell is lined this very minute with such folks as these."

"Yes," he agreed. "I do believe they are more cruel here than in Georgia."

"I've not seen such cruelty in Georgia or in Alabama, yet I know it's everywhere in the South. But I tell you, there are more slaveholders in hell tonight for treating niggers this way than for all other sins put together, and I know it." The good mother lamented.

"Be careful, I say. They'll hear you, and it will make trouble. It's their property. It's none of ours," Joseph cautioned.

"I don't care! Niggers are human beings and have feelings as well as other folks. There's that little nigger down the street they hired from Dr. Webb. They whip him and pound him about, and they'll kill him some day. And I think somebody ought to report to Dr. Webb how they are treating that young nigger. He is a mighty nice-looking boy. He is almost white, and they've got him all scarred up."

"Well, what of it? Dr. Webb himself is no better. About three months ago he kicked his boy Tom, who was pitching wood down into the cellar. Then he jumped down and pounded him to death with a wood billet. Two white men passing by saw the whole affair. The coroner judged Tom's death, a result of excessively harsh punishment. Dr. Webb was arrested, put into jail for a few days and walked free after paying a $500 fine."

"Is this the doctor we've been sewing for?" Mrs. Springer asked with an angry edge in her voice.

"Certainly," her son-in-law replied.

"I'll say it again! Hell is lined with such people," Mrs. Springer mumbled and groaned aloud. Mrs. Springer's ranting made me think of St. Clair in *Uncle Tom's Cabin,* as he went "cursing up hill and down" frightening his old maid cousin. I grew fearful that at any minute a member of the proprietor's family would march in and call us to account.

Thankfully they did not. The next day while we were sewing, we heard another argument erupt between Aunt Winnie and the Shears. Mrs. Springer asked. "Mrs. Smith, do you hear this quarrel"

I nodded, and she continued. "Poor Aunt Winnie will catch it now. There, just hear those blows! They sound like they're beating the table. Joe Shears will kill her."

Aunt Winnie, the Shears's cook and housekeeper, had just informed her mistress that she was too sick to complete a large washing for the family and boarders. Mrs. Shears began to curse her and I heard her say,

"Winnie! Damn you! You lazy slave! You could do it if you wanted!"

Joe walked in and demanded. "What's all this fuss?"

"Oh, it's Winnie again. She says she's sick and can't do the washing this week."

"Sick! I'll see how sick she is." Joe took up a billet of stove wood, beating her on her head and shoulders yelling, "I'll give you something to be sick about!" It sounded like the whole kitchen was rattling apart. We heard the sounds of tables, stools and pails clanging against the walls. The clatter and Joe Shears cursing continued for quite some time.

Mrs. Springer's rage had reached a boiling point once again, "Hear that? What devils they are! Don't you believe Aunt Winnie will die? Why, I can't hold still!"

Acting as indifferently as my body could muster, I responded, "What can we do now? Remember what thy son-in-law said?"

On the brink of tears Mrs. Springer remarked, "I know it. But there isn't a particle of humanity about them. I feel as if I want to give the whole Shears family a dose of their own medicine." Soon there was deathly silence.

"I believe Aunt Winnie is dead, don't you?" Mrs. Springer cried.

"I think not," I said looking down.

"I am going in there to see." With purpose in each step, Mrs. Springer picked up the pitcher for water, and started pumping near the kitchen door. And there was poor Aunt Winnie with one eye swollen shut, staggering to the door, trying to keep a cloth around her bleeding head.

Mrs. Springer summoned for me to bring another pitcher to the pump, so I, too, could see. Holding her off, I said "I'll wait a bit. I don't want Mrs. Shears to think we're just snooping on Winnie."

"Poor thing, I know she came to the door on purpose to let me see her." Mrs. Springer paced back and forth until I could take it no more. I drew the next pitcher of water where I, too, saw poor Winnie, reeling in the doorway with her hand holding the cloth saturated with blood on her head. Seeing Winnie after this merciless beating, I could not sleep. I spent the night weeping and praying to God who hears the cries of the oppressed.

Aunt Winnie approached Mrs. Springer a few days later and asked if she would make a suit of clothing for her. Her husband had given her seventy-five cents to get outfitted. She whispered to Mrs. Springer "Please don't let my mistress see or know for my husband is going to take me away three weeks from next Saturday night. 'Cause the people are so hard here, he says I shan't stay here any longer."

Mrs. Springer explained, "I felt so sorry for her. I told her to come in when the Shears family is gone and I would take her measurements. Then once I have it ready to try on and fit to her, she can come in after everyone is in bed. I'll keep it right here under this sheet. I told Aunt Winnie, the only ones who should know will be my daughter and you, Mrs. Smith."

"What did she say to that?" I mused while holding one of my patterns up to the light.

She said, "'It's all right. I know her by her face.' You know how quick these black people read faces!" Mrs. Springer remarked.

One day, Joe Shear's wife entered the sewing room while Mrs. Springer was working on Aunt Winnie's sacque. To avert her attention Miss Springer pointed out the back window where Jack was chopping and said, "I don't reckon your Jack is going to live long."

"Why?" She asked. "I'm sure he eats hearty."

"He looks so bad in the eyes. I watched him a couple of days ago, and I noticed he sort o' staggers, and he don't talk natural."

The young Mrs. Shears looked out at him, jumped up and within ear shot, immediately reported to her mother in law. "Mother, Miss Springer says Jack is going to die."

"What makes her think that Jack is going to die? I don't see anything that ails Jack." The elder Mrs. Shears rebutted.

Miss Springer let out a little chuckle. "I thought I'd scare her a bit. I wish I could scare them to death, so they would treat their niggers like human beings."

"Well, you've got her out of the way long enough to get Winnie's suit hidden before our Joseph comes in. He's so mighty fearful we'll get into trouble. I know he'd scold us if he knew what we were doing," Mrs. Springer replied.

I felt guilty living among these extremely cruel slaveholders. And here I was, a superintendent of the Underground Railroad. Little Rock was a starting point for one of our Underground Railroad networks. But now I served as a silent listener, merely asking questions to understand the perception of these people.

I asked, to everyone's surprise as well as my own, "Where can slaves like Aunt Winnie and her husband go?"

Mrs. Springer reflected. "I don't know. They go somewhere out of the way of their owners, though slaveholders keep up a mighty hunt for a long time. A good many of 'em are never heard from again. I don't know where in creation they do go, and I don't care. I just hope they get away from these hyenas that have no more feelings for their niggers than a wild animal." She halted in her response and then continued on. "I just wonder sometimes why the niggers don't turn upon 'em and kill such devils. I know I would if I were in their place."

"Yet aren't there those who treat their servants kindly?" I queried. I felt compelled to be indifferent. My words fell on deaf ears, and with no response our conversation ended.

Later that day my contact for Ann, Charles McCain's sister, passed by my window. Waiting a few minutes, I took a break for a short walk as we each did throughout the day. I caught up with my informant friend and she said, "Ann wants to see you following this afternoon's tea. Her mistress will release her to walk with a close friend for about a half-hour to her aged slave parent's home." Her parents had been given freedom due to failing health, and Ann was allowed to help them with chores after her work was completed. She led me to the place I was to go, her parent's yard, protected by shrubs and fruit trees.

At the appointed time I returned to this solitary nook when three bloodhounds approached. Their sight reminded me of stories I have often heard about bloodhounds being freed after sunset, reconnoitering the plantation's premises. Remembering that a stern and steady gaze would disarm the animal of its ferocious intent, I resolved to try it. The three formidable enemies had begun to circle around me with a low growl, hair on end, showing their teeth. The largest among them, their leader was as big as a yearling calf. I fixed my eyes fiercely upon the sparkling eyes of the leader as he came within six feet. He then stopped. Soon the growling ceased as the lips dropped over the long tusks, his hair smoothed back and he walked away with his slightly smaller companions following close behind.

MRS. HAVILAND AND THE BLOOD-HOUNDS.

Trembling for several minutes after this threatening encounter, Ann's contact came running towards me. "Did the hounds come to you?" She gasped.

"They did," I said, barely above a whisper.

"Did they hurt you? What did you do?"

"I stood perfectly still," I responded, still trembling, "and looked into the eyes of the leader. They calmed down and walked away."

"Oh, Mrs. Haviland! That was the only thing that saved your life. If you would have stirred an inch, they would have torn you to pieces. I was so anxious to have Ann see you, I forgot the hounds until I started back, and I almost fainted, for I know they are awful. I wanted to scream out 'God have mercy on that dear friend,' for I was most sure I'd find you killed," She said, visibly shaken herself.

"Oh, no, the Lord has preserved me, and I am not harmed." I spoke trying to calm her. It took some time for both of us to regain composure. But I thanked God, knowing that He is always present for His trusting children.

We made arrangements for Ann to head North, warning her that if any suspicion surfaced, she would have to scratch the plan and defer until a later time. She seemed to understand, yet begged to go with me on my boat. Word came back to me that Ann had been overheard asking to borrow a shawl from a friend for a trip. I sent her word to abandon her plan of going immediately.

Ann had to wait several years after her mother's death before she obtained freedom. As difficult and painful of a trip as it was for me, I did not waste the lessons learned. I had certainly seen the true essence of slavery in its own demonic playground.

Immediately after our plans for Ann had been abandoned, I was on the first boat home. On my trip I befriended a young slave family traveling with their boy slave owner. The couple had been separated from several of their older children by this young master. They were frequently in tears. Some of the other passengers noticed and made cruel remarks.

"Look at that nigger cryin'. I don't see what she's cryin' about. She's got her young one and a man to her heels." A heartless woman spoke.

Now that I was far from the very difficult role of being an indifferent observer, I went out of my way to speak to the sad couple. They were sitting on the rear deck where I was close enough to inquire where they were headed.

"We don't know! Our young massa got to frettin', an ole massa gib us to him and some money, an' to le him to go. We lef' three bigger chillum behin'. We never 'spects to see 'em ag'in. I wish he'd buy a plantation somewhar, so we could go to work. It 'pears like there's no comfort for us poor people; only when we's got work, an' stops thinkin' so much."

As they huddled together the tears poured out without warning. I took their hands and said, "Dear friends, Jesus is the friend of the poor. He knows thy sorrows; and if thee will pray, He will comfort thy broken hearts. I also will pray for thee."

Nodding towards his wife he said, "She knows that, and I wish I did."

Soon this heartbroken couple and their boy slaveholder left our boat at Pine Bluff.

Three weeks in this environment was more than enough for me to learn about slavery in its own home. I certainly felt its sting of death. Finally in Cincinnati, where I could breathe deeply the air of freedom, I embraced dear friends. Staying only two days, I needed to get home and share my adventures. The prevailing feeling arose in the North that only the "cannon and sword" could destroy this hideous monster of slavery.

Finally home, another refugee found my place. Here is his story.

Sharing supper with him, I asked what brought him to me.

He explained. "Two men six miles from here said you was a frien' to my people, an' I thought if folks knew you six miles off, I would be safe to come to you, 'case I wants to go to Canada right soon."

"Good," I replied.

Sighing, he continued. "I started once before, and traveled three nights by the Norf Star. As Indiana is a free state, I thought I would stop and buy some bread; the people was mighty kind and said I could rest a week. They would pay me for the work I did, to help me on to Canada. But firs' thin' I knew my master come for me, an' I seed him pay them money s'pose 'twas reward."

Escaping a second time, he said, he was determined not to talk with any living soul until he knew he was in Michigan. Michigan folks are considered to be friends of colored people. Six weeks away from Kentucky and he was still afraid to talk with folks. He found my house by asking the colored gardener in Mr. Bailey's yard.

Looking him over, I said, "Your coat and pants are too ragged and need repair." Giving him a towel, soap, a pail of warm water, and a pair of Joseph's clothes to wear while I would mend his, I said, "Now, go upstairs and take off your shirt."

When he returned he still had not taken off his coat or followed my suggestion, I said, "Thou must listen to me. I am not thy mistress, but thou must clean up."

Tears began to roll as he slowly pulled off the coat revealing his torn and bloody shirtsleeves. There were long scars and sores on his arms that were far from healed.

I asked, "Are these the marks of the slave whip?"

He nodded, as the tears continued to fall.

"When was this done?" I asked.

"Two nights afore I lef'."

"What was thy offence?"

"Dis is what I got for runnin' off, an' I fainted an' master dragged me in my cabin, and didn't lock me in, 'case I's so weak. I reckon he thought I's safe. But I got an ing' on to rub over the bottoms of my shoes so dogs couldn't foller me, an' I got four loaves o' bread and a big piece o' boiled meat, an' crawled into the barn an' tuck dis bag an' buffalo-robe for my bed, an' dragged it into the woods, and tuck my bes' frien', de Norf star, an' follered clean to dis place."

"What did thee do for something to eat?" I kept asking questions.

"I tuck corn in de fiel'. When I foun' log heaps an' brush burnin' I roasted a heap to las' a few days, but I was weak an' trimbly to start, an' kep' so all de way."

After this brief history, I had him take off his vest at well. He did so very reluctantly and gingerly with cries of pain. Ahh! What a sight! A big scab came off as I gently helped him remove his shirt from the waist, leaving a mass of open flesh! Opening his collar, I helped him very delicately remove the shirt off his shoulders. It appeared to me that his shoulders and back must have been slaughtered into one mass of raw flesh. There were still very large, unhealed sores.

I wanted my son and son-in-law to recognize the severe actions of slaveholders. So I asked him if he would permit them into the room. As they gazed on this poor man's back and arms, my son-in-law, Levi Camburn, cried out. "Mother, I would shoot the villain that did this as quick as I could get sight of him."

"But Levi," I rebutted, "the villain is not fit to cause such violence in thee."

"Yes, but the quicker he goes to the place where he belongs, the better. Indeed, I would shoot him as quick as I would a squirrel if I could see him," Levi continued.

Joseph agreed, "I think Levi is right, mother, the quicker such a demon is out of the world the better."

"I know this is a sad sight for us to look upon; but I did not call thee here to encourage violence. That is not the Quaker way," I emphasized.

I felt I was still fighting the mentality that even my own son-in-law maintained, that I was severe in judging all slaveholders by the actions of a "supposed" few unprincipled men. After this encounter with our severely whipped and beaten fugitive, I never once heard my son-in-law remark on my severity in judging slaveholders.

Doing my best to relieve this poor man of his pain, I furnished him with healing salve for his journey. I wanted him to rest with us a few days, but he would not feel safe until he was in Canada. He wanted to sleep on the floor in my kitchen, stating that he did not want to sleep in any bed until he was free. I insisted that he take the bed in the room over the kitchen. Very few fugitives would sleep in homes, but I knew mine to be the first home where several of them dared to fall asleep after leaving their house of slavery.

Sending him off with a note of introduction to the next station and a bit of pocket change, it was several weeks before I heard back. A friend of mine, George Wilson, said of him. "The first two weeks he seemed to have no energy at all. But then he went to work, and quite disappointed our cynicism. He is getting to be one of the best hands to hire in Windsor."

The year 1861 seemed to be a determining year in the fight between threatening attitudes from both the North and the South. The future of the Raisin Institute was threatened, as well, though we prospered with many of our students professing new spiritual life. It wasn't long before our ranks were broken, and in the end, seventeen of our students would enlist in the Civil War. When the 75,000 men who had been enlisted by President Lincoln were simply not enough to suppress the slaveholders rebellion, our male students felt bound to go.

Our school was not exempt from the dark battle of the war, during the time of the Battle of Bull Run and the attack upon Fort Sumner. We grieved the cloud looming both over the school and the war. We somehow continued to operate until the third year of the war, 1863-1864, until all seventeen of our young men were taken into battle.

Keenly aware that severe suffering afflicted our troops in need, I offered my service of nursing to my country. Gathering close to 2,000 garments and supplies for the war's makeshift hospitals, I carried with me the credentials of Michigan's governor, Austin Blair, and Congressman F.C. Beaman. Once again, I was leaving my sweet home and loved ones.

My son, Joseph drove me to the depot. On our way Rev. B. Powell met me, and when I revealed I only had fifteen dollars, he offered to gather funds for my journey. However, I would have to wait a couple of days to leave. The offer was tempting, but I politely declined, sharing my reason. "I have arranged for all my supplies to go on today. There are three or four boxes waiting for me at Hillsdale, and I wrote them that I would be there tonight. I have not asked for money, but for supplies. I have a free round trip pass to Chicago, and if I can get the same to Cairo, I think I can get along. Perhaps lives may be in peril during the time I would be waiting here for money."

"Will you telegraph me if you do not succeed in getting the passes in Chicago?"

"I will," as I waved my farewell and moved on to the depot.

Joseph took my hand as I was about to enter the train car and said, "One promise I want thee to make for me, Mother, and make it so strong that thee will keep it. Promise that thee will stop and rest once in a while and think about thyself. Thou art going among the suffering and dying, and I know thee so well that thee will keep going and doing until thee will drop before thee will take time to rest. If thee will make me this promise, I will feel better about thee going."

"Joseph," I said, "I will promise to do this." We embraced as I parted. As I traveled looking out the train window, I cherished my son's kind, loving words and knew the roles were beginning to change. My son was turning into a loving parent.

PART TWO

Service During the Civil War & Reconstruction Era

Chapter Fourteen

Enlisted!

In Chicago I marched into army headquarters to meet General Chester Arthur, requesting a free rail pass to move supplies in and out of the ports connecting to the Ohio and Mississippi Rivers. General Arthur granted my pass after an intense interrogation of my motives and abilities. The honored request surprised all of my new found military friends. Such passes were rare, and General Arthur was not easy to persuade. The encounter proved to be a very important one for me. Twenty years later, I would find myself once again indebted to this esteemed man who acquired an even greater stature as our President of the United States. But for now I was on my way to Cairo!

Arriving in Cairo, Illinois, with my official government papers and railway pass in hand, I was saddened by the horrific scenes of wounded and dying soldiers. Soon I traveled to Mound City, along the Ohio River, where the military planned to move the Freedmen's camp to Island No. 10. While waiting I visited the United States Hospital in Mound City. I held the hands of many and listened patiently, sharing God's love and forgiveness to each one. Oftentimes a groan would represent the regrets of a vile-lived life or that of failing to express love to someone. Miraculously, many of their groans would grow calm, and sorrowful sighs turn into a smile after a prayer and reading the promises of Jesus. I carried my writing utensils, meticulously writing names and addresses of loved ones on a tablet, promising to write their families. In the evenings I found myself pouring over these letters, praying that they would be a comfort and hoping that these soldiers would live long enough to see their families again.

While visiting with the freedmen in the city, I would reinforce what the soldiers continually said. "You are free! Never again will there be a day when you will be sold away from your family!" Of course, they thought me a bit odd because I used Quaker speak and said instead, "Thou art free!" Yet, this wonderful reality did more to move the camp of 3,000 to Island No. 10, as the soldiers requested, than any clothing I could give them.

I daily witnessed so much suffering in the freedmen's camp. I tried to do my part as the official seamstress of the camp. Many of these poor folks were almost nude. I would have them come to my tent, where I found clothing or material with which I could make a suit or dress for them to wear.

One poor woman came to the captain weeping. "My poor baby is dyin' an' I can't leave him. He is the only child left me." The captain's reply was quick and brisk, "Go back and I'll see to it." Turning to me he said, "Go see about her, who knows if she's telling the truth." I followed her down to her slab hut, where her words proved true. An hour later her eight year old son was dead.

"Oh, missus," she cried out to me. "I can't go an' leave my dead baby for de wharf-rats to eat, an' de boat goes out soon at three o'clock." I reported the death of the child and her mother's distress to the captain. His words, "Tell her we will see that her child is buried this afternoon. I want her to get on this boat." Being the ambassador at hand, I repeated the captain's desire for her and then gave my word, "I will see to it, ma'am, that thy child is buried today."

"Oh, missus, it 'pears like I can't leave him so; they'll leave him here tonight, and' dese wharf-rats are awful. Da eat one dead childe' face all one side off, an' one of its feet was all gnawed off. I don't want to leave my chile on dis bare groun'."

What grief! It was most distressing. The poor lady had no idea what had happened to her husband and three older children who had been sold from her two years prior. And now her only other child. . .such sad separations were hard to bear. She finally allowed me to console her and consented to go, with the promise that I would see her child buried before nightfall.

I made haste back to the captain, who appeared very indifferent about the whole matter. "What is the difference if that child is buried this afternoon or whether wharf-rats eat it or not?"

I said abruptly, "Thee promised to have it buried this afternoon, and I told the poor woman I would see that it was done! I see no other way than for thee to keep thy end of the promise. I shall meet her on the island, and I must report to her."

"Mrs. Haviland, you won't allow such things to break your heart after being in the army a little while. You will become used to seeing our soldiers buried in a ditch with no other coffin or winding sheet than the soldier's dress. We bury hundreds just that way. When from five to fifteen die in one day, as sometimes is the case in these large camps, we cannot make coffins for them. We are forced to roll them up in whatever we have. If we can get a piece of board to lay them on when we lower them down in their graves, we do well."

I calmly replied, "But we have lumber and carpenters in this place that can make a plain coffin for the dead, and I do hope one will be made for this child. I told the mother I would see that a coffin was made for her child and have it buried this afternoon, and I will do it."

Immediately, he called the sergeant, and while I stood there the order for a soldier to make a coffin was made. I watched throughout the afternoon and noticed with a thankful heart the pine board coffin, with the child in it, heading out to the burial grounds before sunset.

The art of co-existing with the troops who were responsible for the freed men and women was no easy task. At times I learned my lessons the hard way. I was grateful for the kindness of those who made my work possible. I began to realize that they appreciated my efforts in support of their cause and my care over those lost souls who were displaced, battered and devastated.

Needing permission from General Taliaferro to carry my supplies to Memphis, Tennessee, and on to Island No. 10, I appealed to my new friend Colonel Thomas, as well as the captain already mentioned. They shared the uncertainty of Taliaferro's approval for my request, and further informed me that he was a cross old bachelor who made the claim to never give a woman transportation in the army. Colonel Thomas said to the captain in my presence, "I think she will be more likely to succeed if she goes herself without any word from us."

The following day the car-load of supplies arrived. I was beginning to regret that I had not waited a couple of days longer at home for that $100 that had been offered by Rev. Powell. That would have given me some emergency money for transportation.

Thinking these thoughts, I entered General Taliaferro's office requesting an interview. I introduced myself by placing my papers in his hands. He looked them over and asked me in a pleasant manner, "What can I do for you?"

"I am hoping," I said, "to secure transportation to Island No. 10 and to Memphis, Tennessee, for myself and the supplies referred to in these papers."

"Well, madam, I think your papers are worthy of attention, and I will grant your request."

He said this with such a kind demeanor that I concluded this man had been misrepresented to me until he called for his assistant in a demeaning tone. The assistant instantly stood by his side and Taliaferro demanded, "Go tell my clerk to come here."

He jumped to obey and returned quickly with the word, "He is gone, Sir."

"Gone, where has he gone?" the general demanded.

"I was told he left a few minutes ago to attend church, Sir."

"Gone to church? He has no business going to church or anywhere else, without my permission. He has no right to leave his office without my order." His voice grew louder and more intense!

I found myself wishing to be out of earshot from this vociferous general's voice.

Suddenly he reverted and conversed with me in that original, mild demeanor, "Mrs. Haviland, you don't want transportation tonight. You come tomorrow morning at nine o'clock, and you shall have the papers."

I expressed deep gratitude to the general as I left his office. Colonel Thomas and the captain were waiting for my return, anxious to learn about my experience.

"What is the news?" The captain asked.

"The general granted transportation for me and my supplies to the Island and on into Memphis," I replied gleefully.

Clapping their hands in joy one would have thought they were celebrating a great army victory. I realized they felt some responsibility for my success, as they had solicited my support in getting the folks to follow them to the island.

With the morning's dawn, I panicked as I found the boat leaving before my promised transportation papers would be supplied at nine. Thankfully another captain of the army, standing by, heard my plight and offered to take me and my supplies. He knew General Taliaferro was good to his word and that we would be able to get the promised transportation from the general in Columbus, Kentucky.

Arriving in Columbus, I needed help adjusting to the army's protocol of paperwork. After several mistakes, I confessed. "I'm completely ignorant when it comes to this army red-tape." Thank goodness the army captain came to my rescue, filling out my papers and providing me with a pass from the provost marshal. After this episode I knew and was always prepared to follow the correct protocol.

At Island No. 10, there were 700 freedman working 250 acres of available plow land. Their 25 plows, harrows, hoes, axes, rakes and garden and field seeds were all donated from Indiana and Ohio. There was a well-kept orchard with three hundred peach and apple trees. Chaplain Thomas was the overseer who informed me, "I have never seen a more willing and obedient people than we have here."

There were few buildings, with only a few more temporary dwellings being erected. A dilapidated old farmhouse and a few log-huts that had originally been occupied by slaves were now the homes of Captain Gordon and Surgeon Ransom and their families. They were in charge of four companies of soldiers. The hospital on the island was in good repair, with an air of comfort and neatness.

The soldiers explained to me the appearance of the battleground as we strolled over the deep furrows plowed by terrible shells. Some of the furrows were large enough for a horse to be buried. There were seven or eight feet deep "Rebel rat-holes," as the soldiers called them. They were covered with planks, yet still maintained two to three feet of ground where the soldiers dropped to reload after firing. I picked up a cannon ball the size of a small tea-cup.

An officer informed me, "Mrs. Haviland, I saw twenty-five Rebels killed with one discharge of these balls."

I cringed as I responded, "Oh, what needless slaughter of human life!"

Shuttering, I returned to my tent, from which I dispensed my supplies of clothing, bedding and other household items. On leaving my tent I handed out tickets with an explanation of what I had to offer them. This, of course, seemed very strange and new for the freedmen. The United States Government provided a physician and a dispensary for the freed fugitives. Like most of the other regimental hospitals in the army, a tent served as their makeshift hospital.

Meeting appreciative people who were basking in the reality that they were no longer the property of someone else was a rewarding experience. As I fitted folks for clothes, finding something I had that would fit or measuring them in order to alter a piece of clothing, I heard many, many stories. One young man had attempted to flee for his freedom a year earlier, but he had been captured and shot by his master shattering the bone six inches above the ankle. He had to have his leg amputated and was just now beginning to get use from a wooden leg. His master was taken prisoner by our troops a few days earlier. He, along with 100 fellow slaves, had fallen under the care of the Union Army. I had him fit for a whole suit. This was the exception, because our general state of destitution and supplies could not provide that much for everyone.

I know our donors would have loved to see me open their boxes, taking out each and every garment, measuring and delivering them to these homeless slaves. Fifty to a hundred at a time would present their tickets and then lift up a gracious, heart-felt "Than' kya" and "God bless ya!" as I presented each one a garment.

One morning, an adjutant informed me of five little boys who were almost naked. They belonged to some of the Fort Pillow families. The soldier, himself, had given a young boy a pair of his own pants. I asked him to bring the boys to my commissary that morning. I would make sure we provided some clothing for them.

As we started our work for the morning, measuring, fitting and handing out clothes, one little 8-year-old boy stepped up. He was wearing "tall man" pants. They were rolled over many times at the bottom and one of the suspenders was tied around him. The other was placed over one shoulder to keep the pants up.

His eyes sparkled when I threw a new suit over his arm, and he called out, "See here, Johnnie, what I got!"

"Yes, look at mine!" was Johnnie's delightful response.

In the adjacent aisle, a little girl exclaimed in surprise, "Oh, Milla, my dress has a pocket, and look what I found in it!" She pulled out a two-inch rag doll. There were probably close to a dozen other little girls in the room at the time and they each found similar treasures searching their pockets. I recognized the dolls coming from sweet little girls back in Hudson, Michigan. I wished they could have seen these happy girls stepping on tiptoe with excitement.

As these sweet children's comments were flying around the room, the staff officer entered the tent. Talking to the children and laughing through his tears, he asked in all seriousness, "Have you ever thought of the Savior's words, 'In as much as ye have done it unto the *least* of these, ye have done it unto me?'"

I replied, "Indeed. That's what brought me from my Michigan home."

"Doesn't this pay you," he continued, "for coming all this distance, to see those sparkling eyes and light hearts dancing with joy?"

"Oh Yes! It proves the words of Jesus true. 'It is more blessed to give than to receive,'" was my reply.

A woman standing by listening to this interchange asked me, "Missus, whar all dese clo'es come from? Does gov'ment send'em to us?"

"No, these clothes are from individual families and small group of ladies who have donated them for thee."

After listening to my explanation she asked, "An' don't gov'ment pay you for bringin' 'em to us?"

"No." I replied. "But I am in need of nothing."

When she had finished asking questions, she sat quietly for a moment as if deep in thought. Then she surprised me by saying, "De Norf mus' be mighty,

mighty rich to send so much money down here to carry on de war and send so much to eat. Den da send so many clo'es an' keep so many men here, too. Indeed da mus' be mighty rich."

I spent over a week on this beautiful island, and as my work here had come to a close, I found it hard to leave. I was excited to learn that the army was going to open a school on Island No. 10. The teacher would carry on this work and mine as well, disbursing clothes and supplies.

On my way to the steamer, I was hailed by a female voice. "Missus, missus, don't passby dis yere way." When I turned to the direction of the call, there she was, a very old, large woman, clad in men's shoes, coat and hat, but wrapped in an old parched skirt, sitting on a log. I took her bony hand into mine and said, "Oh, my dear! Thee is in great need. Tell me thy story."

She replied, "Can't tell how ole I is, only I know I's been here a great while. You see dat white house over de river dar? Dat's been my home great many year; but massa drove me off, he say, 'case I's no'count, gwineround wheezin' like an ole hoss. He snap a gun at me an' say he shoot my brain out if I didn't go to de Yankees. An' missus come out an' say she set fire to my cabin some night an' burn me up in it. 'Go long to de Yankees. Da wants niggers, an' you ain't no 'count no how.' An' I tole 'em, 'Wa'n't I 'count good many years ago? But da say, 'Clar out wid you.' An' I seed some boys fishing' on de bank, an' da fetch me over."

As she looked down so did I. She had no stockings and she said, "Missus, I ain't had a suit o'clo'es in seven years." I told her I would see that she had a woman's garment. "The good folks in the commissary will see that thee has a suit of clothes," I promised.

"Tank you, missus. God bless you!"

It was difficult to get the giant old lady's image out of my mind. Her head was bleached white from eighty or perhaps ninety winters. As I waited for the steamer on the gunboat, I shared my story with some of the men. One of them turned and said to another soldier,

"That's the same strange-appearing old woman we brought over," and he repeated verbatim the story she had just told me.

Another soldier remarked, "Such slave owners ought to be made to bite the dust. Her master took the oath of allegiance to save his property. He has no more moral principle than a hyena to turn out such an old white-headed woman as that to die like a brute."

Late in the afternoon I sailed off for another field. On board the ship were a unique diverse group of people, military officers, three women who were also ex-slave owners and me. The conversation of the officers had been fascinating and all of us had listened in as they discussed establishing schools for the freed slaves and bringing freedmen on board the army as soldiers.

When the officers left the cabin, one of the women passengers pulled her chair over next to mine and asked me in a subdued tone.

"Do you believe it is right to set up schools among niggers?"

"Certainly I do." I asserted. "They have as much a right to become intelligent as any other class of people."

"Do you think that it is right to make soldiers out of niggers?"

"Certainly, it is if it is right for any other class of people."

Looking from side to side to see if there might be an officer listening, she continued, "And do you think it right to rob us of our niggers, as the Yankees are doing?"

"Certainly I do, if robbery to thee means allowing Negroes to go where they please."

I responded in my everyday, common tone of voice, yet the woman seemed to be frightened by my answers. Once again she would gaze in all directions for an officer before she continued on in a low tone.

"I tell you it is mighty hard. My pa paid his own money for our niggers; and that's not all of which they've robbed us. They have taken our horses and cattle and sheep and everything."

I read to her, from the Bible in Revelation, the story of God destroying Babylon and taking . . .'fine flour and wheat and beasts and sheep and horses and chariots and slaves and souls of men.' "See here," I continued, "these are the very articles thee has named. And God is the same unchanging Lord today."

Shaking her head she claimed, "But I tell you, madam, it's mighty, mighty hard."

Our Southern woman closely watched the officers, raising her handkerchief to her face while talking to me. This was an attempt to tone down the sound of her already stifled voice. I could relate to her, though. Six years earlier my thoughts could not even be echoed in a whisper, while slaveholders carried the thought of the day. They enjoyed intimidating, threatening and cursing the abolitionists. How the tables had turned! Now I could shout all that was in my heart on the sin of slavery. It was the slaveholder who was hushed. How our country had changed!

Once in Memphis I made my rounds through the hospitals, inspecting them for cleanliness and healthy food. I found the hospitals were flooded with wounded, sick and dying soldiers. The hospitals were all in better condition than I had anticipated except for one, the Jackson Hospital. The Jackson was the largest hospital in Memphis. It needed desperate attention. It suffered from a lack of good care.

I arrived at the Jackson Hospital, hailing the guards to gain entrance. They responded by saying they had very strict orders to allow no one in without permission.

"Very well," I replied, "please inform me where I can find the clerk, and I will secure a permit."

It just happened that the surgeon in charge was passing by the front entrance, and the guard introduced me. I shared with him my desire to visit his hospital.

He inquired of me in a surly manner, "Have you a son here?"

"I have not," I answered.

"Then why do you want to enter? This hospital is no place for a lady to step her foot over the threshold."

"I expect thee and I disagree on that, but if thee doubts my fitness to visit thy patients, here are my papers from the governor of my state, as well as from a member of Congress and others."

"If you have no son here, I don't see that you have any business here," The surgeon charged.

Undaunted, I replied, "Every soldier is some mother's son, and I wish to visit them. Here are my official papers. Thee can read them if thee wishes."

Begrudgingly, he threw his hands up in the air and said, "Come on in."

He decided to follow me as I traveled through the hospital, staying close by my side.

In spite of the surgeon, the half dozen men that had the opportunity and means to do so sprang to their feet and stood by their cots while we were in the ward. I realized that it was expected, in pursuance of an order. I tried to shake hands with each soldier who was awake and conscious as I passed by. Yet the surgeon hurried me so, I barely had the opportunity to speak except to a handful.

I saw one poor skeleton of a man. He was bolstered against his cot, eating dinner with a spoonful of cooked onion on his plate.

"Where did you get that onion?" the surgeon protested.

"I paid my own money for it, doctor."

"Who said you might have it?"

"Dr. Spears."

Without another word we passed on.

My frustration and anger were ready to spill over. It mattered little to me if he wanted to browbeat me, but to treat a poor, dying soldier in such a manner of disrespect was wrong. I could hardly contain my indignation. From then on it was very tense between us.

"I would like to pass through thy kitchen," I insisted.

"Very unfavorable time, madam-*very unfavorable,* it's about dinner-time."

"Very favorable," I thought as I marched in. At a glance it was obvious that the large pot of potatoes had boiled half an hour too long. The bread looked decent, and I hoped it was good. As we passed out of the hospital with pencil in hand I began to ask questions of the general and take copious notes.

I said, "This is a very large hospital. How many will it accommodate?"

"Fifteen hundred patients, madam, very few, very few at present, only 484," he answered.

"How many nurses are on staff here?"

"Twenty-three nurses," he replied.

"No female nurses?"

"No, madam, as I told you, a woman has no business stepping inside of a hospital."

"As I told thee, we evidently differ in that respect, I find judicious female nurses create a more home-like atmosphere where soldiers feel more contented," I exhorted.

"Very few, very few judicious female nurses," the surgeon retorted.

"They exist, notwithstanding. How many surgeons serve here?" I asked curtly.

"Only four at the present time"

"Ist thee the surgeon in-charge?

"Yes."

"Please give me thy name."

"My name is Surgeon Powers, of the Seventh Missouri Regiment."

He was telling the truth because his name and figures were plainly recorded.

And then Surgeon Powers performed a dramatic feat of double-speak. Bowing at the waist, he concluded. "Madam, I hope you will call again sometime. Call in the middle of the forenoon or afternoon, but meal-time is very unfavorable."

"If I remain a week or ten days longer in the city," I replied, "I shall do so."

"I would be very happy to have you call again, madam, very happy to see you again. Good Day!" Surgeon Powers schmoozed and swooped me out the door.

With a heavy heart I entered the army base health office in order to get more information about the hospitals. The office was filled with officers and generals of high rank. I introduced myself, handing my papers to Dr. Warrener, the health agent.

"You are visiting the hospitals, with supplies, etc., are you?" He asked. "I am glad to meet you, as we have had few visitors from the North. How did you find them?"

"I found them in better condition than I anticipated, with one exception," I answered.

"Have you visited the Jackson?" Dr. Warrener replied.

"I have just come from there."

"Today is not the visiting day. Did you see Surgeon Powers?"

"I did."

"Did you get into that hospital without trouble?"

"We had a parley."

"What did he say to you?" Warrener asked.

Sharing my objections regarding Surgeon Powers in a low tone, I was fully annoyed that the doctor repeated my every word aloud so as to be heard.

"You certainly could have given no better reason than that every soldier is some mother's son," he continued. "What do you think of Surgeon Powers?"

The room was full of these officers and I was a bit hesitant to speak my mind at first. On second thought I decided that if the President himself were in the room, I would want him to know. So, I frankly replied.

"I think he is a tyrant brandy-cask! Why is such a man allowed to occupy the responsible position of surgeon in charge of hundreds of sick, wounded soldiers?"

Dr. Warrener replied, "We tried once to get him out, and failed. You need to report this to the medical director who is in the city." After giving the information requested, I thanked him and left.

I was very weary, and remembering my promise to Joseph, I returned to headquarters and spent the rest of my day writing letters home for soldiers.

Early the next morning, I resumed my visits to the hospitals. While on the street I met an officer who reached out his hand with a smile, and said, "You do not recognize me, but I recognize you as being the lady in Dr. Warrener's office yesterday after visiting the Jackson Hospital."

"Did thee think I was severe in my remarks concerning Surgeon Powers?"

"No. No. Not at all! I had two sons in that hospital for six weeks, and they both declared they would rather die in the open field than be under the care of that drunken tyrant again!"

"Why do the authorities permit such a surgeon to have the care of sick and dying soldiers?"

"Well, it is difficult for us to make that change from within, but that is the medical director just ahead of us. Walk with me and I will introduce you. He is very much a gentleman."

After my introduction to the medical director and his perusal of my papers and instructions, he asked, "Have you visited the Jackson Hospital? And did you see Surgeon Powers?"

"Yes, I was there yesterday," I replied, "but was hurried through in such haste by Surgeon Powers that I could not speak to any of the soldiers."

"What do you think of Surgeon Powers?" He keenly watched me as I answered the question.

"I think he is an unfeeling tyrant. The white of his eyes had the color of red flannel, and the unmistakable brandy breath made standing near him very unpleasant. His rough, morose treatment of helpless soldiers indicates his entire unfitness for the position he occupies. If the milk of human kindness is more loudly called for in one position than another, it is with the surgeon in charge of sick, wounded and dying soldiers."

"We know, Mrs. Haviland, this is true. We made an effort to replace him once and failed. The medical director over our entire division, next in rank to General Grant himself, is determined to hold him here. But if you will make your report, giving a recommendation to replace him because of the endorsement from your governor and congressman, we can make that happen this time. Make your report as strong as you please."

Cordially thanking the medical director, I left and my report was soon in his hands. On my second visit to the Jackson, Surgeon Powers was courteous and polite. A few weeks later I received the good news that Surgeon Powers had been relieved of his hospital duties shortly after I had left Memphis. Sadly, Powers filled a drunkard's grave just a few months later.

Another interesting experience in a Memphis Hospital was meeting Charlie, a female soldier. She had marched in both battles of Bull Run and four additional battles. Enduring the long marches was extremely difficult for her. She became violently ill with typhoid fever. During this illness her gender had been revealed. She was a rather large, coarse featured woman with an indomitable will. Charlie now wanted to go home. She intimated to me that her betrothed had been killed in battle, and she no longer desired to serve in the army, as he had been the reason for her enlistment.

While supervising hospitals in the Memphis area I stayed at Camp Bethel with the army. I had constructed a little frame bed for myself in one corner of the commissary tent. All military personnel were asked to have lights out in the tents after dark. As our camp occupied the weakest point at our post, we needed to be ready at a moment's notice to move to Fort Pickering. We were prepared before dark each night for any such call. As the enemy was threatening to retake Memphis, the soldiers kept ready for action.

One morning, excitement swept through the camp as a telegram arrived from President Lincoln. The President ordered 400 colored men to enlist for service. This greatly disappointed the masses of colored men who wanted to serve in the army. Colonel Eaton enlisted the required number, and reported that many left in tears because they were not needed.

In the early hours of one morning I heard a loud cry outside the window close to my cot. "Halt!" This was quickly followed by a still louder cry, "Halt! Maybe you don't know who I is? I holds a gun, an' she's ready to go off."

"Well, I only want to come to you. I don't want to go further."

Once again the soldier cried, "Halt!"

The officer in command responded, "Right! If I had taken one step further after you cried halt the third time, you should have fired no matter who I was, even if I was the President himself!"

At the breakfast table the next morning, Colonel Eaton remarked, "A number of our new colored soldiers on picket guard last night were on trial, and not one sleepy head was found among them. Good job, men."

While I visited the hospitals during the day, I would often read portions of Scripture to the patients. There were times I knelt by the cots and appealed to the Great Physician for these suffering and dying soldiers, imploring for the healing of their souls. I wrote letters home for some of the poor, homesick boys, which I found very gratifying.

One evening as I was passing by, one of the convalescents called out, "Frank, here's that woman you wanted to see!"

Frank came running to greet me.

"Is thee from Michigan?" I asked him.

"Not quite," he said. "I am from Ohio, but I've been in Michigan and that is its next neighbor." He seemed as glad to see me, as if he were meeting his mother. "Oh, how much you remind me of my mother! Your advice to us boys is almost the same as my mother gave me when I left home." His tears spoke louder than any words of appreciation for my visits.

I also spent time visiting the camps of the freedmen. Some days 2,000 or more freed fugitives would enter a camp. One afternoon forty came into Bethel Camp and I went out to meet them.

I asked the first man I met, "Has thy first taste of freedom brought thee into a Union camp?"

"Freedom?" The man said looking up in surprise.

"Yes, doesn't thee know that President Lincoln has proclaimed all slaves free?"

"Is dat so?" he asked.

"Certainly, thou has heard about it?"

"No, missus, we never hear nothing like it. We's starvin', and we come to get somfin' to eat. Dat's what we come for. Our people at home tell us Yankees want niggers to kill, and' da boils 'em up in great caldrons to eat, 'case da's starvin'. But all de white men gone into de army an' lef' us all wid missus, an' da locks de bacon up, an' gib us little han'ful o' meal a day, an' we's got weak an' trimbly. An' I tole my people we's gwine to die anyhow, so we'd try de Yankees."

They seemed to be in a state of shock over the idea of freedom and would hardly believe me until it was confirmed by some of their own people. We fed the hungry with our rations. I asked the man, "This does not look like killing off colored people, now does it?"

"No, missus, dis 'pears like makin' alive, instead of killin,' God bless sich people as dese, if dis be Yankees."

When my work in Memphis concluded, my travel plan was to go to Cairo, checking in at Island No. 10 and Columbus on the way. When I returned to the Island, many people were waiting for the remainder of my supplies. The number of refugees had increased to 3,000.

At Fort Pillow I met a company of 37 ex-slaves who had just made their escape. Mesmerized by their stories, I continued to ask questions. "What time did thee start on thy journey?" I asked one extremely tired women. "Early moonrise," was the reply. They had traveled all night and made haste to reach our lines before dawn. Yet most of them walked twenty-five miles to reach Fort Pillow. It had been a fearful trip for them. Several in their same neighborhood had been shot and killed in their attempt to leave.

Boarding a steamer I returned to Columbus, Kentucky. Soon after arriving I encountered a large funeral procession of colored folks and military personnel. I joined in the procession and soon learned the funeral was for the only son of a slave mother. As the son had heard that colored men were now accepted as soldiers he wanted to enlist in the Union. She and her son had made their escape from the plantation and were nearly half way across the river when their young master called out in a demanding voice. "Return or I'll shoot you!" The son decided to push on to reach the other shore.

A ball passed through his right arm and broke the bone above his elbow. The old mother grabbed the oars and pulled with all of her might. But a second ball entered her son's lungs. They reached the shore, where they were met by soldiers who delivered the young son from the skiff to the hospital. He received the best surgical support, but all to no avail. Much sympathy and condolences were extended to this poor, bereaved mother. Yet, sorrow was no new trial for her. She told me her husband had been sold down the river a few years before. She was left with two little girls.

I asked, "Were these three children all of thy family?"

"Oh, no, honey; I had two big boys sold jus' afore the war. Don't know whar they went. An' now my poor boy is shot dead by that young massa I nussed alon' with my own boy. They was both babies together. Missus made me nuss her baby, an' set her little girl to watch me, fur fear I'd give my baby too much. It never mattered how hard he cried. Many times I wasn't allowed to take him up, an' now that same boy has killed mine."

The poor mother buried her face in her faded calico apron, sobbing until it was drenched with tears. A soldier, so moved by this sad scene, said they were only waiting for the word from their commander to strip that plantation just as they had many others. He said all of the soldiers felt deeply indignant for the poor mother.

Walking over to the Soldier's Home, one of my stomping grounds, I noticed a white man with a chain on his ankle carrying a ball and a brick in a wheel barrow. He was wheeling towards the soldier's camp and the irony was he was being guarded by a black soldier. As I stood looking at this unusual scene an officer informed me, "Madam, that prisoner you see wheeling back to our camp is a strong secessionist. He was a hard task master over a large plantation with more than 100 slaves. Then he was taken prisoner, and all his slaves came into our camp. The younger men enlisted as soldiers, while the old master made an attempt to escape. But we put him in irons and set a black soldier, one of his own slaves, to guard him."

"What a turning of tables!" I exclaimed.

"Yes, you will find this same reversal of roles within our lines all over the South."

Moving to the door of a tent, I saw a large, square block of iron. It must have weighed sixty to eighty pounds and was attached to a ring. I asked the colored man standing by about the purpose of this iron.

"When the plantation master had a mind to punish us he ordered us locked to that block. From one to a dozen of us were locked to it with a long chain. When we hoed corn we'd hoe the chain's length, then the one next to the block had to tote it the length of the chain, and so on till we did our day's work. Since we've been here we've seen nine of our masters chained to that same block and made to shovel sand on that fortification yonder. There were forty of us that belonged to our plantation standing in this yard looking on."

"How did thee feel to witness such a scene?"

"Oh, I can't tell you, madam, but I cried like a baby."

"Why did thee cry?" I asked.

"Oh, to think what great things God is doing. Man could never, never do it."

"Do the others feel the same?"

"Oh no, some laughed, and one man said, 'Ah ha, you see now how sweet 'tis to tote the old block now, don't you?'"

"Did he say that in his hearing?" I inquired.

"Oh no, we's five rods off."

In Kentucky, I found the hospitals at this post cared for well. One exception was a regimental hospital where there were too many sick and emaciated soldiers to be cared for properly without desperately needed supplies. They had no pillows but their haversacks, no covering but their overcoats and they pitifully begged for milk.

Their spirits were very low, and I wondered why I could not take them quilts and pillows. Inquiring of the surgeon I wondered why boiled milk could not be used to help alleviate their camp diarrhea. "Madam, you can bring them milk, or anything you've named, but I tell you, if you undertake to listen to all the soldiers whining you'll have your hands full. And like it or not, they'll trade whatever you give them for whisky the first chance they have."

Getting the permission I needed, I could not rest until I had delivered these supplies. Two soldiers traveled with me carrying the milk, quilts and pillows for the sick. Despite the words of their surgeon, their tears of gratitude said it all. Each personally thanked me. I returned to the Soldiers' Home quite content, though weary and sick. My cough had been following me for more than a month, and I knew it was time for a return to my dear home for some rest.

Chapter Fifteen

The Call to Natchez

After a few days of rest in my Michigan home, I found a traveling companion in my dear, devoted friend, Letitia Backus, and we quickly began to prepare for a return to the field. Believing our war relief work needed formal organization, we joined forces with the Freedmen's Relief Association in Detroit. With the appropriate documentation from our state leaders and a train car load of supplies, Mrs. Backus and I left our homes to provide relief in Natchez for the fields of greatest suffering.

Natchez had been the largest slave trading center in the region, a vibrant mainstay for the Natchez economy. Over 340 planters individually owned at least 250 slaves. This created over 85,000 slaves who were displaced and in great need during the war. That's how we knew our call was to Natchez, Mississippi. Our living quarters, being the exception to the everyday realities of war life, was a story in its own right. Lieutenant Thirds and his family invited us to share a home with them in Judge Bullock's three-story house. The Judge, a strong secessionist and all too unexcited about making peace with the Union troops, offered his parlor and beautiful third-story rooms as an offering of good will and insurance against confiscation. His cooperation was to protect his wife, their assets and property.

What an irreconcilable paradox to find comfort in a Rebel judge's home while working to alleviate horrible suffering created by him and those of his ilk.

Thanks to Colonel Young we obtained the usage of a good-sized store on Main Street to display our goods. Unfortunately, there were 4,000 freedmen all pressed together in condemned tents. These tents were so leaky that after heavy winds and rains, the camp would suffer five to fifteen deaths in a day due to exposure. There was constant work for head, heart, hands and feet.

Few days passed without hearing the roar of battle close by. We could often see the cloud of blue smoke. A few days after the horrific Fort Pillow massacres, a battle fought by our brave black soldiers came within two miles of our camp. Our troops fought valiantly. And when asked to stop, a number of soldiers continued to reload, and one was heard to say, "I hear no cry from headquarters at Fort Pillow," and fired again. Again, they were ordered to stop, and finally did so, but only at bayonet point. The enemy had been mowed down like grass.

I understood how the men felt about the awful Fort Pillow massacre. It was wonderful that not one of our boys was lost or even wounded. A white regiment of soldiers was in reserve if needed, but they were not. The colored soldiers even resented the idea that they should need any type of assistance at all. Great excitement came over the camp after this victory. One woman, who had a husband in the battle, asked him. "Why didn't you shoot on as long as one was lef'?"

"Our officers commanded us to stop," Her husband replied.

"I don't care, they need killin', everyone," She lamented.

I asked her, "Thee wouldn't kill the women, would thee?"

"Yes, I would," she answered; "for they's wusser'n the men."

"Well, there are the innocent little children, thee wouldn't kill them, would thee?" I queried.

Hesitating a little, she said: "Yes, I would madam; for I tell you nits make vermin."

This same woman and her entire family had been the slaves of Judge Bullock's wife. Still working for the judge's family and living in the same log cabin, she helped us with our washing and gave us insight into her experiences.

She said the judge was much more difficult to please than his wife. But Judge Bullock became deathly afraid of the Union Soldiers after they had taken Natchez. He hid in the family garden within a thicket of bushes for days. They had to take him his meals when no was in sight. He expected the Yankees to kill every man they met. Finally, when he realized that was not the case, he came back to the house and began talking freely. She said their slaves were mostly house-servants and treated far better than most. Judge Bullock was originally from the North, but had married a wife from the South, inheriting the slaves.

In the Natchez Freedmen's Camp were signs of great cruelty. Men with broken shoulders and limbs were more prominent here. It was heart-sickening to hear their stories of injustice at the hands of slaveholders.

I asked one man in our camp with only a shred of an ear, how it had been torn. He didn't say, but one of his fellow slaves told me the story. "It was at the order of our master that he had been stripped and fastened to a tree by a large nail driven through his ear. The overseer was directed to whip him on his naked body until his writhing tore his ear out. That alone ended his punishment."

Week after week I kept at my work. As tedious as it was, it was also heart-warming. I worked at preparing bundles of clothes for those in need of clothing and nearly naked. As new refugees were flooding into our camp, the officer found it necessary to form a new camp across the river, behind Vidalia, Louisiana, on the Ralston Plantation. A few hundred had already gathered there, and we found them destitute. They had become so discouraged. Most of them had family members enlisted as Union soldiers who were ready to desert.

One of them said, "They say we are free. What sort of freedom is this, to see our families without a board, shingle or canvas to cover their heads? We are going to leave our regiment and build something to shelter our wives and children. They haven't got a place to sleep at night except in the open field."

We subdued and calmed them, promising they were our first priority. We asked them to give us a chance rather than to leave hastily. Thank goodness Brother Reed, one of the teachers, offered to support me in this cause. He had no official papers or transportation, and no time in which to get them. Flagging down a passing general, I explained my need for help and our Brother Reed's dilemma. He said he would allow Reed to come and go if he could do it while he was in command and before the firing of the sundown gun. He said, "Just do it!"

Our work took a slight change on a cold, stormy day when Captain Howe sent a sick woman and her two children in an ambulance. We needed to get the ambulance to the hospital, but there was much work to do along the way, and everyone believed the lines had been closed for travel. There was no provost marshal in sight and we were at the weakest point in the post, where we could see the smoke of Rebel fires off Lake Concordia. A recent struggle indicated that another attack was imminent. Brother Reed and the ambulance driver doubted that we could get back across the river. "For if the lines are closed," Reed said, "the President himself would not be permitted to pass."

But I said, "We don't know the lines are closed, so we had better cross."

"It is your load, and if you say go, we shall go," said Brother Reed.

"I say go!"

Shortly we found ourselves in front of the provost marshal's office, but no provost marshal. No one knew where he was. At my pleading the entire office conducted a lengthy search. Finally some of the guards found him and brought him back, flailing his head of long hair decorated by feathers and straws. I stood in his office and read him my papers, holding them right in front of his face in the same way I would read to a two-year-old child. After I had explained my purpose, I made the request to pass his lines with my supplies.

"Who - who's there?" The drunken marshal reeled.

I introduced him to Brother Reed, explaining his offer to assist me in the disbursement of the supplies. I told him the general's advice of taking Brother Reed, and how the general said he would pass him if he were in charge.

"Well, well, I don'-don't-li-like –this-whole-whole-sa-sale business."

"Please sir, I beg of thee! Think of the children, the women, those poor suffering souls. They are in desperate need of our provisions. . .Think about it, sir." I could not remember begging in such desperate tones.

I mustered up politeness, as not to show the true disgust boiling inside of me. As he mumbled, stuttered and shook his head, his headdress of feather straws were waving in all directions. Finally, he took his pen and scribbled a pass that was almost illegible. When I reached the next line of guards they hardly knew what do until I told them that the provost marshal was drunk.

"Oh, yes, and it's no new trick. Go on."

Thankfully, we finally reached the group of sufferers, who were freezing and shivering as if in a fit of ague. I gave each family two blankets and quilts. I could see the numerous children crawling between them in minutes. Because of the intense suffering for the women, I gave them each a suit of men's clothing. I gave them several rag carpet blankets that they could put underneath them for protection from the elements. All the while remembering my dear Michigan friend, who after listening about the great suffering from these camps, took up her own rag carpet and cut into four pieces, sending it with us.

I wished these refugees would have remained in their old homes for just a little longer. Because of the bare elements and lack of shelter or provisions to sustain them, it was difficult to care for them. I know they had suffered from great cruelty, but surely they should not come out here to die like this.

A little girl came on behalf of her mother for assistance. One of her little brothers was dying. They were stationed in an old blacksmith shop, a temporary hospital. As I entered the shop and listened to the groans of the dying, once again I thought to myself, "Oh! If only they had waited a little longer!" Four other little boys were sick with pneumonia. The mother of the sick boys was managing as well as possible. I gave her ground mustard and showed her how to mix the poultices and ginger for those with chills. The miserable shelter did not leak so much, but the one side and end had such a large opening, you could throw a hat through the wall.

Over by the dilapidated cotton gin a pile of irons and a double jointed ring caught my eye. Placing my foot on the strange double-jointed contraption, I asked, "I wonder what this sort of a double-jointed ring could have been used for?"

"That's a neck iron," said an old woman standing near me.

"A neck-iron! What does thee mean?"

"Why, it's an iron collar to wear around the neck."

"But thee is certainly mistaken," I said, picking it up. "You see these joints are riveted with iron as large as my finger, and it could never be taken over one's head."

"We know. Dat's Uncle Tim's collar. An' he crawled off in dat fence-corner," pointing to the spot, "an' died thar, an' Massa George had his head cut off to get de iron off."

"Is it possible for a human being to become so brutal as to cut a man's head off when he is dead?"

Looking at me as though I had doubted her word, she said: "It didn't hurt Uncle Tim when he was dead as it did when de iron wore big sores way down to de bone,

The Call to Natchez

and da got full o'worms afore he died. His neck an' head all swell up, an' he prayed many, many prayers to God to come and take him out o' his misery."

"How long did he wear it?"

"'Bout two years."

"Two years! It is impossible for anyone to live that length of time with this rough heavy iron," I exclaimed.

"We work'd two seasons anyhow, over in dat cotton fiel," pointing to the 200-acre cotton field on the right.

I took up another iron, and inquired, "What sort of an iron is this?"

"A knee-stiffener to w'ar on de leg to keep 'em from runnin' off in dat swamp," She was pointing to the dark swamp that borders Lake Concordia. It was so thoroughly draped with long Southern moss that it was difficult to discover anything three feet into the thicket.

I asked, "Did any of this company live on this plantation before the war?"

"Yes, missus, Six of us live here. I live here seven years."

Before leaving I said to the ex-slaves, "I want this collar and the other heavy iron a woman called a knee-stiffener. This plantation is confiscated, and these irons belong to thee as much as to anybody. Will thee give them to me?"

Everyone was speechless, looking and waiting for the others to respond, but at length the one to whom I had mostly directed my conversation said,

"I reckon you can have 'em, for we's had all we wants ov 'em."

"If thee can find any other slave-irons in that pile, I wish thee would pick them out for me. I want to take them home to Michigan just to show what sort of jewelry the colored people had to wear down here."

245

SLAVE IRONS (IN POSSESSION OF THE AUTHOR).

Before I knew it they were scavenging through the heap and showing me all sorts of iron horns, hand-cuffs, etc. They explained to me how each was worn. They also had to show me where the iron rod, which had a suspended bell on it, was cut off of Uncle Tim's collar.

A crippled man in the group walked with two canes. His clothes were so tattered they were hanging like icicles from his arms. I found a whole suit for him, as well as a soldier's overcoat. He changed in the rear of the cabin and returned weeping.

"I come to show you," he said; "dis is de best dressin' I's ever had in my life. An' I thanks you, an' praise God."

As I was returning to my Natchez post, there before my very eyes standing on the bank of the river were thirty or forty men dressed in Rebel gray waiting for their return ferry. Fear crept over my heart, but thankfully, there were enough Union bristling bayonets close by to intimidate them. Fighting the lines, the crowds, the storm and helping the suffering along the way, we finally delivered Captain Howe's sick woman and two small children to the hospital.

As I arrived at my camp following curfew, the guard said, "Madam, you cannot enter without a permit from the officer for the night."

I said, "Sir, I have been all day without a fire."

He said, "Yes, I know the storm continued late into the afternoon."

I explained, "We could not get the ambulance for the sick woman through the lines this morning," and I held my papers up for him to see.

Holding up his lantern to look, he caught sight of my pass, and immediately said, "Go on! I know who you are. I've seen your picture before." Retiring to Judge Bullock's third story, I was so grateful to have accomplished our feat for the day. I felt greatly relieved, though very chilled. I knew that I would never forget the horrific scenes of suffering and dying that day.

Early the next morning, peering out my third story window, I saw a twelve-year-old drummer boy march into camp with seven ragged and weary barefoot prisoners under his command. This unimaginable image caught my attention. Interestingly enough, many Rebel prisoners acted relieved to be taken by the Union camp, where they would receive food, clothing and comfortable accommodations. One entire Rebel company turned themselves in after a few had been given a Union mark and a badge of national colors to wear under their coats in order to go out and bring the rest of their group in safely.

Many of these men were tired and exasperated and did not actually realize the true object of the war. Had they known it, they never would have joined the Rebel forces, or so they said. More than half had never even owned a slave, and they had been given erroneous information about the rabid nature of Northerners. Similar lies had been shared with slaves. The converted Rebel soldiers found their needs were supplied, and in turn they provided needed help to the Union.

Spring 1864, the wheels of justice were set in motion! Judge Bullock complained he couldn't go to a meeting in Natchez without a pass, the same passes once required of the 6,000 slaves now roaming freely in this City of Refuge.

Painters were actively repainting all of the slave sale advertisements throughout the city of Natchez. The painters were on a mission, as they knew these signs were offensive to the eyes of their new Northern leaders. Yet on many signs the white paint was "too thin" to hide their original messages. One sign read, in spite of the white-wiped washing, "Slaves, horses, mules, cattle and plantation utensils sold on reasonable terms." My fear is that many Southern hearts were just as frail as the half-covered white washed signs.

Mrs. Backus and I set up our supplies and rations on the Ralston Plantation. There we met many needy families and handed out supply tickets, telling them the place and time to meet again. The squalid wretchedness of the slave families was appalling. The next afternoon we scheduled a time for orphan children; 122 arrived. Placing them in two rows, boys on one side and girls on the other, and finding an assistant for each row, we worked tirelessly measuring and handing out clothes that were close to their size. We kept each of them in their respective places until we had given each child something. Hundreds of families had their needs supplied for the moment; yet, we felt discouraged that we really could not meet their overall needs.

I met Milla Granson while working on the Ralston. Milla was one of two black teachers in the area. There was no more fascinating journey than the one she shared. She taught hundreds of black children and adults to read and write through her night schools, though she had been closed down more than once.

In the midst of the most pitiful, despicable scenes of sorrow, we found many little scenes of hope and cheer. Sometimes men and women from the South would confess that they never really believed in secession. One confessed that he had never been convinced that slavery was right, in spite of the many arguments. He had inherited a few slaves, but he could never bring himself to buy or sell one. All of his slaves remained with him, though he had released them. They remained, and he began to pay them wages. At sixty years of age, he was able to avoid serving in the Confederate Army, but found he had to keep quiet about his views. Completely against war, this conscientious Christian believed the Lord would not prosper such folly.

This Confederate soldier had a very different spirit from that of Judge Bullock, who one day carelessly spouted in my presence, "I think you have only one class of men in your North. They are the most despicable I have ever known." Holding my tongue, I could not help but think and share with Mrs. Backus later, "Who does he think he is? Judge Bullock is a Copperhead, slippery snake too dastardly to come down and help us fight, but too pusillanimous to fight for their own side!"

Providing supplies and rations to war-weary refugees required endless hours of labor. But little quips of joy and good news along the way made it bearable. Stories of freedom and reunions of family, though bittersweet, were pearls of joy in the midst of the quagmire of pain and suffering. Most days we walked four to six miles to make our deliveries. Fresh arrivals, of those sick with pneumonia and those near death because of wind and rain exposure, kept us extremely busy and required our constant attention.

One day while Sister Backus remained at our store opening boxes and barrels, sorting and arranging their contents, I rode with a load of supplies on a recently confiscated stage-coach drawn by mules into the camp. The colonel was concerned about me riding, as one of the mules was a bit unruly. But I thought, "what could a little ole' mule do to harm me when we had an experienced driver?" So, not only did I ride; but I took in a poor crippled man along the way. He had just arrived at the camp clad in a few cotton rags patched so completely with old stocking-tops and bits of tent cloth that one could not detect the original fabric. His garb was quite a spectacle.

Tromping down "Paradise Road" to the camp in Natchez at the bottom of the hill, the unruly mule began to prance, kick and rear until both mules were completely out of control. The galloping mules had kicked up such a cloud of dust we couldn't see a thing. If we would overturn at the short curve near the base of the hill, I knew we could be dashed to pieces especially if we were to strike one of the many large stumps. I prayed for a guiding hand, as there was no way to avoid a fall. As the wagon went down amid the stumps, we were drug several feet beyond the coach. The canvas covering broke free from the wheels. Our driver landed several feet further over the canvas while my crippled friend and I were attempting to crawl out from underneath it. By the time a dozen men reached us, I had crawled out and was hauling the canvas off the groaning, crippled man. His head and face were covered with blood, and I whistled for one of the men to run for a pail of water. I just knew the poor man must be dying.

"Oh, no, it's all right! It'll make me a better man," he said weakly, while catching his breath and wiping the blood from his mouth.

"You had better sit down, Mrs. Haviland. You are badly hurt," said one of the men.

"Oh no, I am not hurt," was my reply.

Still trying to help wash the crippled man's head, I found a little child's shirt that helped do the job. Looking down I realized the front of my dress was torn open, though I had to throw back my bonnet to see it. I knew, however, nothing was broken. Although we had turned many somersaults in the air, I never felt quite as vigorous. I had requested someone to send for the surgeon to check out my wounded comrade. Yet I knew he was in good care as I saw one of the men carefully washing the large gash in his head. Learning the driver was going to be fine, as well, I left to find the surgeon myself, holding my torn dress-skirt in my hand. Reaching his office, I found him mounting his horse, and seeing me he cried out in surprise.

"Why, Mrs. Haviland! I just this moment received word that you were nearly killed, and I was coming to check on you."

"I am all right," I said; "but I wish thee would go and see the crippled man that was with me, for I am afraid he was nearly killed."

"Very well, but I shall look after you first."

In spite of my protests, the surgeon gave me a rough, but thorough, check, pressing all over my body. I was convinced he had either found or made some extra sore places. But he insisted that I be taken in his ambulance to headquarters, where morphine was prescribed. I knew I did not need it and refused to take it; but I promised him I'd ask for it if necessary. Thank goodness he dropped the issue and let me go without it. Too sore and lame to resume my work for several days, it was at least a month before I was back to normal.

Chapter Sixteen

3,000 Soldiers

Mrs. Backus and I also spent time in Baton Rouge and New Orleans serving our troops and freedman by providing food, clothing and supplies. We heard many first hand stories of the wounded and suffering. As the tables of justice began to swing compassionately for the freed slaves, so the Rebel voices began to cry foul. It appeared the greater the wins of the Union, the louder the whining of the Rebel. I was thankful that my hands and mind could remain busy with caring for those in great need. Never in my life could I have anticipated to see such great changes for people of color. I wished my dear Charles and Elizabeth Chandler could have been here to share this sweet victory. Yet, I sensed they were rejoicing with me.

Arriving at our temporary New Orleans home on April 6, 1864, our accommodations were most comfortable. A grove of fig trees rested beneath our windows, and here we found shade and the kindest friends. Mrs. Brice, our lovely hostess, was also the teacher of sixty scholars in one of the ten colored schools in New Orleans. We joined the Brices and spent hours eating delicious oranges, listening to their personal experiences with fanatical and wild, hateful attitudes towards the Union. Though greatly terrorized, they were able to stand strong against the torrent of opposition before the war. Mr. & Mrs. Brice had struggled with this bitter hatred towards the North for close to five years, all the while contending for the Union goals in all forms of civil, political and religious life.

Mrs. Brice touted with a tear creeping unashamedly down her cheek. "When the 'Yankee' soldiers arrived on their gun-boats, marched up the streets, the poor terror-stricken and misguided children ran home and started screaming the Yankees have come to kill us. While at the sight of the 'red-white-blue,' others cried out for joy." She continued, "Schools were dismissed and businesses closed. Unfortunately, the bitter opposition between the two sides continues to prevail."

Meeting kindred spirits was a rare treat and as always seemed like an oasis in the dessert. At one New Orleans love feast service there was "breaking of bread," weeping, singing whirling, jumping, and shaking hands. Some exclaimed tearfully as they shared one with another, "Praise God for this day of liberty to worship Him!" There was such joy and exhilaration!

One sister said to another as she hugged her neck, "Oh sister, don't you 'member when da tuck us over in dat jail dat night, an' said da would whip us if we didn't stop prayin'?" Together they laughed, jumped and shouted, throwing their hands in the air.

One elderly man placed his hand on the pastor's shoulder and said, "Bles' God, me son, we don't hav' ta kep' watch at th' door fur feer' they tak' us to jail. can't no longer fine' us $25 fur prayin' and talkin' o' th'lov o' Jesus. Oh no! We's FREE!" He clapped his hands and shouted, "Glory, glory, Hallelujah!" and many others joined in, "Glory, Hallelujah to the Lamb forever!"

The release of such emotion, the long pent-up feelings, continued and then settled into a reverent silence. The pastor exhorted each to share their specific remarks briefly. After an hour of hearing their gut-wrenching experiences, the meeting closed with singing.

"The jubilee has come; And we are free, we are free!"

At the conclusion of the service, once again they joined together in expressing the joy and excitement of freedom overflowing their hearts. This people had been oppressed for so long that this great victory was truly beyond their comprehension.

We had visited many New Orleans schools, some opened by missionaries and government aid workers, one in a confiscated college with more than 400 students. One school visit in New Orleans surpassed them all. Their school was held in an old slave-pen, the same place that thousands of slaves had been sold away from their families to the highest bidder. One could almost hear the cries between mothers and children parting that had been ignored, and the sounds of whips lashing out as husbands and fathers pleaded to keep their families together. Now these heartaches, sorrows and groans lived on only in haunted memories and nightmares. This place of torture had been transformed into a building for education, culture and religious learning for black children. Union flags hung proudly in the old pen along with a large portrait painting of President Abraham Lincoln, which hung on the wall behind the teacher's desk. Unbelievable! Tears of joy mingled with pain streamed down my face, assessing the reality of it all.

Calling at the Christian Commission Room (CCR) in New Orleans one day, Brother Diossy, the chaplain there, said, "If you are hunting for destitute places, I wish you would go to Ship Island, in the Gulf of Mexico. There are soldiers and many prisoners there that have no chaplain or agent to look after their condition."

Pondering his suggestion, I was torn. I would have gone had I been by myself, but Sister Backus felt it better for us to return home. I told Letitia I would never try to force or manipulate her into going anywhere against her better judgment. The weather had finally turned warm and we were quite fatigued from our months of toil. The more I thought about it, she was right. We were worn to a frazzle.

Yet, after attending a soldier's prayer meeting, I felt impressed by God to head towards Ship Island. At the end of the meeting one soldier stood, looked at us, and said, "I thank God for the privilege of knowing ladies like the two of you who remind us our dear mothers far away at home." He was overcome with emotion and could say no more until finally he was able to speak these words: "You may call me weak, and if this be weakness, then I am weak." Before we left, another had requested prayer for his sick brother soldier, as well as for the continuing welfare of the Northern ladies who labored so faithfully among them.

I started calling at the transportation office daily, but was given no hope that a steamer headed that direction would surface for perhaps two weeks. General Banks had called for nearly every boat on the Red River to support his fleet. Then it happened. I saw it, a steamer, *Clyde,* had landed and was heading to Ship Island in four hours. I immediately made reservations for two, not even thinking about what I had done.

Walking into our boarding house, I asked Sister Backus, "Dost thee think, Letitia, that a little bit of sea-breeze could do more to bring thee rest than the labors would to bring weariness?"

I'm not sure what she really thought, but she consented to go along for the ride. I'm sure she could have questioned my judgment and promise not to coerce her, but she did not do so. Rushing to prepare in short notice, we barely managed to bundle ourselves down with a half a bushel of reading materials from the CCR. We were most fortunate to secure the aid of two soldiers who carried our books to the streetcar and further onto the *Clyde.*

That was when poor Letitia Backus discovered there was no sleeping berth for us. The crew was thoughtful enough to provide us with a couple of blankets, but there was only enough space for one of us lie down at a time. Taking turns we were able to sleep. The next morning, April 8, we arrived at Ship Island. From a distance, the white sand along the coast could have passed for a beautiful white blanket of snow.

Once landed, we settled under a few scrubby trees and close to a cactus plant that spread out and looked like a dinner plate. Ship Island is only eight miles in length and about a half-mile wide. The captain said he would not leave until late afternoon. We worked hard, making the best use of time accordingly. It wasn't long before we drew a crowd with our large market-basket full of New Testaments and other devotional materials.

The gunboat boys and prisoners surrounded us like hungry children. Some of these prisoners came in their irons. Holding the iron ball in one arm while reaching for a New Testament with the other, one said. "Please give me a Testament. I lost mine in battle." Another said, "Please give me one. I lost mine in a long march." Yet another said, "Please give me something to read. I lost my Testament in a rain-storm." At one point it looked like there were thirty to forty hands reaching over the shoulders of others. Our basket was empty in less than an hour.

Since we had an extra hour before our boat's departure, we decided to gather sea shells along the beach. Finally, we took our remaining rations to the hospital. Visiting with the officers, we learned what they needed us to bring on a return visit from New Orleans.

That's when we discovered our boat had left us. Poor Sister Backus was so distraught at being left behind. We spied the boat almost a mile away before we realized it. I tried to comfort her saying all was not lost, assuring her the Lord would provide for us as He always had. Returning to the place we had left our satchels, Mrs. Green, an officer's wife, heard our dilemma and interjected. "Yes, you shall have a place at my home. I have plenty of bedding, and I'll dress up a bed for you two. My husband can find a place with some of his comrades, and I'll make a bed for myself on the floor till the boat comes back."

"There, Sister Backus," I said soothingly, "the Lord is already providing for our needs."

With a catch in her weak voice she whispered, "I shall doubt no more."

Mrs. Green, a prim and proper, tidy mulatto woman, prepared a beautiful dinner presented in the best possible style, with fine linen and china, a solid silver pitcher and tableware. "Mrs Green, I have not seen such a richly set table in my time of serving the army," I mused. She laughed and with a tilt of her head nonchalantly commented, "Oh, Mrs. Haviland, both my father and Mr. Green's father were wealthy planters, and we were recipients of a fine inheritance.

"How very fortunate for you," Sister Backus replied, wiping her tears and trying to accept our circumstances cheerfully. Lieutenant Green arrived for dinner, and we found him a kind and congenial conversationalist. As dinner was being served, Captain James Noyce called for us and requested that we stay with his family while we were on the island. Of course, we shared Mrs. Green's kind offer and he replied, "I know that Mrs. Green has the nicest things of any one on this island, but my wife and I want you with us. I will return after dinner to help you collect your things."

Bidding farewell to the Greens, Captain Noyce accompanied us into their home. We were most comfortable, realizing our lot had been cast in a pleasant place. By this time Letitia was completely calm, and Mrs. Noyce a very pleasant hostess. During our visit Sister Backus happened to notice a newspaper circular on the life of Orange Scott.

Holding up the paper Sister Backus exclaimed in surprise: "Sister Haviland, here is the life story of Orange Scott! Isn't this home-like way out here in the Gulf of Mexico?"

"Do you know anything of Orange Scott?" Mrs. Noyce inquired.

"I guess we do. We know all about him," Sister. Backus responded.

"You are not Wesleyan Methodists, are you?"

"Indeed we are, both of us." Letitia Backus actually sounded happy.

Mrs. Noyce flew towards us, grabbing both Sister Backus and myself in an embrace. "I don't wonder! You seemed so much like relatives. Orange Scott is my father, and Mr. Noyce and I are Wesleyans," she cried and laughed all at once.

It was obvious that this overjoyed, homesick woman desperately missed her Northern family. Standing by her husband's side on Ship Island many years, she was experiencing military fatigue. Her husband feared that she was struggling from poor health, yet she would not leave his side. Our joyous time was a healing balm with kindred spirits sharing to gether.

Walking on the beach the next day, we were pelted by thick, drifting sand. Mesmerized watching the waves as they lashed from the gulf against the bars of sand, we stood paying our respects at the soldier's cemetery. A briny spray stuck to the soldier's graves like frost in the early morning. I couldn't help but shed a tear thinking of those brave soldiers who had left their homes and loved ones to serve their country, never to return. Reflecting on this while listening to the solemn moan of the ocean, my heart ached. Yet I sensed God's presence of peace and love, remembering the words of an old poem. "He plants his footsteps in the sea, and rides upon the storm."

On Ship Island, we met many prisoners who impressed us with their Christian character. Because I labor among prisoners, I never question any of them regarding particular crimes. I always pray and direct their thoughts to the Lord Jesus who loves all sinners. Yet, in this case I had an uneasy feeling, and I felt a great sympathy on behalf of these held by irons.

One day, I broke my own rule and inquired of Captain Noyce. "What crime have these soldiers committed that they should be confined so in these chains?"

"No crime," he responded.

"Then please tell me," I asked, "Why are they here?"

"They were sentenced for drunkenness, being late to roll-call, absence without leave and selling government property. Most of the offenses include exchanging rations for groceries such as sugar and tea."

"Is this possible?" I questioned. "Wherever else I have served, such trivial offenses are settled in their own regiments."

"So they have wherever I have been, until I came here. But you seem to question my word. If you would like, we can step into my office and examine the record. You will find these men sentenced from one to 38 years for the offenses I have named."

"I have no reason to doubt thy word, but I will thank thee for the privilege of examining that record. Who pronounced these sentences?"

"Judge Attocha," Captain Noyce replied.

"Who is Judge Attocha?"

"He was a Rebel captain until New Orleans fell into our hands. He took the oath of allegiance, and General Banks promoted him by giving him the position of judge advocate."

"That man is a Rebel still!" I exclaimed. "He is doing more for the Rebel cause than when he was at the head of his Rebel ranked company. Dost thou say over 3,000 have passed through your hands here and on the Dry Tortugas?"

"Yes, Mrs. Haviland," Noyce calmly replied.

"We read in the paper, an order from President Lincoln to draft men, and here are three whole regiments sentenced out of commission. Are these all Union soldiers? This is a grievous situation," I groaned.

"They are all Union soldiers. We held only one Confederate soldier sentenced to one year for murder. He was here only three months, before he was pardoned. On your return to New Orleans you may see him walking the streets free as a bird."

"Holding these 3,000 men is a flagrant wrong! Can thee report Judge Attocha?" I questioned.

Hesitating, Captain Noyce admitted. "He outranks me, and should I presume to report him, I would be put into a dungeon myself and probably be left to die there without an investigation."

This state of affairs troubled me deeply, and I was thankful that Captain Noyce stepped back into the office and brought out the long roll, a record of offenses that had been documented on these soldiers. The roll measured the length of a man's height. As I unrolled a few feet at a time I read each name, his regiment, company, the offense and penalty for each soldier. They included the following offenses: 1) drunkenness, fifteen years of hard labor attached to a ball and chain, with no wages save three dollars a month; 2) selling government property, eight years hard labor with the same affects as the prior offense. The sentences were not all the same duration, but each included the same forfeitures and everyone was chained to the irons. A man who was from my home state of Michigan, near Battle Creek, was sentenced to life. Why? What was his crime? "Suspicious character" was the reason given. No other offense.

Reading through this unjust record with Sister Backus, we were laden with heavy hearts. What could be done on behalf of these poor men? Some of them were sick and dying. Scurvy was a deadly killer. I couldn't sleep that night, thinking and praying. My anguish went out to the One who hears the sighs of each prisoner. I prayed that God would lead me to the one who could break the chains for these 3,000 men in irons.

Thank goodness, Captain Noyce was a very kind-hearted man. It comforted me to know that in many cases he would allow them to go without the chains. He charged the men to be careful and not allow him to see them in order to keep his own record clear. He did everything he could to favor these men because of the injustice of their sentences.

I awakened to a clear beautiful morning, Sunday, April 10, 1864. The first comment from Sister Backus was, "You are either sick, or very weary, for you groaned in your sleep all night long."

"I am not conscious of having groaned, but I did not sleep a wink. I am distressed, and have spent the night praying for a guiding hand to open a door of relief for these prisoners. I must see them before I leave this island. I am bearing a heavy heart this morning!" I lamented.

"Try and dismiss it if possible," Letitia soothed. "Captain Noyce has appointed a meeting for us in the regiment, and I presume there will be an opportunity for you to see the prisoners."

All day long I tried to dismiss my heartache for the prisoners, but could not. Sister Backus and I held a special service at a Ship Island church that included several officers and many gun-boat soldiers sharing together in the peace of our Redeemer's love and spirit of freedom. At the end of the service, Captain Noyce approached me. "You must certainly be too weary to visit the prisoners now."

"Oh no," I was quick to respond, "Not at all, if thee will allow me that privilege."

"They are in large barracks, and it is an unpleasant place for a lady to visit; but if it is your wish, the gun-boat officers wondered if you have any objections to their going along," Noyce continued.

"No, I'm not tired in the least, and anyone is welcome to join us," I replied.

Arriving at the prison barracks with Captain and Mrs. Noyce, the prisoners were packed six men deep all the way around the barracks, leaving only a three foot aisle in which to navigate. Every bed was full. Everyone was in irons, either handcuffs with a chain, or an ankle clog with a ball and chain. I'll never forget the scene before me, nor the sounds. At the slightest move there was a chain reaction of clicking irons. Our group walked midway through the long aisle. I could not get this image out of my heart and mind. The men, filthy and ragged, with bugs and fleas crawling all over them, were a desperate sight. Many had been there for over a year without even as much as a change of clothing.

I had been asked to speak and yet the words were slow to come. I certainly could not discuss the injustice of their punishment.

"Men, I encourage thee to envision the day these chains will fall from thy ankles, the day that thee will walk out of these doors. When thee will rise from this place of affliction, and walk into noble, higher and holy aspirations! I know right now it seems as though thy prayers to heaven sound like brass and the whole is a great prison filled with chains. But hold tight, look up, God has not forgotten thee!"

After speaking for a few minutes, I turned to Sister Backus for her thoughts, but I could tell by her tears she was choked and unable to speak. So, I offered a closing prayer as we were ready to leave. As I knelt, the sound of the clinking chains was deafening as each man in turn kneeled. It took a moment for the sounds to reverberate through the barracks. While praying, my heart overflowed with thankfulness for a room full of men who expressed such reverence to God.

Two prisoners stepped forward as we were leaving and said, "On behalf of our fellow prisoners, thank you for the kind words you have spoken to us. We pray God will grant you safe travels to your Northern homes." We left them with many tears in our eyes and theirs. After this stop we traveled to several other quarters equal in size, all with very similar experiences.

Early the next day a prisoner approached me, asking if I would take a petition from the Ship Island prisoners to General Weitzel, the former commander of seventy of the prisoners. Hearing that he was currently in New Orleans they thought that he was the one commander who could possibly do something towards their release. He was remembered by all as a very kind officer. I agreed to the prisoners' request, and his eyes filled with tears as he thanked me.

Making a few more calls on the prisoners, we prepared to return to New Orleans. Sister Backus and I joined the soldiers for dinner at the request of their wives. While there, I poured over the official roll, writing down the alleged crimes and penalties given to many of the soldiers so I could share this with authorities. Another prisoner brought me their petition, which I promised to deliver to General Weitzel. It read as follows.

>SHIP ISLAND, April 12, 1864.
>
>MAJOR-GENERAL WEITZEL: Sir, We whose names are affixed, prisoners on Ship Island; respectfully beg our release and that we be allowed to return to our respective regiments. We are here for various military offenses, and for nothing criminal. Nearly all of us have participated in the engagements under your lead in this department, both on the battle-field and on the long, wearisome marches we have been called to undergo; and we have always followed cheerfully wherever you have led. We naturally feel that you are the proper person to appeal to give us one more chance to redeem ourselves. And we solemnly assure you that we never will, by any unsoldier-like act, give you any occasion to regret any act of clemency that you may exercise toward us. Many of us are already suffering from that dreaded scourge – the scurvy, which will increase to a fearful extent

in this tropical climate as the season advances. And now that the campaign is open and advancing, and men are needed, we hope we may be permitted to return to the field, and by future faithfulness in our country's cause be able to return to our homes with what all good men so highly prize – *untarnished characters.* Should you exercise your influence in our favor in procuring our release, rest assured you will ever be remembered with gratitude.

Moses Fuller

Fuller had been sentenced to three years hard labor with belt and chain and the meager salary of three dollars per month. His sentence was to appease his crime of selling government property, exchanging his surplus rations. Judge Atocha, the official of this court, would not allow witnesses in his case. Sixty-nine other imprisoned soldiers with similar crimes and sentences included their names in an appendage to the petition.

Anxiously awaiting, our steamer, the *Clyde,* finally sailed into view. Too windy for it to land until noon of that morning, I made one final call on Colonel Grosvenor, the commander of the post. I was thankful he appeared to be a kind-hearted officer and approved our petition. Sailing for New Orleans on the *Clyde,* after spending one week to the day at Ship Island, we watched the island recede from our view. Thankful that all had gone well while stranded in the Gulf of Mexico, we knew our Heavenly Father had a plan and a great adventure. The great adventure had just begun.

Chapter Seventeen

"Red Tape"

Arriving in New Orleans, we searched everywhere for General Weitzel, as well as any news on the state of the war. Participating in a mid-afternoon prayer meeting, we heard from two chaplains who had returned from engagement in the war. One had traveled through Arkansas, and gave exhilarating accounts that his regiment had encountered triumphantly over the enemy. The other chaplain had just come from the dreadful flight of the Union Troops at Alexandria up the Red River. The report was General Banks had received a flag of truce from a Rebel general who indicated that if the Union would withdraw the colored troops that he would take no prisoners and give no quarter. Banks, indeed, withdrew the colored troops and accepted the Rebel's terms of peace, only to be deceived by a horrible slaughter of Union troops.

This continued to demoralize the colored troops as they found themselves, more times than not, doing all types of manual labor and yet generally inactive in the war efforts. As we had traveled the length of the river fortifications, Sister Backus and I noticed that colored soldiers were the ones that kept the cities and streets clean, but were kept away from the war effort.

Visiting army offices and following each lead available in our search for General Weitzel, we grew discouraged. Continuing the search, we didn't know what to believe. Some said he was with General Banks assisting up the Red River. In spite of our completely fatigued and blistered feet, we finally found him. Handing him my official papers, I introduced myself. "General Weitzel, I am Laura Haviland from the Detroit Freedmen's Bureau."

Scanning my papers, General Weitzel gave a courteous nod and asked, "What can I do for you, ma'am?"

With deep emotion betraying my voice, I exclaimed. "I hope thee can do something toward releasing 3,000 of our soldiers now confined on Ship Island and the Dry Tortugas, seventy of whom served under thee! Here is a petition from them."

Taking the petition, he began perusing the names listed. He could not have read for more than a minute when his voice, also filled with emotion, resounded. "Mrs. Haviland, these are noble soldiers. I don't think Moses Fuller, or any of these others, is capable of doing a wrong act. They are the most conscientious men I have known. Judge Attocha should have no right to give these sentences! He obviously has no business judging our Union soldiers!"

"Can thee do something towards their release?" I implored.

"If I were in command, I would tell you 'Yes,' very quickly, but General Banks is the one you must see."

"I am aware of that, but he is beyond my reach up Red River. And I've been told a petition similar to this one was sent three months ago, and they have heard nothing from him."

"I will do what I can toward getting a committee to investigate and report these documents," Weitzel acquiesced.

"Dost thou think thee can accomplish anything in their favor?" I queried.

"I fear it is doubtful, but I will do what I can," Weitzel sadly admitted.

Exhausted and discouraged, there was nothing more to do. Leaving the general, I entered the Christian Commission Rooms (CCR) weary and frustrated, hoping to find some inspiration. I often found these rooms filled with officers, and in particular, generals of high rank duly noted by the eagles and stars on their shoulders.

"Here comes Mrs. Haviland, just returning from Ship Island. How did you find things there?" asked Brother Diossy.

"Sad enough," I responded with a shrug of my shoulder. Handing him a copy of General Weitzel's petition, I highlighted for him the record, offense and penalty of the first fifteen prisoners. This aroused the interest of the other officers, and they all gathered around to see and hear what this petition was all about.

"This is bad," one commented.

"Can't any of thee do something for these soldiers?" I queried.

"I wish I could, but I can't leave my post," said one.

Another replied, "It is a pity someone doesn't."

Turning to him I asked," Can thee do something for their release?"

"It is the same with me," he muttered. "I cannot leave my post."

"Someone ought to see to their release. Can't any of thee do something?" I implored as the pitch of my voice rose in intensity.

"I tell you, madam, it is hard to do much for each other," one admitted.

Addressing these officers of high rank, I ranted.

> Gentlemen, I have learned one thing thoroughly since being with the army, and that is, it is almost impossible to get one officer to touch another's red tape! But position or no position, head or no head, these flagrant wrongs ought to be revealed to the entire country! An order comes from President Lincoln for drafting men,

but Judge Attocha has cast 3,000 good soldiers in chains, when all they ask is to be permitted to return to their respective regiments. That man is serving the Rebel cause more effectually than when at the head of his Rebel ranks, by decimating the Union army from within. Here we have it, proof in a tangible form. I am informed that Judge Attocha was a Rebel captain. He is a Rebel still, and in the exercise of this authority is banishing thy soldiers for trivial military offenses, in irons, with forfeited wages for which their families are now suffering.

After this passionate outburst I recognized that all eyes were upon me. Suddenly feeling very self-conscious, I realized I was talking to them as though they were a group of ten year old boys, forgetting the honor and respect owed them by the straps on their shoulders. What will they think of me? I wondered as my face felt red hot with embarrassment. As I cast a sheepish glance towards them, I was dumbstruck and surprised to see tears flowing. I realized at that moment that these ranking officers were not unfeeling.

Turning to Brother Diossy, I asked. "Can thou leave thy position, and get another to occupy thy place here?"

"Yes, I could, if it would avail anything; but it would be impossible for me to accomplish what you have already done on Ship Island."

"Why does thou say such a thing? It's perfectly preposterous," I said out of exasperation.

"I will tell you why," Brother Diossy continued. "There is too much red tape in the troops. I would be suspected of trying to displace an officer for a position for myself, or for a friend. Consequently I could not have examined the record as you did."

"That is true." Another general joined in, "I presume there is not one of us who could have had access to those records for the reason that Mr. Diossy has given. They know you have no such object in view, but see you as a soldier's mother type. Records, or any sort of investigation, would be opened to you, but they would be closed to us."

I was stunned by their responses.

Then a man of large stature, 6'4", stepped towards me in an official manner and asked as if in command. "Mrs. Haviland, what do you propose to do with these facts gathered from Ship Island?"

As he towered over my 4' 9" stature, I felt more than a little overwhelmed.

"I say, madam, what do you propose to do with these papers?" He asked again.

"I can hardly answer intelligently. I'm not sure," I responded with hesitation. "But I will tell thee one thing I propose to do. I plan to take these facts from one officer to another until they reach the highest official at Washington. Justice needs to be done for those poor soldiers in irons!"

"Yes, it ought to be done," He said in a relieved, low tone walking away.

Though I never learned the officer's name, his commanding presence and memory comforted and motivated me when I grew discouraged on the journey to free the 3,000 soldiers.

Attending an afternoon prayer meeting, Chaplain Conway, my dear friend, said he would meet with General Weitzel and see if anything could be done on behalf of the Ship Island prisoners. He said if he received a favorable response he would write me at my Adrian home, as Sister Backus and I were planning to return there. I asked him to send the letter on two boats as guerrillas were actively involved in robbing ships and destroying mail and other cargo. We agreed that if no letter came from him within two weeks of my return, I would accept the fact that nothing could be done by General Weitzel for the men.

Colonel Hanks gave us a tour of his Sabbath-school with 700 students at the Medical College. Then as if God himself had picked me up and placed me exactly where I needed to be, I made a connection that began to set into action the course of justice for our 3,000 prisoners. Late that afternoon in a service at the Medical College I met her, the wife of General Banks, Mary.

Unexpectedly, Colonel Hanks called me upfront to address the school and the folks there with a few words about our work. I said, "Friends, please pray with me for a very serious concern in Ship Island. There, on our mission's journey, we found 3,000 soldiers who are serving time in the Ship Island prison without due cause!"

Immediately following the service, Mrs. Banks came forward and Colonel Hanks introduced us. "Mrs. Haviland, this is General Banks's wife, Mary. She is very concerned about your comments."

"Indeed!" Mrs. Banks spoke commandingly. "Please tell me more about this travesty on Ship Island. I know that Nathaniel will be quite upset, as Judge Attocha made a commitment to my husband that he would do all in his power to promote the Union cause. Is this his way of repaying my husband for the promotion he was given to serve as a judge? No, Mrs. Haviland, do tell me all you know!"

We visited for close to an hour when Mary Banks finally concluded, "Oh dear, I will never remember all of this. Please write out these facts. I need something tangible to hand my husband."

I wrote down everything I could remember from the petition and my notes. I denoted the high levels of punishment with the low level of misdemeanors that had been leveled against the men. I reinforced General Weitzel's comments about the men being some of the best who had ever served him. It was a relief to have finally found a sympathetic and influential ear. One that could do something that just might reverse the adverse and unjust sentences. Perhaps it would come to nothing. Yet, I knew I had given my best, both with my statement to Mrs. Banks and with the petition handed to General Weitzel. I now felt free to return home, for which my heart was longing and my body ached.

Following this encounter, Sister Backus and I traveled to the Red River and witnessed 500 prisoners of war that the Union soldiers had captured. Many of these were citizens of New Orleans. Our journey home began on the hospital steamer *Thomas.* It was bound for Cairo. On board were eighty wounded soldiers from the Red River expedition that had gone badly for General Banks and the Union. These soldiers were all headed home, either discharged or furloughed. The medical inspector on the *Thomas* gave us a state room for our temporary stay on the ship. Right after breakfast we began dressing wounds. The worst problem was flies; constantly swatting flies away we worked on the soldiers' wounds. The stench was unbearable. The poor soldiers had wounds that required intensive care. These included the horrible mangling due to saber cuts and all sizes of bullet wounds to all parts of the body. The sight was atrocious! Trying to hide my tears, a few still crept down my face regardless. But once back in our stateroom, Letitia and I cried our eyes and hearts out!

The trademark of these Union men was their patience. They were such an inspiration to us! Mrs. Backus and I were thankful for the many kind and loyal soldiers we met on our travels. We had to smile and thank God for his protection and special acts of comfort and kindness that often came our way. This seemed incredible to us, as we were often surrounded by bitter Rebel opponents.

Our ship's first stop was supposed to be in Baton Rouge. It was my hope that the ship would make a quick stop at Plaquemine, LA, so I could pick up a little girl, Matilda, and take her to Eliza, her mother, who was a former slave I had helped escape several years earlier. I was busy nursing when suddenly I was informed the ship was stopping and we were at Plaquemine. Without thinking I grabbed my shawl and bonnet, hastily told everyone farewell and jumped ashore only to look back and see a small group of friends, Letitia and the surgeons waving their handkerchiefs.

Instantly realizing with a sinking feeling, my portfolio with all of my official papers and pass were still on the *Thomas* and on their way to Baton Rouge. Ah...what had I been thinking? In the hustle and bustle I had completely forgotten them. But what could I do but keep moving.

Searching for Matilda I found a colored soldier who recognized me from Detroit. He pointed me in the right direction to find Eliza's sister, Matilda's aunt. Knocking on the door of an old two-story brick building that served as boarding rooms for newly released slaves, I found Eliza's two sisters and Matilda. She was wild with delight when she saw me. I had been visiting with them for a short time when my soldier friend knocked on the door, bringing with him several other soldiers whom I had helped in Detroit. It was a great reunion! Eliza's sisters told us the quite complicated and lengthy stories of efforts to recapture both of them. We were thankful that their efforts turned out to be idle threats.

Everyone was quite concerned that I would have a difficult time crossing to Baton Rouge because the commander was a cross man and known to limit transportation along the river. So I went straight to his office, told him my business and my dilemma. "Sir, on leaving the *Thomas* in haste, I simply jumped off without my portfolio and pass. I understand that thee has nothing to judge my statements by, but I need to find a way to get this little girl and myself to Baton Rouge."

"Well, I think your motherly face will take you to Baton Rouge," he replied. "There is a regular packet running to that city, and I will send a note by you to the captain that will secure you passage, although it is not a government boat. The captain has received favors from me, and I will gladly make this return." I was elated as he handed me a signed request for ship passage, including a stateroom for the two of us, and my heart cried out, "Thank God!"

Matilda and I rushed to board the packet *Bank* on a beautiful April evening. Once Eliza and Matilda were reunited, I was released to move forward in our work. What a relief to be reunited with Letitia and my personal belongings that she had held in safe keeping.

It was good to see Brother Merrifield again. He accompanied us on a visit through the jail so we could pass out our New Testaments and tracts. They were gratefully received by most. One Rebel captain, who was a rebel in the strongest possible sense, boasted. "If I get out of this place, I will go after my regiment and we will fight to establish the one true government. 'Long live the Rebels!'

Handing him one of our New Testaments I said, "I'm afraid the only true way to peace for thee is through the truths thee will find in the Scriptures. Read them carefully. Pray thoughtfully! If thee will drink in the Spirit, thee will begin to find peace and a pure walk with God that is beyond imagination."

"Madam," he declared with flushed face, "if I thought reading that book carefully and prayerfully, and accepting pure and undefiled religion, would lead me to lay down arms in defense of my Confederate Government, I would never read a word in it or take one thought of religion, not to save my soul!" His face then turned completely pale and he stumbled away. We learned later that he had been the captain of a guerrilla band, sentenced for execution, but the sentence had been commuted.

Two days later arriving in Natchez, we rejoiced together with old friends. We also grieved as we met much resistance here. Rebel leaders and sympathizers were causing havoc all along the way. They schemed and made every plan possible to drive the refugees back into the arms of their slaveholders and their old plantations. Worse yet, the Union Army itself worked against the refugees through an infamous Health Order.

The Health Order demanded that every unemployed colored person was compelled to enter a "corral," or colored camp. People of color were doing all they could do to provide work for those of their race in order save them from the "corral." Yet, all to no avail. What the order did not say was these persons had to have a white employer.

The soldiers, on the day the order took effect, hunted all of these good people down. It had been indiscriminately determined that no colored party would be considered a responsible employer. To my dismay and horror, 250 persons of color were marched through the streets of Natchez on a cold, rainy day into the camp of four thousand who were living in condemned tents.

Driven under Union bayonets, the fugitives were tantalized by Rebel sympathizers, "Come back to us! Come back to us! We never would have done this to you!"

One colored woman standing by with tears streaming down her face said, "I was paying this woman wages, and allowed her and her three children to live with me in my home. Did the soldiers listen? No! They paid no heed at all, pushing her out into the mob parade in the pouring rain."

The women marched weeping, while an old colored man in the group, comforted them, saying. "Never min', there's a better day a comin.' Twould be strange if Uncle Sam din't have a few naughty boys."

Feeling outraged at these abuses and excess when they clearly ran counterproductive and inhumane to all other Union's efforts, all we could do was pray. Word came that a skirmish occurred close to our camp. All we knew was a group of Rebel scouts had fired at our pickets and then hastily retreated. Blue smoke billowed some four miles away as the skirmishing of war continued. It was unnerving to see and smell. The smoke made the shooting seem much nearer to us than it was. I had to think about how those in our free states understood so very little about this terrible war! Overcome with a chill and feeling homesick I was ready to head home.

Sister Backus and I met Delphine, a 17-year-old mulatto slave girl, as were preparing to return to Michigan. Weeping as she walked the street, I asked, "What's wrong, honey?"

She replied with tears still flowing, "My owner, Mrs. Morehead, just beat me as does daily."

"Why does thee remain with her?" I asked.

"She keeps my baby locked up and says if I leave, I shall never have him." She continued sobbing.

"Delphine, go to the provost-marshal and he will order thy mistress to give thee the child." This brought great relief to her anguished face. Having promised to go with her, we entered the marshal's office together. The marshal verified my words and offered her protection. Leaving the office she said, "I'm goin' to go pack a few things in my old trunk and then watch for a time when the mistress is gone to bring my baby to the Freedmen's store."

Once the child was out of sight and in safe surroundings in our headquarters, I sent for a soldier to carry her trunk. Yet we didn't tell a soul about her situation. A short time after Delphine had arrived hiding little Charlie, Mrs. Morehead appeared searching up and down the street for Delphine.

Charlie's sad story began before the war when Mr. Morehead had purchased Delphine away from her mother in St. Louis. Purchased to be their hotel dancer, Charlie's father was her master, Mr. Morehead. The child bore such a strong resemblance to Morehead that he was frequently mistaken by strangers as the child of her mistress. Delphine was 66% Caucasian. The skin of the child was pure white and would never give anyone the least thought that he had one sixteenth part of African blood. Delphine just wanted to go home.

Securing transportation for Charlie and Delphine to Cairo, I paid for her trip to St. Louis. Saying good-byes to our kind friends, we headed towards the wharf with Delphine and Charlie by our side.

Unfortunately, Mrs. Morehead found our whereabouts and followed, crying out, "Delphine! Delphine!" Thank goodness we had boarded the boat before she arrived. Delphine was trembling like a leaf, but at least she had the presence of mind to grab the babe and hide.

"Delphine, where are you?" she wailed. Finally Delphine came out of hiding and asked me with misery in her eyes, "What shall I do? I would rather throw myself and baby into the river than go back to her."

Jumping up and down, her mistress yelled. "I tell you, Del, I've got an officer to come and take you to jail for stealing."

I calmly stated, "Delphine, thee has nothing to fear, none of the officers will trouble thee. They informed me earlier they would ignore her threats and complaints, no matter what they were. The police have had more than a little trouble with this Rebel family since they moved to town."

With Delphine's frail body shaking and her lips quivering, I continued. "Go ahead. Leave Charlie here on the boat. Then, go out to the levee and tell Mrs. Moorehead clearly that thee is going to thy mother in St. Louis."

Delphine followed my instruction. Her mistress cried, coaxed and frightened her for over an hour. All the while, the poor little waif of a girl continued to tremble with fear. I was thankful Mrs. Moorehead did not have an officer with her, otherwise I believe Delphine probably would have thrown herself and the child into the river. Unfortunately, Mrs Morehead did not leave but came on the boat. When Delphine recognized that she was on board, she picked up Charlie and ran to the back of the boat with the mistress chasing behind.

Once again she cried, "Mrs. Haviland, what shall I do? I calmly stated, "Sit down here beside me and hold thy child. She will not dare touch thee." Delphine's trembling increased as though she had fallen into a fit of ague.

Looking squarely at me, her mistress said in a rage, "You came into my kitchen with an order and took her, when she was doing better than you ever dare do!"

"I have never entered thy kitchen," I calmly replied. "A soldier went with Delphine for her trunk. An officer also called on thee for the child. It was Delphine's request."

"It's a lie! Delphine lied about me!"

Letitia Backus, sitting close by, responded. "I shouldn't think you would want such a person of low character about you, if that is true."

"Well, the child is so close to me. I've always had the care of it." Stomping off in a fit of rage, she left us with these parting words. "I will return with officers to take Delphine to jail for stealing."

That was the last we saw of Mrs. Moorehead. Thank goodness! We arrived in Cairo the next day and boarded the *Kennet,* starting the final leg of our journey. Delphine clapped her hands for joy as we pushed away from the shore and said, "Now I know Mistress Morehead can trouble me no more. Thank God, I've got my Charlie too!"

Arriving at Vicksburg on the following day, Letitia and I ate our breakfast at the Soldier's Home and took in the sights of the war around us. We were excited to meet Governor Harvey, their former governor, who was a true friend to the soldiers. We consoled a lady transporting the body of her brother home to Iowa for burial. He had been killed in the Red River conflict. As Vicksburg was in the midst of war full of soldiers and tents spread massively across adjoining fields, we spent little time there.

Eight weeks later the city fell into Union command, and we received the following report. An old man, very confident in the Confederate Army and its success, Said, "God will not let it fall; and if the Confederate Government shall fall, I will never believe in God again." After the gun-boats arrived, he was informed that the city had been taken. Shrugging his shoulders, he would not believe it until he rose from his chair and saw the marching columns of soldiers with their bayonets glowing in the 4th of July sun. He immediately fainted back into his chair and died!

Leaving Vicksburg, we boarded a boat, *The Baltic*, but it ran aground. Three hours later we were able to set sail again. Many passengers were dressed and ready to jump off in order to make an escape if we were shipwrecked. The water at one point had risen to three feet in the hull. Thanks to the valiant efforts of the men on board, we pumped the water out. Being a very large boat, we moved very slowly. Thus we spent two extra days with a variety of passengers: soldiers, officers of all ranks, preachers, missionaries and, believe it or not, a few secessionists. General Hunter was also on board for these two days.

A smuggler of goods on the *Baltic* steamer was identified and arrested as he came through the lines on the boat. The prisoner, hands tied, was led to the rear of the boat, when a dozen people of color expressed great excitement over his presence, until they heard the major take charge. The major asked the offender, "Have you taken the oath of allegiance?" The smuggler responded gruffly, "No, and I never will."

The major then continued to ask many other questions concerning his trade and activities on the *Baltic*. He replied, "I will tell you nothing about it, if I stand here till I die! Go to hell!"

Angry tempers flared on the boat. One colored man blurted out: "Let him stand there until he dies!"

Ironically, it seemed the angry mob sentiment of the crowd scared him enough to confess his sins. The major examined him there in the presence of all these witnesses, including General Hunter himself.

After the excitement had subsided the next day, I introduced myself to General Hunter, sharing with him my portfolio. He responded with a kind interest. "How long have you served our army? How far have you traveled?"

Sharing a short sketch of our work, I included some of my struggles, such as General Tuttle's sanctioning of Dr. Kelley's infamous Health Order, the many wrongs we saw among the colored soldiers and in particular my quest to free the 3,000 prisoners of Ship Island and the Dry Tortugas. I shared with him that other missionaries had advised me to never mention these wrongs, no matter how flagrant. I also mentioned the printed order that there should be no report, either verbal or written, of any movements within the army.

"General Hunter," I asked, "should I keep quiet about my concerns within the army, such as the 3,000 prisoners, the Health Order and the unjust treatment of colored soldiers? Or should I report it?"

"Mrs. Haviland," General Hunter thoughtfully replied, "I am glad you have served the army this long, and have come so far. Let me explain that order to you. You have observed movements of troops from one place to another on the eve of battle. These are the matters you are not to report. The wrongs you have met along the way you may proclaim upon your house top when you arrive at home."

His thoughtful answer was a great relief to me. "Thank thee, General Hunter. That is such a helpful explanation."

The general still seemed troubled. After pacing back and forth across the cabin he returned to me in a few minutes and asked. "Mrs. Haviland, we have done a great deal of sifting in the army, and more must be done. Did General Tuttle see those papers you gave me?"

"He did," I replied.

Hearing this, General Hunter responded.

> Copperheads have no business exercising authority in the army. General Tuttle ran for governor on the Copperhead ticket in Iowa last year. What right has a Copperhead to be in his position where loyal men are needed? I believe the only way to crush this rebellion is to emancipate and arm the slaves. I would have proclaimed freedom to the slaves as fast as I reached them. The strength I could have gathered from the slave population would soon have reached 200,000 men, and that number was all that I asked. But the vacillating policy of the government would not permit it. I saw clearly this was the only policy that could prove successful, and I thought surely everyone else could see it when I first proclaimed it in South Carolina. Unfortunately, others took a different view, and my order was superseded.

Intently drinking in General Hunter's words, Sister Backus commented. "General Hunter, you have the satisfaction of knowing that your policy was right for our nation."

"O yes," he hesitantly admitted, "but it is with regret that thousands drafted could have been avoided. There was no necessity for the draft."

Letitia continued, "Yes, we certainly should have armed colored men. They make as good soldiers as white men."

A man standing by, who obviously had paid no attention to our conversation, suddenly chimed in. "I don't know that colored men make as good soldiers as white men, they are not nearly as intelligent. I presume you will say the same thing. Is that right General Hunter?"

General Hunter, looking directly at the man, countered. "I shall say no such thing. Black men make the best soldiers. First, they are kind and docile. Secondly, they are apt to learn. They learn military tactics very readily, and ought to have the same wages as any other soldier. All along this river I find one continued series of wrongs inflicted upon the Negro."

Reaching the mouth of the infamous Red River where so many Union Troops had been slaughtered, we paused in silence, remembering their loss and the atrocities of this war. Here three women of business prowess came on board. They had received permission to board from a gunboat officer. The women said they were looking to hire men willing to gather cane and weave it into reeds. One of the ladies confidentially reported to Dr. Long that she had been watching two ladies on the boat whom she was concerned might be spies. They seemed to do a great deal of writing. Dr. Long, a friend of ours, happened to know these ladies carried the reputation of serving as spies themselves Thankfully, we were able to travel unharmed as he protected us from their accusations.

Continuing our journey upstream, we found the next day miserable and cold. We stopped once again in Columbus, where we finally found a paper. We had heard about the terrible slaughter in Fredericksburg and wanted to get the straight account. The rumor was that 15,000 were wounded and killed. Lee had been pushed back some thirty miles. Grant and Butler were pushing on to Richmond, the Rebel capital. It was thought they were less than a day's march on this advance. If General Hunter were a signal to their success, it would be a good one. He believed confidently that Richmond was soon to fall.

It was difficult to leave our newly-made dear friends. But after this five-day journey we arrived home, welcomed by dear children and wonderful friends. We realized then why the soldiers we met were so excited to see a Northern face, as it brought many thoughts of home. What a blessing to be home!

After sharing our project to free the 3,000 soldiers, the intercession began in earnest for those banished off the Gulf Islands. The mail brought me nothing from Chaplain Conway in New Orleans. I understood from this that nothing could be done on the soldiers' behalf by General Weitzel. I wrote a full account of my findings that included the unjust suffering these soldiers had to endure and handed it to Congressman Beaman. As Congress was still in session, I urged him to present their case before the War Department.

Immediately heading for Detroit, I gave a report of our work with an account of the 3,000 prisoners from the Tortugas and Ship Island. As B.F. Wade the Chairman of the Committee on the Conduct of War, was in Washington D.C., a scribe tediously penned my words so they could be forwarded to him.

The scribe responded, "You should go to Washington and report these facts to the committee in person." I shared that I had already sent a fully detailed report with Congressman Beaman, and I believed he would do all he could on their behalf.

Encouraging me further, he said, "I shall send these items to B.F. Wade, and the letters will make good opening arguments. But the living tongue will do more than the pen."

I replied, "I am ready to go anywhere or do anything that I can for these men's release." Preparing to depart for Washington, I received a letter saying,

> The exhibition of these letters before Secretary Stanton has proved sufficient. Judge Attocha was dismissed immediately. A committee is to be appointed to investigate and release the prisoners at once. There is therefore no necessity for Mrs. Haviland's

presence on that score. General Tuttle is already relieved from his duties, as well.

Writing an account of these facts for the Detroit Tribune, I mailed a copy of the article to Captain J. Noyce. He replied that my communication was the first he had heard of the reversal. He wrote, "I sent the letter and paper to the prisoners, and they eagerly read them in all their companies, until I doubt whether a whole sentence can be found together." It was but a few weeks later that I received a joyous report from Captain Noyce, saying that an investigative committee had arrived and only one out of seventy-five men was still being held, while the others were released at once. It wasn't long before all of the soldiers returned to their regiments. I was thrilled!

The word that Calvin Fairbanks had been released from his Kentucky prison brought cause for new shouts of joy. My thoughts went back to my adventures twelve years earlier in Louisville with Colonel Buckner. I wondered if he had been the one to unlock Fairbanks's chains. How could the chains of bigotry imprison so many and still further justify the chains of slavery?

Chapter Eighteen

Kansas–1864

Exciting changes were taking place in our Freedmen's Aid Commission in June 1864. The commission's purpose was to serve the newly freed refugees in Detroit when suddenly a great call of distress came from Kansas. General Price's raid in Missouri, along with Colorado Lane and Jennison, opened the floodgates, causing thousands of freedmen and poor whites to flood into Kansas. Due to the influx of slaves across the state lines into Kansas, the Detroit Freedmen's Aid Commission created a Kansas Freedmen's Commission to serve the needs of those fleeing over the pro-slavery Missouri border into Kansas, a free state. I enlisted Mrs. Lee of Hillsdale, Michigan, to serve as my assistant in this work. With a carload of supplies and $400 in hand we made our way to Leavenworth, Kansas.

The Kansas Bureau Board of Directors hired me as the first paid agent for their Freedmen's Commission. Never having received a salary for my work, it seemed unusual to receive a paycheck. The rewards of my work, seeing prisoners set free, unfaithful officers relieved of their duties and finding a solace for the dying and suffering remained the same, priceless!

J.R. Brown, under the command of General Curtis, met us there. He operated a soldier's home in Ft. Leavenworth. Two hundred occupants lived in the soldier's home, comprised of two, large two-story frame buildings. Brown and I shared an office in one of these buildings. Brown was in charge of the care for both black and white refugees. His passion for the anti-slavery cause was equal to that of his deceased half-brother, Captain John Brown of Osawatomie, though directed through non-violent means.

General Curtis telegraphed for my goods and gave me transportation passage to and from Fort Scott. My job was to determine and provide for needs in all the intermediate towns where these refugees had gathered. General Curtis authorized me to determine the amount of aid needed and to order the appropriate amount of rations per family.

Because these supplies had not arrived, J.R. Brown immediately provided me with two large trunks of goods for those with the greatest need. With these goods in hand I boarded the stage for Quindaro, a small town, built around deep ravines and rocky bluffs. Years earlier, speculators deemed Quindaro to be an important stop on the Mississippi. It had served as an integral station for the Underground for thousands of refugees escaping to freedom.

Quindaro's simple stone homes were filled with refugees, black and white, consisting mainly of women and children. The men who were able served in the Union Army. Surprisingly, some of the refugee families had men serving in the Confederate Army. Others were victims of General Price's October raid or leftovers from Colonels Lane and Jennison's Jayhawker rebuttal. These stone buildings were terribly crowded, with every niche of space occupied.

What squalid wretchedness! With an achy body and queasy stomach, I attempted to serve 23 wretched souls found in one of these homes. Eight children had measles, three had died and two others looked as though they would not survive! Their feet were exposed to the mud and snow. There was not a single piece of furniture or dish in their gloomy home.

How they slept, I could not guess. But I was shown a rag-carpet that hung on the fence. This was their makeshift bed acquired by doing one of their neighbors washing. It was spread before a large fireplace and all but two of the 23 slept there at night. The other two kept the fire and watched over those sleeping keeping them safe from the fire. Their home was next to a wood land, and the owner kindly gave them permission to use all of the wood on the ground needed. Unfortunately, they had to borrow an axe to chop it. The four adult women, two with pneumonia, husked corn and chopped wood to keep everyone alive during the winter. They were almost completely out of corn and very anxious about food. Ordering rations for them I measured their poor scarred, bare feet for stockings and shoes. One of the women accompanied me to the post office where my trunks were stored. I gave them all I had in stock, two pairs of shoes, four pairs of stockings, six pairs of drawers, six knit woolen socks and four army blankets. The poor woman broke down, weeping for joy as I piled these articles in her arms.

The postmaster asked, "Is this your business here?"

"It is," I replied.

I noticed a tear rolling down his cheek as he said, "Tomorrow morning the ground will be frozen, and I will go with you where most of these poor people are."

Lodging with Widow Johnson, she lamented my mile and a half walk from the log-house in the field and back to the post office, as I had not eaten since early morning. But as I shared with her the blessing I received in alleviating some of this family's suffering, she, too, rejoiced with me. Her son, who had traveled with Captain John Brown's party during the border-ruffian skirmishes, shared many stories.

The kind postmaster accompanied me early the next morning to point out the greatest poverty and destitution in the Quindaro area. Climbing rugged rocks and descending steep cliffs until the afternoon we finally returned for dinner. Reporting the need for 81 rations to the commander in Wyandotte, the postmaster and Mr. Johnson organized teams to distribute rations for the needy. If they found other needy folks, they promised to report it to me on my return trip.

Running late, I barely caught my designated stage to Wyandotte. Arriving late in the evening, Mrs. Halford, my hostess at the Garno House, commented. "Mrs. Haviland, I wish I could help you, but my many duties here are overwhelming. I'm glad to board you, however, and introduce you to my friends."

Mrs. Halford, true to her word, introduced me to a group of benevolent ladies who promised to assist me in my investigations. They felt sure that I would not find the suffering in Wyandotte as I did in Quindaro. One of the ladies, Ruby, decided to accompany me to a neighborhood where I had been alerted to find new arrivals of refugees.

It was late October in Kansas, and this particular season was extremely cold. With the ground already frozen, we found many dying from cold and hunger. Entering sheds and stables we found destitute humans, both black and white, crowded into stalls like animals. Ruby wept herself sick as we listened to their tragic stories of flight from their homes in Arkansas and Missouri. Here are a few stories of those we met.

Melinda Dale with six small children and a very sick husband had fled for their lives. The children's father was sick with fever; the children were sick for lack of food. Melinda, sick with grief, had sewn together a few pieces of old tent-cloth they had salvaged from a campsite for their bed. Giving them several loaves of bread and a blanket, we prayed and shared Scriptures of encouragement with them.

Next we met Lieutenant Miller's wife and five small children living in an old Sibley tent. The lieutenant was being held in chains at a Rebel prison, and Mrs. Miller was greatly concerned over the uncertainty of her husband's welfare and her children's starving condition.

Another example of the agony and suffering we witnessed was Barbara Stewart. Her husband had been murdered by guerillas because he was known as a Union man. We ordered rations for Mrs. Stewart and her two children.

Green F. Bethel left his Arkansas home with a large family; his wife, aged mother and nine children. After passing Fort Scott they, unfortunately, contracted the measles. Bethel lost his mother, an infant child, two sons and finally, his beloved wife. Having buried them by the roadside, he cried out in grief, "Oh, what sorrow is mine! One-half of my family is gone!" He told me, "The light of my household has been extinguished! Were it not for the help of my Lord I should have fainted under this sweeping affliction. My wife and mother had been Christians many years, members of the Cumberland Presbyterian Church."

Poor Green Bethel was overtaken by a hard chill and a high fever when we found him. Yet, he managed to work on alternate days by doing little jobs of hauling with his team. In that way, he kept his surviving children and team alive.

"Why didn't thee tell someone in town of thy need?" I asked.

He sighed and continued to share his tale.

"No one knows me! Who could I trust? In Arkansas our lives were threatened by Confederate Soldiers. The rope was placed around my neck once, but thanks to the entreaties of my wife and children the Rebels concluded to let me live. They left me with the threat that if I did not join them in supporting the Confederate government, I would be hung or shot. We hid in the woods three weeks before we left in the night for the lines of the Union soldiers. Starting with two wagons, nine horses, and three cows, we lost all except the young, best team. I have a good farm in Arkansas, but if we are ever permitted to return, it is doubtful we will find one building left."

Green and his children wept freely. Amy, his seventeen-year-old daughter, leaning her head on my shoulder said, "We could all bear this furnace of affliction much better if our dear mother had been spared us."

I prayed with this dear family who had suffered so much. I told Mr. Bethel that he would need to call on head-quarters to pick up the rations I was ordering for the six in his family. Taking my hand he begged of me, "Dear sister, please continue to pray that the Lord may open a way for us where there now seems to be no way."

Promising to do just that, Ruby and I left the Greens. Ruby lamented, "My head aches with weeping, in witnessing these heart-rending scenes. I must decline going with you further this afternoon. I shall be obliged to take to my bed. I do not see how you live. You meet similar scenes so frequently."

Arriving late due to these long visits, I was thankful Mrs. Halford had dinner waiting for me. She sat beside me, interested in my report of our morning calls. "Mrs. Haviland, I am shocked that such suffering and destitution exists in our fair Wyandotte!"

Resuming my work after dinner I met a sick, poorly dressed woman shivering and weeping. I asked, "Honey, why is thee so sad?"

"I'se been huntin' for somethin' to do, washin' anythin' to feed my poor little children. They hasn't had a thin' to eat all day!" I promised her that I would bring her bread before night. I met her later in the day on the street, carrying her eight-month-old infant with two small children crying and clutching at her skirt. Sharing with them a few loaves of bread, I also gave an order for rations for her family. The poor lady was trying to provide for the family since her husband had been recruited into service. The army had taken him without even giving him the opportunity to tell his family good-bye. She had not seen or heard from him since.

Another man walked twelve miles roundtrip each day to support and feed his six small children. Losing his beloved wife, he had to leave his children in the care of the oldest, a ten year old. Another dear mother of six children was waiting to hear from her Union Army husband. She had not heard a word in countless months. She greatly feared that he was being held in a Rebel prison.

On my way into the Wyandotte Dry Goods Store I found a crippled, colored soldier hiding between two store fronts. He told me he had just been discharged and had not eaten for at least two days. Entering the store I purchased plenty of crackers and sugar to provide some energy for the mothers, children and other poor sick ones that I had just met, including the soldier.

Agnes Everett, a mother of five children, fifteen months old to twelve years of age, approached me that afternoon. Her youngest children were starving. She lamented that the baby had been so sick that she had not been able provide food for the others. Her twelve-year-old son had been doing little jobs such as sawing wood for cold vittles or a pint of meal that the mother cooked into porridge.

The little baby, Fannie, was fed this porridge. She was one of the worst case scenarios I had ever seen. Emaciated, with sunken, glassy eyes, her baby face looked like that of a wrinkled ninety year old. Her hands appeared more like bird claws than human hands. "Don't, Clarkie! Poor little Fannie is so sick she must have this." The mother chastised the hungry toddler who was mesmerized by the bowl of porridge. He used every opportunity to grab a floating lump from his baby sister's bowl.

Aghast by the appearance of these famished children, I wept with them. Agnes's husband and grown son were serving in the army, due to send her money any day. She had been waiting for several months, yet no word. Giving them two loaves of bread for their supper, I directed her to meet me the next morning. I had six half rations I could give her and that should provide them enough food until hopefully she could hear from her husband.

My visit with Agnes was the last for the day, and there were just as many visits in the afternoon as there had been in the morning. Returning to the Garno House, Mrs. Halford said, "Dear Mrs. Haviland, I'm afraid that Ruby has taken sick. She can't quit crying, or get the picture of these destitute families out of her mind."

The next morning I met several families at the post office and gave the quarter, half and whole rations, as well as the limited amount of clothing I had with me. Agnes Everett arrived as planned. Handing her rations to her, I strictly charged, "Agnes, feed those two little ones little bites at a time. Don't give them too much, or let them eat all they want. The baby, especially, will die if thee allows her to eat all she wants."

"Thank you, Mrs. Haviland! I will follow your instructions," She said with the tears rolling freely.

As she left, a group of gentlemen who had been visiting in the post office approached me, tipped their hats, and one cordially asked.

"Where are you from, ma'am?"

I'm from Michigan working for the Kansas Freedmen's Bureau," I replied.

Following introductions, Dr. Speck was the first one to speak, "I just met with a family whose youngest child starved to death three days ago. They called me when he was dying, but it was too late to save the child." He continued, "There were two other families who would have died soon if the citizens had not rendered the aid needed. Now, we can see there would have been another death by starvation before we would have known it, but it took you to come from Michigan to find it out."

Lawyer James spoke next, "Mrs. Haviland, there is a family on the hill opposite the ferry I wish someone would call on. So many families have crowded in here lately. It seems that we have done all we possibly can do to help these folks."

I said, "Well, General Curtis has granted us authority to order rations for these refugee families."

At this news all of the men gave out an audible sigh of relief.

"That's great news!" said James.

Speck replied, "It's about time!"

Dr. Wood, the third gentleman, commented, "The freedmen are seeking work, no matter what kind. But those white refugees are the most do-nothing set I ever saw."

"Yes, unfortunately, that seems to be the case," I agreed. "I worked with a poor white family in Quindaro who had been asked to help a sick neighbor. There were three grown women in the family, a mother and two adult daughters, so it was assumed that surely they could do something to help their neighbors for a few days. Yet, the mother with a toss and tilt of her cocky head drawled out contemptuously, 'I reckon we hain't come down so low yet as to work.'"

"That's unfortunate," replied Dr. Wood. "What did you do about the situation, Mrs. Haviland?"

"I told her, 'Until thee raises thy point of view to be high enough to work, I can't do a thing for thee.' Then I walked off leaving them to rot in their own rags and filth. General Curtis ordered me carefully to give rations to no one who could work."

They all cheered my words with a hearty "Here, here!" And we walked out of the post office together. Ordering 104 rations for Wyandotte, I was grateful to have participated in this timely relief for many.

Lawrence, my next stop, was the stomping grounds of the late Captain John Brown. The town had passed through great turbulence in 1863, with two terrible raids during the war. Thankfully there was no need for a Union force now. Having determined that the suffering and need for rations were being met locally, I moved on to Fort Scott.

Riding the stage coach to Fort Scott on Confederate General Price's track, we were advised to hide watches, jewelry or any article of worth, as guerrillas could be lurking in the woods ready to rob stages. Being thus advised, we were a little leery when a group of Indians on horses darted in and out of view. Actually, we were terrified. "We are all for the Union," one man on our stage shouted out. Though we feared them, we later found they thought we were the guerrillas who had stolen their ponies. They were just as afraid of us as we were of them.

Arriving at Fort Scott late at night, my first stop was to see Colonel Blair commander of the post. He and his wife very kindly offered me a place in their home to stay while I remained in their town. The Blairs introduced me to Dr. Slocum. He described to me the horrific plight and destitution of the 40,000 refugees and freedmen who had passed through Fort Scott. The next day he accompanied me on a visit to many destitute families.

I found a great number of poor whites called "clay-eaters" because they grumbled about the government giving rations to colored folks. I heard one of these grumblers say, "if niggers would stay with their masters where they belonged, we would have more white bread and beef."

I replied, "Well, it's my understanding that many of thy husbands are fighting against the government, while the husbands of many colored women were fighting to sustain it. I certainly favor those who are on the side of the United States Government." Having paused a few minutes to let my words make their impression, I then asked, "Why did thee uproot and move here where there's really nothing here for thee?"

"We came cause our men was conscripted," was the reply of one who shrugged.

Two white women, a mother and her eighteen-year-old daughter, who I attempted to help, lived in one of the most unsanitary environments I had ever visited. Each had a filthy bed quilt wrapped around their shoulders. Their swarthy, dirt smudged faces were so dark that the contrast between their faces and teeth and eyes were similar to those black refugees. Their four-year-old boy had no shoes. Having a pair that would fit him, I asked the mother to wash his feet so he could try them on. "Sal, bring me that cup thar," the woman commanded. The boy brought the drinking cup with water. "Han' me that rag thar," She said while she dabbed at the mud on his feet ever so lightly. I insisted, "Ma'am they are not clean. Look, the mud is still on the bottom of his feet and between his toes!"

"O, yez'm," she drawled. Once again she tried to clean the boy's feet. When the shoes were on, the poor boy could not even walk without hanging on to someone! They must have been his first pair of shoes ever.

Spending most of this day visiting such folks, this low white class, I found them degraded, ignorant and listless. On my return and report to Colonel Blair, I could not help but vent concerning their uselessness while I also gave my description of their filth and ignorance. Colonel Blair asked in response, "Mrs. Haviland, what would you do with them?"

Without a blink of the eye, I instantly responded. "I would keep their body and soul together till Spring opens. Then load them up in thy great army wagons, take them out to the rich prairies and dump them, saying, 'Root, pig, or die!'"

These so called "clay-eaters" would do nothing for themselves. And that's what made it so difficult to do anything for them. I found the freedmen were willing to do anything their hands could find for them to do. What a contrast!

After three days at Fort Scott, I boarded the Monday morning stage returning to Leavenworth. Once there I mailed packages of clothing to designated friends at each destination, with a specific request that our clothing was not to be given to anyone who refused to work. During the month of December we were able to support 444 families.

On New Year's Day, 1865, I discovered a poor woman in Leavenworth who was dying and in the last phase of consumption. She could not speak a word and was extremely weak. I hired another poor woman to care for her needs, giving her a place to sleep and providing clothing for her and her children. As I left them, they were all in tears and the dying woman said, "We thank you, honey, and praise God. When my poor mother died in that old out-cellar, neither father nor anyone of us was permitted to give her a cup of cold water. The last words she was heard to say was, 'I'm going home to die no more.' Now, I'm goin' home to meet her."

With our supplies running very low and all our money nearly gone, a letter from the Ladies' Michigan State Freedmen's Fair crossed my desk. The chairman of the event was soliciting relics of the war in order to raise funds on our behalf. J.R. Brown felt that I should attend the fair and take his brother's (Captain John Brown) sharp-shooter. Brown had carried this weapon through the border-ruffian conflict in Kansas and during his time at Harper's Ferry. Reflecting on this idea a few days, I decided to go. General Curtis sent me with his blessing and a round-trip pass to Detroit.

In Detroit at the Freedman's Fair, the John Brown gun served its purpose well. It brought a crowd, creating great interest. At the fair we displayed the fifty pounds of slave-irons, including Uncle Tim's collar collected from those deserted plantations in the far South. A petition from Lenawee County was sent to the Freedman's Commission requesting that they place $1,000 in my hands to alleviate the suffering in Kansas. I thanked God for this money, as I had no doubt in my mind that many lives were saved and much suffering was alleviated.

While in Michigan I sold the Raisin Institute and its ten acres that included an excellent orchard to the Freedman's Aid Commission to be used as an orphanage. I gave $300 of my proceeds to this orphanage project, stipulating that the money be used for the orphanage only. My friends named the orphanage the "Haviland

Home for Homeless and Destitute Children." My desire was for this home to serve as a starting point for a state orphanage. The aftershock of the war created a serious need for these homeless children.

The opening of the "Haviland Home" created yet another shift in my service. Returning after two weeks to my Kansas office bearing supplies and resources for the refugees, I completed my service in Kansas. I received permission from the Freedman's Commission to send children and mothers to our new orphanage, the Haviland Home in Michigan. One of my final responsibilities in Kansas was to place a teacher in Oklaloosa in Jefferson County, Kansas. There I met Dr. Nelson, by whose kindness we secured a house for the school to train the colored refugees there, as well as a place for our teacher to live. Through the good doctor, I also discovered a poor woman sick with five children. She had been ordered out of her cabin home because she had no more money to pay the rent. Like so many others, she had not heard from her husband who enlisted in the army since he had left. Dr. Nelson interceded on her behalf. After she recovered she and her children made the trip back with me to Leavenworth and would also make the long journey with me to the Haviland Home.

We celebrated the end of the war on April 9, 1865, in Kansas, but it was to be short-lived. Nothing could have ever prepared us for the sad news that less than a week later, on April 15, our dear President Lincoln was assassinated! Everywhere, houses and businesses were draped in black. We were a nation in mourning; such loss was difficult to absorb. President Lincoln had communicated in his two-minute Gettysburg Address the guiding force of the Almighty God that our armed forces had spent several years defending. I feared without our dear President's resolve and commitment, our friends of color would not be considered equal.

As we mourned the loss of our great president, we continued to live out his words from the Emancipation Proclamation and Gettysburg Address. Yes, dear

Kansas–1864

President Lincoln was gone. His words will live on forever. With them came this new birth of freedom. All men are created equal. We could not stop our work now. It was needed more now than ever!

The Freedman's Commission had provided the train fare for 75 individuals, 68 children and 7 women from Kansas to our Michigan orphanage. Continuing my preparations to close the two refugee buildings in Leavenworth, I planned to accompany the remaining women and children on this journey.

Encouraging the white "clay-eater" women who lived in our refugee facilities to seek new homes as our facilities prepared to close, was no easy task. I offered them the best dresses we had on hand to rally them for this cause. Unfortunately, these women had no desire to find new homes for themselves; and they ignored my incentives and made no effort to move.

Finally, I turned to General Curtis exasperated from wasting time and energy. "General Curtis, I've threatened them with eviction. I don't mind helping those in need, even the most degraded. But these women have lowered themselves to maintain a "house of ill repute" on government property, and I am at a loss of how to proceed."

The noble general immediately replied, "I will give you a good honest guard day and night over that building,"

His actions did more than I could have ever done to scatter them. They swore and cursed my name, saying "I will not be controlled by that Yankee woman ever again." One by one each of them left, much to my great relief.

A dear old woman, Aunt Phoebe, came to me begging to make the Michigan trip with me along with her four grandchildren. Her story was heart wrenching.

The father of her grandchildren ran away to enlist in the Union Army, but his master followed, caught him and ordered him to return. The poor man refused and the master shot him dead. Receiving the word, Aunt Phoebe's daughter, the man's wife, screamed and fainted away. Her owners were extremely cruel, whipping her severely for making such a fuss. That's what they called her grief, a fuss! She was crushed under such severity that she died, leaving a week-old infant and their three older children under the care of Aunt Phoebe.

Jerry, her oldest grandson, had fallen ill with small-pox. He had not been close to the other sick children, and Dr. Carpenter hoped the others would miss it. I rolled Jerry in two quilts and quarantined him to the pest-house. Poor Aunt Phoebe wept bitterly, thinking she'd never see her good boy Jerry again. "He was always so good to help with the other children," she lamented. Aunt Phoebe herself came down with lung fever, and I had to hire a colored woman to nurse her. Within a month, Jerry was better. After a thorough recovery and cleansing, I returned him to his grandmother, who wept for joy.

Before my grand trip home, I revisited all of the places I had served: Quindaro, Wyandotte, Lawrence, Fort Scott and Kansas City. Unfortunately I acquired a severe case of pneumonia in Kansas City. Calling the army surgeon, I ordered mustard that I plastered in the middle of my pain. I could hardly breathe as the pain had become severe enough to attack my every breath. The mustard alleviated some of the pain. Yet, I was unable to rest, but simply had to pace the room.

In spite of my physical condition I made arrangements to catch the boat to Leavenworth and for a carriage to meet me at the dock to take me to our headquarters. I returned with a high fever to Dr. Carpenter, who said I should not leave for Michigan for at least thirty days. Yet, I continued to make arrangements in spite of my condition. Next, I took a hack to General Curtis's office, where I secured transportation for 75 persons that included Mrs. Lee and me.

Doubled over with pain at times, I was determined to make the trip home. Admitting three children to the hospital who had more severe illnesses, we still carried three sick children whose mother could travel and care for them. Three other children began to show signs of chills and high fever soon after we left. Their illness turned into full blown measles once we were traveling. Against Dr. Carpenter's judgment I decided to lead our group of 75 to Michigan within a week's time. I prayed non-stop for guidance and felt safe in the Lord's hands.

Chapter Nineteen

Needed in the Northeast

Awaiting the train at St. Joseph, Missouri, I received a delightful, unexpected visit from Susan B. Anthony, who walked in carrying a picnic basket overflowing with delicious treats for all. Her visit was a pleasant reprieve from my current concerns. Mrs. Anthony and I discussed many interests, the plight of the freed blacks and their restoration, and the hopes for women's suffrage.

After Sister Anthony left, folks at the train station were mumbling about our large caravan, with all of its movement and excitement. One commented, "I reckon she's got a big plantation to stock with a picked set of young niggers, she's going to train to her own liking."

Another said, "I am going to ask where she is going with them."

I pretended not to hear until one man addressed me directly, "Excuse me, madam, where you are taking this large company?"

"I am taking these orphan children, who have been picked up off the streets, to an orphan school in Michigan," I replied. "By order of the State Freedmen's Aid Commission, they will be sent to school until good homes can be secured for them. They will be taught the fundamentals to improve their intelligence, habits of industry and a good work ethic. We in the North think they will learn if the opportunity is provided."

This answer pleased him greatly. He began to spread the word around to the other bystanders. Before long many approached me with kind words and a "congratulations on our good work."

An ex-slaveholder told me he wished that the children of his slaves could go with me. "I know it will be a long while before schools will be provided for 'em."

Once our train departed, Mrs. Lee watched the sick children by night, and I had their charge during the day. This gave me the needed sleep to overcome my cough.

In Quincy, Illinois, I had difficulty getting the coach to Chicago I needed for 75 passengers. Finally on board, four drunken men repeatedly attempted to burst into our sleeping quarters. Reaching the night policeman, he guaranteed that we would have no further problems with these men, and we didn't. Behind schedule, our train arrived in Chicago only thirty minutes before the train was to leave for Adrian. Purchasing tickets for four omnibus cars, the crew was determined to cram our caravan into two. Moving 75 children and adults is no easy task, and it became even more difficult when the train crew attempted to downsize our quarters. While they were placing our little children on the top berths, I immediately ordered them down.

"We are capable of taking care of these children, madam," said one of them. "Why don't you take this berth below?"

"I'm capable of taking care of them and all of thee as well," I remanded. "I thank thee to remember that I paid for four omnibuses, and I must have them."

"My! My! Stand back everyone. Mrs. Haviland will take care of all of thee," one of the crew hands mimicked. Though they made a great deal of sport over my countermand orders, they stepped back and allowed us to take care of the children. And finally we were on our way in four omnibus cars.

Arriving in Adrian on June 1, 1865, we met the director of the "Haviland Home" at the train station. He had arrived with teams of wagons for the women and children. Finally, I could release my heavy burden and find the much needed rest I longed for, spending time with my children.

Several weeks later, with health restored, I visited our state prison. One of the refugee convicts there, Thomas Lean, requested an interview with me. He appealed earnestly on behalf of his family, his wife and two children that I should assist him in securing a pardon. Lean had served seven of the fifteen-year term given him for stealing $42 from the mail.

I said, "I will make an appeal on thy behalf, but thee must realize these efforts have been tried twice before. I cannot promise a successful outcome."

Thomas replied, "Oh, thank you, Mrs. Haviland. I know they will listen to you!"

Drafting a petition, I secured fifty names and provided three letters of recommendation, from Governor Blair of Michigan, Judge Ross Wilkins, who issued the sentence, and from the prosecuting attorney who acted on behalf of the United States in Lean's case. Mrs. Campbell and Mrs. Pappineau, from the Detroit Freedman's Aid Commission, squeezed $600 in my hands, and I left for Washington, D.C. on August 3, 1865, to serve my country again.

Stopping in Baltimore, I identified six other Maryland convicts who had aided slaves and included them in my petition along with Tom Lean. The Maryland governor believed these were just as worthy for release as ten others who had already been released, as the weapons of these six were used in self-defense, and the horses had only been taken to the river and released. Receiving letters of support for these six, I was once again on my way to D.C.

Along the way I visited the Virginia State Penitentiary, housing 500 inmates. There I was introduced to the warden. He granted me a tour through the prison shops and an opportunity to speak with the 68 female convicts. Most of the prisoners were black and sent there by former owners for the most trivial offenses, such as stealing a dress, a pair of shoes, perhaps a dollar or two. Everyone knew they were there simply because their masters did not want to set them free.

One intelligent octoroon woman was in prison because she whipped her mistress. After hearing the Emancipation Proclamation, she felt empowered and whipped her mistress with a cowhide that was often used to whip her. For this, she received a nine-year prison sentence. One of the guards said the mistress claimed the girl had almost killed her. Yet he had seen her out riding shortly after the violent whipping, and the mistress looked just fine to him.

One dying white woman called for a visit. I read the Scripture to her and at her request I offered a prayer. She said, "I'm going to meet my Judge. I trust in my Jesus and he hears my cry." It was beautiful to sense her confidence. The next day the chaplain asked me to conduct the woman's funeral service. She died just hours after I left her. At three o'clock that afternoon I led a special service for the dear woman. The chapel was full as I shared her words of trust and peace. Many of the convicts were touched by her faith and expressed interest in finding this same peace for themselves.

Reaching my destination of Washington D.C., my visit to the White House was overrun with pardon-seekers from ex-slave states. Visiting with a number of congressional officials, they felt Thomas Lean's chances for pardon were slim, as the severity of his sentence made it look bleak.

Doing the best I could for Mr. Lean, I shared this with these legislative leaders:

> Perhaps thee knows of the case where a man had robbed the Post Office of $5,000 and was pardoned in three years even though his sentence was ten years. The difference is he has influential, wealthy friends acting on his behalf. Poor Tom Lean has taken $42

out of the mail, and he received a fifteen-year sentence of which he has already served seven. Of course he is poor and his wife is also in bad health. Yet she is working to support herself and two small children.

The legislators, hearing me out, advised me to take my letters and petition to the Postmaster General Dennison. After obtaining the signatures of all of the Michigan members of the House and Senate, I secured a letter of recommendation for Lean's pardon from the Postmaster General, as well.

Finally, I made my way to the front door of the White House. Mr. Wade, the President's house-keeper, ushered me into the President's office, where I was seated with a room full of southern pardon-seekers. With little time to admire the colonial architecture, I soon handed my letters with the petition to President Johnson.

The President looked up at me and replied quickly, "I will refer these to the Attorney-General, and he will do what seems best."

He looked down as if in dismissal, and I was instantly ushered out of his office by a butler. Standing outside the White House, I shook the dust off my feet as in a ritual of disgust. In all my days I had never envisioned an audience with a sitting President to take place in such a dismissive, detached manner. Also, I never dreamed it would be in the presence of so many adversaries that our Union had so earnestly fought and defeated. Alas! Andrew Johnson was no Abraham Lincoln! It was quite a disappointment after the many hours of hard work that had been enlisted on behalf of these prisoners.

Walking back into the Postmaster-General's office, the chief clerk informed me, "Come back early next Wednesday morning. We will know about his pardon on that day." Fearing the worst, I didn't arrive until late that Wednesday morning. When the clerk saw me, he raised both of his hands in excitement. "Your man is pardoned! Come and read the notice in this morning's paper." He shook my hand heartily after telling me the good news.

Surprised, I replied, "I never realized thee was interested in this case."

"I have had an interest from the first time you walked into this office." He said, smiling.

After my return home months later, I received what looked like a tear-stained note from Thomas Lean thanking me for his freedom. I was grateful that another burden had been cast aside. I whispered my own thanks to the tender Healer of broken hearts.

While in Washington D.C. I had the privilege of meeting our country's Secretary of War, Edwin Stanton. Stanton empowered me in our work of alleviating post-war suffering with a permit to trade at the government store. Sending me to purchase $2,000 of supplies for $500, we were able to provide relief for the sick, crippled and aged refugees in the Washington D.C. area. Thus, I stayed a while longer to distribute these supplies.

Being aware of great suffering in Harper's Ferry, I accompanied $400 in supplies there. Boarding an early train to Harper's Ferry, I was seated across from Dr. Davies, a Presbyterian minister. His servant, seated next to him, was very attentive to his every need, bringing coffee, books or any item he requested.

"How far are you going on this road, madam?" my interesting dignitary asked.

"Harper's Ferry," I responded.

"Have you friends there?" he inquired

"I have," I slyly responded "but I haven't seen them yet. They are the poorest of the poor, the sick, the lame and the blind of all classes, black, white, red or yellow."

"Madam, that is a noble work, and God will bless you in it. I am now on my way to Vicksburg where I once owned a plantation and forty slaves, but have since set them free. They are now as free as me. Madam, I tell you what your duty is. Go to New York, Philadelphia and Boston, gather up $50,000, and follow General Sherman's track through to the Gulf. You will find plenty of suffering to relieve among both white and black, and you can do it. Those cities I have named are wealthy. It's your duty, madam! God will bless you in it." He concluded with an unbecoming air of aristocracy and insistence.

Believing he had been inspired with power from on high, he repeated his command as I departed at Harper's Ferry.

"Do as I have told you, madam! God will bless you. Good-bye," he adamantly emphasized. I often wondered thereafter why the good doctor did not implement this divine plan himself.

Finding my goods had arrived, I made arrangements with the post commander to store the supplies and obtain transportation as needed. I was sent to Mrs. Johnson's home to seek a boarding place for several days.

"Where are you from?" Mrs. Johnson asked skeptically.

"From Washington," I said, "with supplies for the poor freedman and whites who are suffering."

"Oh! You are a Bureau woman! I can't board you; we don't have nothin' to do with Bureau folks," she said, closing the door in my face.

Inquiring at two other boarding homes and receiving similar treatment, I realized finding a place to stay was going to be an all day job. After making eight more inquiries and chatting pleasantly at each home, I was told everywhere that not a soul in town would disgrace themselves by boarding or even speaking with a nigger teacher. The sun had set on my unsuccessful day's work when I met an army surgeon sitting on his front porch.

"Have you found no place for dinner?" he queried.

"No!" I replied. "I have been amusing myself over the Confederate fever that runs too high for good health in thy town. Thy neighbors must think I am John Brown's sister!"

Laughing, he said, "Mrs. Haviland, my mother-in-law is away, but my wife and I will give you her room to-night, and we will see that you have supper at once." Relieved and thankful, I was able to stay with his mother-in-law for the remainder of the week.

Attending a Methodist Episcopal Church meeting in Harper's Ferry, I officially introduced myself, reading aloud my papers from the Michigan Governor, members of Congress, and several distinguished ministers. Following this, I cordially received and accepted a number of invitations into homes. These social invitations gave me the platform to share my first day's experience in their town. One society lady replied, "Mrs. Haviland, Horace Mann's sister snubbed white folks when she arrived and associated exclusively with colored people. She was even unwilling to make calls on white people. Instead she taught in colored schools and lived with them." Still, my new friends did concede that those whom I had called upon were Rebel sympathizers.

Harper's Ferry, like other places, contained folks who experienced extreme suffering. Many afflicted people were too sick to care for one another. One very sick Union soldier's wife had no firewood. She relied upon her three-year-old daughter to gather boots and shoes from an old camp in order to build the fire. Many other children stepped in to help their adult family members. Fortunately, we were able to relieve many of these cases.

A dozen injured refugees called for my assistance. A few nights prior, a mob had devastated their grocery store, breaking windows, taking sacks of flour, meal and crackers, and strewing pies, cakes and other goods all over the street. They crashed through, breaking their tables and chairs, swearing, "No nigger will ever own a business on Main Street!" As if this were not enough, the bullies also threw stones and brickbats into homes. These poor refugees ran to the Union soldiers for protection. They had bleeding wounds and bruises, which I bound during the time of my visit. What a sad image they presented with not only broken furniture, but injured bodies as well.

One of their leaders asked, "What use is there in rebuilding? You see our lives are in danger as it is. When the troops withdraw, what shall we do?" Fortunately, as if in direct answer to prayer, a Free-Will Baptist preacher arrived in Harper's Ferry and opened a mission school. The school's presence ushered in a new era of stability.

Leaving Harper's Ferry, I had to chuckle at the irony of my departure opposed to the time of my arrival. Walking to the train depot I was accompanied by a number of prominent citizens, all expressing sentiments of appreciation and kindness. Several hoped that I would call upon them on my return. One couple pointed out their brick home in hopes that I would stay with them on my next visit.

Returning to Washington D.C., I found many in our country's capitol sick, aged, blind and crippled. I could endure the most severe trial in caring for these folks. Yet, disloyalty was the one blight on our postwar country I could not stand! Unfortunately, it plagued many in the nation's capital and continues to be the disease working to destroy our efforts. Brash, uneducated women were unbearably outspoken and unjust. Men, who appear to be compliant with the new postwar reconstruction guidelines, cunningly scheme behind the scenes to hoodwink the government. They say behind closed doors, "We'll yet gain by the ballot what we failed to accomplish with the bullet. And we'll do it with the help of Northern sympathizers."

At times I greatly wondered if President Johnson had formed a "more perfect union" with these Rebel sympathizers than he had with the Union. President

Johnson seemed to do everything in his power to reverse the proclamation of freedom that our country had fought so valiantly to gain. By his order soldiers of color everywhere were discharged and released from garrisons and forts, at the request of their former owners, only to be victimized once again by their unrelenting hate. One colored man returned to his master's plantation after two years of service in the Union Army, and the master shot him in the head with a pistol, instantly taking his life. I heard these types of stories in many places, yet there was no response given by state authorities. All of our efforts could not be in vain! Hear our prayer, O Lord!

On September 14, 1865, I visited several large schools in Alexandria, VA. I was invited to speak at a number of these. Two of these schools were held in an area of what had once been the largest slave-pens in the city of Alexandria. In contrast to dehumanizing slavery, here stood 153 black children reciting poetry and reading. They were quick to learn, and listening to them read after only four months of training was quite hopeful. Surely, "there's a better day a' coming!"

On the street I met a woman weeping uncontrollably. After inquiring the cause, she explained:

> "I have been to visit the grave of my only son. His father died a few months ago, and this darling son, my only child, died in the Union army. What does all this terrible sacrifice mean? President Johnson is giving strength to the Rebels. Every Rebel general has been pardoned, and the vast amount of land restored to them is increasing their power. Wherever troops are withdrawn they commit murders, and no notice is taken of it. I feel as though my son's life and thousands of other precious lives have been sacrificed for nothing."

What could I say to this poor widowed, childless woman who was understandably brokenhearted? I did the only thing I could do, wrap my arms around her and lift her heartache before our Heavenly Father. He alone could comfort this widow's grief-stricken heart.

Arriving at Fredericksburg, a town whose many chimneys loomed over the waste places and burned homes devastated by the war, I made a call at a teachers' boarding home and a soldier's hospital. The soldiers were glad to see anyone who looked like their mothers from home. We read the Scripture, prayed and as I left, there were a number of these poor soldier men in tears!

While in Fredericksburg, I called on Major Johnson, who asked me to place a year-old orphan boy at Camp Lee Orphanage in Richmond. Immediately, I traveled there with the boy. The matron of the orphanage, Mrs. Gibbons, had no name to give the child. Smiling she said, "I will name him after you and me, Haviland Gibbons." I visited little Haviland many times, and he learned his name quickly. I often found myself at Camp Lee Orphanage on Sunday evenings with my new friend, Annie Gibbons. She loved all of the children sent her way, including our little Haviland Gibbons. Gathered around the dinner table, they would close their eyes, clasp their hands and at the tap of a bell pray this verse:

"Lord, teach a little child to pray, Thy grace to me impart. Amen."

Serving at Libby Prison, I heard many fascinating stories from the war. A deep, long tunnel built underground by the Union prisoners helped some to escape from the terrible suffering experienced at Libby. The Rebels boasted they would kill as many imprisoned Yankees as there were Confederate soldiers in battle. The desperation of these prisoners spoke volumes about the risks they took in their effort to escape. As hand-cuffs were removed from the emaciated prisoners when

Richmond fell, these prisoners rejoiced when the gates of Castle Thunder and Libby were reopened and the hand-cuffs were shifted to their cruel keepers. While there, I stored supplies and resources in one of the prison apartments. Guards helped me open, close and move the boxes and barrels, separating the goods I planned to deliver in the Richmond area.

Visiting another old camp, where a school operated in what was once an old slave-pen, I listened to the stories of those afflicted by cruelty. The stump of a whipping post and the old auction block remained to remind everyone of the atrocities committed here that denied our American freedom. I sighed with the realization that our nation had to experience this baptism of blood in order to end the horrible institution of slavery.

Following my talk with the school children, I visited with the sick and aged. One very old man, Anthony Wilson, said, "Dun kno' how ole I is. White folks say I's more than eighty. Had heaps of ups an' downs; good many more downs dan ups. My big family all tore to pieces two times." I found a good suit of clothes that I could give him, and he exclaimed, "Bress de good Lo'd, dis is de best suit I eber had. Dis I reckon is my freedom suit."

Joe, the freed shoemaker, pointed to a large plantation in view and said: "There lives my old master, who said at the beginning of this war, 'Before my children shall ever be disgraced with work I will wade in blood to the horse's bridle.' He did fight hard as long as the war lasted. But last week he told his sons that they must go to work or die. He came into my shoe-shop the other day with his feet almost bare. I took the best pair of boots I had and gave them to him. I know he thought of the old days, for I did."

Mary Brackson was also a very old woman whom I tried to help. She cared for two of her little grandchildren, as their mother had been "sold down the river." Mary's sad life had been plagued by rheumatism, and she had a broken arm from her overseer's club. Giving clothes for Mary and her grandchildren, I also found a bed-tick, blanket and quilt to keep them warm. Helping four other families, I visited, advised, read Scriptures and prayed with them all. All of which seemed to give them comfort.

Arriving in Ashland I first met Charlotte Boles. After asking her age, she replied. "I dun kno'; missus' specks I's eighty, large old." She had served three generations of slaveholders.

> I's had so many children, I can't tell till I call de names Pomp, Jim, Tom, Sol, Sue, Dick, an' Diley; den some babies I's got in heaven. I seed heap o' trouble in my time. I nursed at de breas' eleven of my firs' massar's chillen. Isaac Wiston, and six of his gran'-chillen. I dress 'em firs' an' some on 'em for de grave. My secon' massar, William Winfield Jr., da have six chillen, an' I dress 'em all firs', and most all at las' for de grave. O my God, I can neber, neber tell de trouble I's had. O how hard I prayed for freedom, an' de Lord come at las'. I's praise his name. De one dat I nurst when a babie ordered me whipped 'case I cried so much when da sole my chillen down de riber. But I hear dat de war free five of my chillen, and' I's prayin' God to sen' 'em to poor me.

Her mind was unusually clear and tears would frequently well up in her eyes and fall in great big drops, displaying her strong maternal affections.

After visiting with fifteen suffering families to identify their needs, I called to have more supplies from Libby Prison delivered to these poor folks. As I made proper connections and distributed the necessary items, the gratitude of these folks seemed greater here than anywhere I had been. Some wept aloud. Others kissed my hands as I left them, but each of these poor, crushed spirits gave me their everyday cheery response, "God bless you, honey."

One officer approached me with an urgent request from two women to visit them in their fine, large brick home. I responded immediately. After ringing the door bell, I was greeted by a lady dressed in black satin. I introduced myself and inquired if she was the one who had sent for me.

"Oh, yes!"

The other woman appeared behind her in the entry way. She, too, was dressed in rich silk.

"What are thy greatest needs?" I queried.

"We want money, madam, and must have it," The lady in black demanded.

"Are any of thy family sick?" I asked.

"No, madam, but money we must have," said the other.

"Will rations answer thy purpose?" I kept asking questions.

"No, madam, we want no such thing," said the lady in black, while the other quipped, "We want *money*, and must have it."

Wanting to laugh and cry at the same time, I worked to control my outward demeanor. "My dear ladies, I have no money to disburse. I only supply food and clothing to those who suffer from destitution as a result of this horrible war," I firmly replied, walking away without waiting for a response or further invitation. I could tell these women were used to making demands and expecting them to be met.

In a few days the captain approached me and asked if I had been able to meet the desires of the two ladies. I laughed and said, "No, after their response to a few questions, I did not think they were worthy of the money they demanded."

He smiled and said, "These two women have queried all of our other officers for money, as well, and as they had not succeeded with any of them, they sent for you." He was not disappointed at my response or the result.

I spent over a month in this area working out of the Libby Prison and sharing supplies throughout Richmond. My partner was Miss Morris, a French lady, who kept me very busy. She was a spy and an intriguing one at that. Morris served with the Union Army, but fell into Rebel hands before New Orleans was taken by Union troops. She was able to make her escape, and revisited New Orleans in disguise, gaining valuable information for our generals. She spoke French and German prolifically, much better than her English. She incorporated her French politeness to a fault, and she could have been somewhat annoying were it not for her faithful assistance.

Morris was willing to go anywhere and do anything to assist anyone in need. She was not afraid to run through back alleys, enter dark, cold cellars or climb rickety stairs. Many of these flights of stairs led us into dark attics. There are many fine Christian women willing to serve or assist in a variety of ways, but none were as bold as Miss Morris. She fearlessly and boldly entered filthy homes, running the risk of acquiring contagious diseases. There was a bond between us with our plain life habits and common immunity to so many diseases. We had both suffered from small pox and every other common disease that should have killed us. I never worried about visiting the sick or of dying in any of the loathsome places I stayed. Many of these filthy places in Richmond, I entered with Miss Morris.

Visiting the Virginia penitentiary again, one of my inquiries in the prison led me to the office of the esteemed governor of Virginia, who shared with me some interesting facts about the economics of slavery in his state. He exclaimed, "Slavery in the mines had made the state of Virginia one of the richest states in the Union. At the present time, colored men are making close to a dollar a day in gold dusting without the enterprising facilities with men of capital." He proceeded to show me an exhibit of each metal: gold, silver, nickel, copper and kaolin, a precious metal of fine quality, and porcelain clay. Then to make his point of the economic advantages of slavery, he shared a report from the *Metropolitan Press* from 1861 that said, "The income from slaves for the last twenty years amounted to twenty million dollars annually, and from all other products, eight million dollars annually." He concluded, "Ah, what a great loss to our economy!"

Leaving his office, I breathed a sigh of relief and thought to myself, "Ah, what a great victory for humanity!"

Times were changing and some might call these times "The Great Reversal!" A.R. Brooks, a slave who bought himself fourteen years earlier, was a wealthy man. He owned ten horses along with six fine carriages and hacks. Yet his owner, Henry A. Winfy, had been reduced to beggary. He had sold his 3,000-acre plantation several months ago for Confederate money that no longer had any value. His wife died, and because the ex-slave owner was penniless, A.R. Brooks paid for her entire funeral. He said, "Praise the Lord, I'm able to do it!" What a shock for Winfy, a wealthy plantation owner, well-stocked with slaves, who now found himself poor and unable to care for everyday concerns.

Every day brought new scenes of reversal and revelations. I often felt that I was a stranger moving through a strange land. But in all of these times I never felt alone. Making contacts with friends and co-laborers, there were kindred spirits everywhere I traveled. It was my dear Savior that carried me through the gruesome and horrific scenes of despair and sadness.

Chapter Twenty

Down-Trodden, Down River
March 3, 1866

Sorting, packing and arranging my supplies, I prepared to leave Richmond for a trip down the James River on March 3, 1866. With purpose in each step, my goal was to provide needed clothing and medications for those suffering in Williamsburg. Stepping outside I saw people gathering in great excitement around Libby Prison. As I was burdened down with supplies, I found it difficult to make my way through the crowd towards the dock.

"Why the excited crowd?" I asked a bystander.

The woman said, "A Union soldier is being executed for killing a man and stealing his horse, buggy and money."

"Oh, how awful," I shuttered.

Hurrying to get out of Richmond before I might have to view or hear this horror, I saw the soldier led from the prison to the scaffold. Seeing there was no way I could speak to the soldier personally, I rushed to escape from the whole sickening event. I shuddered to think that a young life was about to end.

The prose kept running through my mind: "The horrors of war no pen can describe, no tongue can utter, no pencil can paint. The demoralizing influence over the soldier is dreadful."

I was sure the young man had deserted his post and more than likely been caught taking a horse or other valuables for his escape. But alas! Suddenly, the sounds of guns roared through the air and with it a life snuffed out!

Saddened by this loss of life, I sat gazing across the horizon, waiting to board my ship at the dock. My spy friend, Miss Morris arrived with a basket of fresh cakes, oranges, apples and a bottle of bubbly wine, trying to cheer me. Since I never drank, I begged her pardon in not indulging.

"Oh, indeed, you must take it your Royal Highness (her pet name for me), for you may be ill, and may find it quite proper to take a little wine for your 'stomach's sake.' Don't, my madam, refuse your most humble servant the privilege of presenting this basket and its contents, wine and all, to my royal madam," Miss Morris persuaded. Noticing the tear well up in her eye I accepted her gift, as I did not want to hurt her. I had to laugh at her in spite of myself.

Steaming down the river, I noticed the cemetery for fallen Union soldiers, with little hillocks covering the burial markers. These soldiers had shared the hope of saving our nation's soul from the Rebel treason. They fell long before Richmond surrendered to the Union. Passing Bermuda Hundred and City Point, there in view was General Grant's headquarters. By noon we arrived in Jamestown, where three, quaint, dilapidated, half torn-down buildings served as our greeting place. These tottering walls were open-air for the bats and birds to inhabit. Across the graveyard there was a marble slab dated 1626 that had pieces chiseled out for soldiers to take as souvenirs.

I discovered an old brick church close by that was the home of 196 refugee scholars. By comparison, our schools for the freedmen were thriving while

Richmond's historic colleges, William and Mary College and a female seminary, had closed.

Once settled in Williamsburg, I planned to visit all of the freedmen schools and distribute supplies to those in need. Walking two miles to Fort Magruder, I discovered 158 colored scholars in a Quaker school taught by Martha Haines and Maggie Thorpe of New York. They opened a night school in order to accommodate 50 folks who had to work by day, but could attend school by night. In just a few short months, these adults, who before had been unable to call out the letters of the alphabet, were now fluently reading second and third grade readers. A few miles down the road another freedman's school served 30 scholars who were making great progress.

The teachers shared that on the oldest plantation in Williamsburg near King's Mill, there were many older people who needed help. Taking my supplies of bedding and clothing in an ambulance, I made the journey to King's Mill and then set out on foot from cabin to cabin where I visited 27 people from ages 60 to 105. After visiting with them regarding their urgent needs, I selected supplies for each individual.

The old plantation was out of sight set back in a grove of woods. Uncle Bob Jones, the eldest among them, told me, "Missus, all dat woods on dat side I helped clar off when firs' woods was that, beech, maple an' linn wood, only now an' agin a pine. Den we work it till it wore out an' wouldn't noffin grow on it, an' we lef it to grow up to dose pines you see."

"Is that possible?" I asked. "I saw men chopping sawmill logs as I came through that wood."

"Yes, missus," he assured me. "Shure's you are bo'n, my sweat lies dar under dem big tree roots. My Mill an' me was married when we's chillen, an' we's had a good many chillen. De Lo'd know what da' done to da sole down de riber, many,

many years ago. But we prayed to Lo'd Jesus to take keer on 'em all dese years, an' we'll go home to glory soon."

"What is thy age, Uncle Bob?"

"Massa Moses' book say I's a hundred an' five, an' my Milla's a hundred an' three. I might slip counta year or two, but I reckon not."

Never in my travels had I met a couple still active at this advanced age. I found the best quilt I had with me. It was made by a Sunday School class of girls, 8-15 years of age, from Wayne County, Michigan. I gave it to them, showing them how the girls had written their names on their block pieces.

Uncle Bob who could barely see, lit up with enthusiasm and asked, "Missus, did you say little white gals made this? Lo'd blese the little angels! Honey, look at dis; we's neber had sich a nice bed-kiver in all our lives."

Aunt Milla Jones agreed, nodding. "I see it's a beauty. We's neber had sich a kiver afore, missus. Tell de sweet little angels we'll pray for 'em as long as we live."

"Yes, tell 'em we won't stop prayin' for 'em when we gits up yonder in de mansions," Uncle Bob cooed.

They were awestruck at the wonder that white girls would make a beautiful quilt for simple black folks. It was satisfying to watch them and listen to their appreciation. They were ecstatic over their surprise quilt.

Amazingly, Aunt Milla was still able to work in her garden patch, as some of their younger men spaded it on her behalf. Their cabin was clean and neat; and their clothes were also patched nicely. Uncle Bob had only left the plantation two times during his life. How touching to see these sweet, worn-out slaves so joyful over their freedom. They seemed most happy for their children, their future and the generations to come. These old folks had "fought the good fight" through many difficulties. Their faith had carried them through. They were rejoicing that they were soon going to see Jesus!

One freedman brought two cripples in his cart to gather the supplies that I could share with them. He told me of two older men living back in the mill. "One of these men," he said, "was an old soldier of the Jackson War." My driver transported me there, to the first mill built in that part of the country, 150 years ago. Thick moss covered the cedar shingles of that old brick mill.

Inside I met an intelligent mulatto war veteran who had a very bad fever sore that had been above his ankle for many years. While I was dressing it, he shared with me the story of his family. He was the oldest child of twenty-seven, and the only single child, as his mother had born thirteen sets of twins. All had been sold to slave dealers in Southern states.

Captivated by the old slave-soldier's story, I thought he must be one of the most intelligent men for his 60 years of age. His use of the English language was excellent. Serving in the war with General Jackson with the promise of freedom, he suffered even more severely when freedom was denied.

> He said,
>
> My mother's name was Maria Sampson. She lived and died in King William County, Virginia. She had twenty sons and seven daughters, all her own. Yet this wicked master tore each child away from her one by one. He claimed her body for himself, a valuable piece of property.
>
> When my mother died in the cold cellar, I begged to see her, but my old master said he would shoot me if I dared to set foot on his plantation case I'd been with Yankees. She died one year ago without a child to give her a sip of water. My wife and seven children belonged to another man. He said he would shoot my brains out if I dared to come on his plantation. But I prayed God would help my

wife go to the soldiers before they were all gone and get help to come to me with our children.

I was one of the slaves the master promised freedom at the close of General Jackson's war. We were promised ten dollars a month for twenty months besides our freedom due to our service. There were five regiments of colored men. Some got their freedom as promised, but my master and many others were more severe than ever.

On my return home I reminded my master of the promise of freedom by him and General Jackson, but I found it unsafe to say anything more about it. We thought General Jackson ought to have seen the promise made good. He gave us credit for being among the best soldiers he had. But we never would have fought as we did had it not been for the hope of freedom ahead. We pledged ourselves to each other that we never would fight for white folks again, unless we knew our freedom was sure. And never would our people have gone into this war had it not been for the Proclamation of Emancipation by the President of the United States.

Visiting the "Loft," an old brick kitchen in the King's Mill, I met two aged sisters, 75 and 80 years of age. Their 60-year-old brother was insane and lived there with them. Stepping onto the porch I met him first, took his hand and inquired of his sisters. Pointing towards the stairway, I climbed the steps while he slapped his hands, danced and began singing "Glory, Hallelujah to the Lamb." The sisters at the top of the stairs said, "Don't mind him, he's rejoicin' to see a white woman come up these stairs, for it's a new thing. I reckon there hasn't been a white woman up here for more'n twenty years. He don't know how to tell his gladness."

One sister continued, "Our poor brother's family, wife and children were sold away from him down the river over twenty years ago. He wept and grieved for so long. He just 'lost his mind.' Yet, he is most helpful carrying water and wood as needed. He takes care of himself and is good to care for his own clothes, washing and patching them." Finding a very nice suit for him, he tried it on, and as it fit, he began to dance and sing again. From all the sisters shared with me, I was convinced he was a man of extraordinary talent. His sisters had also been dealt the cruel blow of slavery, widowed and childless.

These refugees had faced a hard lot from cruel overseers who would take the life of a slave in the blink of an eye if it would advance their position with plantation owners. I enjoyed my visit with the sweet old, freed slaves. After visiting, reading and offering a prayer, I moved on, never to forget them.

Moving on to Yorktown, I visited two large camps of freedmen hosted by the Philadelphia Friends and the American Missionary Association. The freedmen studied in these Christian schools like hungry children grasping for food. Refugees crowded into the old army barracks to share together. One evening more people crowded inside the old barracks than could fit. People stood around the door and the windows. There were two intelligent colored men who had walked eighteen miles from beyond Fort Magruder to attend the school meeting. Others came from miles around as well. Encouraged by the prospects of freedom and its future for them, some were now being paid by their old masters for their work. Yet, most were still frightened by the Rebel talk that white folks could get all of their slaves back, just as before the Civil War.

One said, "They talk it so strong it makes us tremble. For we-uns think they'd be harder on us than ever."

"Are we sure to come out of the wilderness?" asked another.

"Will this sun of freedom, now peepin' troo de black cloud, come cl'ar out, an' make a bright day?" wondered another. I was very concerned for these young folks. Many feared great trouble as they sensed the nasty head of that snake named "slavery" could revive. Many of them trembled with fear, while others expressed greater faith.

Finally I spoke. "Look at that strong fort built by the Confederates. Didn't you hear them boast that all the Yankees of the North could never take it? And where is it now?" I asked.

Pausing for an answer, the room grew silent.

Calming their fears, I quoted Psalm 127, "'Except the Lord keep the city, the watchman walketh but in vain; except the Lord build the house, they labor in vain who build it.'"

Once again I paused for affect. Then, gazing into their eyes, I proposed, "The Lord will never permit the house of bondage to be rebuilt, for the cup of our nation's wickedness has been filled to the brim. They will never again barter for paltry gold the bodies and souls of those whom Christ died to redeem with his own precious blood. No. Never!"

My words were met with great applause. I continued sharing with these young folks well into the night. Weeping and talking about the past, as well as sharing new hopes for the future, many left saying their long trek to the meeting had been well worth the journey. But I knew their feet would be extremely blistered the next day.

One poor lady, who had lost her children and husband down the river to a slave trading gang said,

> When I heard that Richmond had fallen to the Union 'An' all was cryin', and say da catch Jeff Davis, an' I hurried de supper on de

table; an' I say, Missus, can Dilla wait on table til I go to de bush-spring an' git a bucket o' cool water?'

She say, 'Hurry Mill; an I seed' em all down to table afore I starts. Den I walks slow till I git out o' sight, when I runn'd wid all my might till I git to de spring, an' look all 'round, an' I jump up an' scream, 'Glory, glory, hallelujah to Jesus! I's free! I's free! Glory to God, you come down an' free us; no big man could do it.'

An' I got sort o' scared, a feared somebody hear me, an' I takes another good look, an' fall on de groun', an' roll over, an' kiss de groun' fo' de Lord's sake, I's so full o' praise to Massar Jesus. He do all dis great work. De soul buyers can neber take my two chillen lef' me; no, neber can take 'em from me no mo'.

Her tears fell fast and thick as she shared her story of losing both her husband and children, though she had clung to them with all of her might. She could not stop crying when the trader prodded them into the slave pen and locked them up until it was time to head down the river. Her mistress ordered her to be whipped because she could not stop wailing for her loved ones. No wonder she was ecstatic when she heard that such cruelty should end with the demise of slavery!

One day I met Aunt Sally, an old, poor slave, crippled with rheumatism. She approached me walking with two canes. She asked, "Ma'am, I've heard about your work and was just wonderin' if ye might have a blanke' or quilt for me? Me o' blanke' has been my only bed for seven years."

I smiled and said, "I'll pass by thy house tomorrow and bring thee some things."

She responded, "I mus' hurry back, or missus will fin' me out. You gib' em to the man choppin' wood in de yard; he'll put 'em in de cellar for me. Missus is mighty hard on you alls."

She hobbled away as fast as one can with two canes. Yet her mistress, Mrs. Pendleton, the daughter of our past President Zachary Taylor, did find out that she had come to see me. Aunt Sally had also been our President's slave, and she worked hard to help him rear his children. But Mrs. Pendleton was an extremely cruel slaveholder. Poor Aunt Sally must have been between 75 and 80, and still worked like a worn-out horse. Her reward was to freeze in a cold, dark cellar where she had become badly crippled and left to die.

Delivering my package for Aunt Sally the next day, I could not find her. A man near the back of the fence called for me and pointed to a little cabin across the way. There I found Aunt Sally crying and heard her story. Mrs. Pendleton was so angry about her coming to me that she had kicked her out of her home, the only home she had ever known. Mrs. Pendleton screamed, "Sally, Get out! I never want to see you again. I'll never allow a damned Yankee to set foot in my yard!"

The log cabin where I found her belonged to a colored couple, but they had no extra bed. Trying to calm them all, I gave Aunt Sally her own tick bed with a quilt and blanket, as well as a suit of clothes. Digging through the supplies I gave the kind couple a blanket and other necessary garments to help them. Passing by Mrs. Pendleton's house, a large bloodhound stood on watch, who let out a threatening growl when I gave a slight glance in his direction.

Meeting William and Phillis Davis, ex-slaves over 80 years of age, they shared this about their children. William said, "We think there were fourteen. . .all sol' down the river." And Phillis chimed in, "except for those we's got in heaven. We's glad they's safe, an' we trus' de jubilee trumpet will retch their ears, way down Souf, we don't know whar." William said, "We's cried for freedom many years, an' it come at last!"

Eva Mercer, 75 years old, remembered twenty years earlier when her children and husband had been sold leaving her alone. She needed clothing desperately, not having a single pair of underclothes for seven years! She cried as I gave her a plentiful supply. God bless her!

David Cary, 100 years of age, had three wives and all of his children stripped away and sold down the river, several at a time. He never heard from any of them again. Confessing to be forgetful, he admitted, "I will never forget the grief I passed through in parting with my good wives and chillens."

Following the war, Pross Tabb, A 90 year old freedman, was locked out of his cabin. He approached the army captain in tears. "Massar Tabb turn me out to die by de roadside. I begged him to let me build a cabin in de woods, and he say if I cut a stick in his woods he'll shoot me." Our captain informed Mr. Tabb that if he turned this poor man out of his home again that he would fine and imprison him for violating the post-war martial law. Thank goodness, the poor man was allowed to return. The ex-slave master, J.P. Tabb, owned 12,000 acres of land and had owned over 160 slaves at one time, though all had now left, except for Pross Tabb.

The colonel of the Yorktown post asked me if I would visit a group of freedmen in Gloucester who had no clothing and had been seen half naked. I agreed to go immediately, but he could not find a buggy for my journey. He had offered to pay twice the price, but not a soul would provide this service to a Yankee. Discouraged, the colonel was not willing to send me to Gloucester in a Virginia farm wagon, the only government transportation available to him.

I quipped back, "I frequently see the wealthiest Southern ladies riding on straw."

He replied, "Oh yes! The First Families of Virginia (FFV) do ride that way here. But you look too much like my mother to see you go in that style. I could not bear to have your children in Michigan know that I sent their mother out to ride thirty miles on a bale of hay."

Tears filled the poor man's eyes as he spoke of his own mother far away in their Northern home. I said, "Sir, if I can do anything to help these folks, I am glad to ride in the cart on a bale of hay!" And that's how I traveled. My seat had been rigged from a borrowed small box upon which I laid a sack of clothing, making quite a comfortable seat.

Crossing York River at the Gloucester Point, I walked into a store as I waited for my driver. A Southern style brigadier-general addressed me.

"I reckon you are from the North, madam."

"I am from the state of Michigan," I agreed, "but more recently from Washington."

"You Northern people cannot be satisfied with robbing us of millions of dollars in slaves. They were just as much our property as your horses and cattle. You stole our sheep and horses, or anything else you could get your hands on, yet that was not enough. Now you have a bill in Congress to rob us of our land, and of course it will pass. Then we'll go to work and mix up a little cake to bake for our families, and you'll come and snatch even that away from us," He rudely reprimanded.

I countered, "Thee probably refers to the bill just introduced in Congress. It allows the leaders in this Rebellion no more than $20,000 worth of real estate. The government can then sell land to soldiers and poor people, black or white, on liberal terms, in order to liquidate the war debt.

Pausing long enough to allow these words to penetrate, I continued on. "This debt would never have been contracted had not the South brought on the war. The South fired upon Sumter. Thy Rebels determined to sever the Union. It was a bargain of thy own making. Thee determined to make slavery the chief cornerstone of the Republic, but another stone, Liberty, has ground it to powder."

The Rebel general took a step towards me, but I held my hand to stop him and finished. "We had better accept the situation as we find it, and not call each other thieves and robbers, because thy chief cornerstone is no more. God never designed that we should make merchandise of human beings. In the written Word we find that God made one blood of all the nations of the earth. We find there no lines of distinction because of color or condition. Now let us drop slavery and hold it no longer as the bone of contention, and live henceforward a united nation."

With flashing eyes and red face, he angrily responded. "NEVER! We will NEVER give up our rights. We acknowledge you have overpowered us, but you have not, and never will, conquer us. We shall yet in some way secure our rights as Southerners, notwithstanding all your Northern preaching."

I replied, "Moving forward on thy position, thou will unite with some foreign power to break up our government, or grind our republican form into powder and scatter it to the four winds."

"Of course we should, and you can't blame us for doing that. It is just exactly what we shall do if we have the chance." He continued rambling on.

Fortunately, my soldier arrived and rescued me from any further unpleasant talk.

In Glouchester we visited and supplied the needs of those destitute until our means were depleted. Once again I found crippled old folks just the same as I had found in other parts of the state. I always took my Bible, for many times colored folks had none to read. Most of them had never learned to read, as they were not permitted. Yet, many also shared their thrilling experiences in overcoming slave-life!

Saying good-bye to Glouchester we experienced a spectacular ride along the Chesapeake Bay to Norfolk. There I found a pleasant place to stay with eighteen teachers at the Tyler House. While there I met a white woman who was beaten and cruelly assaulted with a raw-hide by family members because she was friends with teachers in our freedmen's schools. They told her she had disgraced their family name, yet she remained friends with these Christian teachers in spite of this treatment by her own family.

"Oh the wrongs and outrages which the spirit of slavery inflicted not only on the blacks, but also on the white people of the South."

Encouraged by the progress and education the children of freed refugees were receiving in Virginia, I returned to Washington to replenish supplies and receive new orders. These words kept running through my mind, "Da's took de bridle off their heads, an' let us loose to serve God."

Chapter Twenty-One
Forging Forward for the Freedmen!

O nce in Washington, I received a request to accompany 15 orphans to the "Haviland Institute" in my hometown. The Michigan delegation chose me to carry $500 in supplies to support the two orphanages in our state, the Detroit Orphanage and the Haviland Institute for the Homeless and Desolate.

Though chosen by the Michigan commissioners to be the delegate, a majority of the Detroit commissioners, whom I did not know, objected to this money being given to a woman. They lacked confidence in a woman purchaser to select appropriate goods at auction prices. A young man was selected to accompany me and ensure that wise selections were appropriated for the needy, homeless waifs we were serving. Though it could have turned into an awkward situation, it did not. My male companion, knowing of my work, was embarrassed by the board's vote.

He said, "Mrs. Haviland, you have been doing this kind of work all your life, and in particular you've dedicated yourself to it these past three years. You certainly need no help!"

I calmly stated, "I'm thankful to receive $500 in supplies for our Michigan orphanages. I can easily overlook these men's ignorance of a woman's ability. I've worked with such stereotypes all of my life!" The young man smiled and agreed to all of my purchases.

Making arrangements to travel to Michigan with the supplies, 15 orphans and 40 freedmen, we hoped to help families find sustainable work. Several of the men were headed towards Cleveland, Ohio, where friends had found favorable work for them there.

Freed refugees were usually resistant in relocating at a distance unless their families were sure to follow soon. They were not willing to risk breaking the bond that had been so violated during their lifetime of slavery. It was a strong force, a fear of persecution that drove many slave families from their Southern homes to Washington D.C., looking for protection.

Unfortunately, with 15,000 freedmen huddled around the country's capitol, once again starvation was the peril that induced many of these to leave for northern states to find work. Only a few hundred could find work in D.C. in order to earn their rations and ten cents a day. General Howard gave an order for transportation for many car-loads to move into the northern free states of New York, Pennsylvania, Ohio, as well as Michigan. But no matter how much they were bribed or offered, freedmen for the most part could not be persuaded to re-enter their former slave states. Who could blame them? General Howard predicted the northern humanitarians in Christian mission would guide the way of assimilating our colored people into jobs for the able and care for the needy children. He urged me to assist as many as possible.

Arriving at the Adrian depot with these 55 refugees, I found the people of Adrian slightly alarmed by the influx of freedmen needing jobs in our community. It seemed in due time, however, jobs were found, and our transplants found homes as well. Once these needs were met, I traveled with my son Joseph B. Haviland to his home for several weeks.

On my return home I was appalled to find that the Detroit Freedmen's Commission had decided to close the "Haviland Home" in order to fund schools in the South. They had already sold and moved one of the buildings to Tecumseh in my short absence. I was also informed of immediate plans to sell the other buildings and the team of horses.

Furious that the Freedmen's Commission neglected my contractual provision included in the selling of my property to them, I called for a special meeting in Detroit where I spoke directly to the commissioners. "Gentlemen, these actions are a definite mistake and misstep for the Freedmen's Commission in light of our contractual agreement. When I sold this property, my object and desire was for it to become a state orphanage for the children of soldiers and all who were living in our county homes," I insisted, pausing a moment for emphasis. "My research shows from my many travels that more than three-fourths of the convicts in our prisons in Pennsylvania, Maryland, Virginia, as well as Michigan, were orphaned and abandoned as children!"

Mumbling and grumbling could be heard throughout the room, but I motioned for their silence and continued. "Emma Hall, the matron of our female prisoners here in Detroit, says that there is not one girl or woman in her care that had not been left an orphan. In view of these reports, as well as the fact that there are even more orphans following the Civil War than ever before, I propose this orphanage is necessary now more than ever!"

George Duffield, D.D., the president of the Freedman's Commission, stood in response. "Gentleman, how do we know but that Mrs. Haviland's proposal is not directly from the Lord? Think about it! We are finding it very difficult to secure homes for these forty children from the Haviland Home."

Finally all concurred. Given one month to reopen the Haviland Home, I worked diligently selling $10 subscriptions. In the middle of this frenzy, J.R. Shipherd,

Secretary of the Western Division American Missionary Association (AMA) offered to purchase the orphanage from the Detroit Freedman's Association so that it could continue in its present form. The agreement did not include a provision for keeping it as an orphanage in case of financial crisis, but it would pay me $250 of the $500 I had agreed to deduct from the $2,000 purchase if that should happen.

Fearful that once again these children could become a public burden, it was my only option. Shipherd pledged his word, and further agreed to make a $3,000 expansion of the building and grounds within the next two years. I reluctantly agreed. Mr. Shipherd secured a matron, Mrs. Edgerton from Vicksburg, Mississippi. As she could not arrive for ten days I agreed to serve as the volunteer matron, and she finally arrived four weeks later.

In October 1866, General O.O. Howard offered me transportation to Atlanta, Georgia. Once again I left home, and thankfully my dreaded cough, to serve the freedmen, but this time under the auspices of the AMA. Spending several days with my dear friends Levi and Catherine Coffin in Cincinnati, we travelled across the river to Covington and Newport, Kentucky, where several thousand freedmen were living. Meeting a lieutenant in charge, he gave us a tour of the barracks dedicated to the sick and suffering.

On the tour I noticed their bunks were filled merely with husks, hay or leaves in their bed sacks. One poor woman suffering from rheumatism had absolutely nothing in her bed sack. All she had was an old blanket that needed to be burned. Her hands and legs were contorted, thus preventing her from being able to dress herself. I bought hay so she could have her own filled bed sack. I also gave her a warm quilt. Before going to sleep that night, I procured enough thick, red flannel and made her a long-sleeve gown that would cover her feet. The next morning I had her try it on, and she simply wept. Finally gathering her senses, she said. "This is more than I deserve. All the sufferin' I's had all the year is nothin' compared to the sufferin' of my Jesus for poor me."

Her caregiver said this dear woman had the patience of Job, and she'd never seen anyone else as patient in all of her life. I brought her another flannel garment the following day. I found my little niche here sewing suitable garments for others, and I continued on helping out in this way for close to a month.

On New Year's Day 1867, I visited twelve families, taking clothes and blankets to those who were aged and sick. Walking a mile to the ferry I stopped by the mission rooms, where I met E.M. Cravath, a new colleague from the AMA in Cincinnati. He had just arrived from a southern states tour. Cravath excitedly shared with me that my work was greatly needed in Memphis, Tennessee. Making arrangements I set out from Cincinnati to Memphis.

Shortly after my arrival in Memphis I attended a large colored church and introduced myself and my work. I was assigned to work in a Mission Home with thirteen teachers and Joseph Barnum, the superintendent from Oberlin, Ohio.

Receiving boxes of supplies, some from England, I soon became busy in the everyday tasks of my mission work. A dying grandmother, whose little granddaughter had died just a few days prior, was sick and in great distress when I met her. She cried out to me, "Oh missus, do pray for poor me. Can God forgive sich an ole sinner as me? Can I fin' Jesus so quick as my poor Mary Jane did afore she died? I knows she went so happy: I prayed all night, but 'pears like so dark; don't see de place o' de candle."

Reading Scriptures to her about Jesus's forgiveness and even his forgiveness of the thief on the cross, I held her hand and said, "Honey, because the thief repented and had faith in Jesus in his last moments of life, he was forgiven." Kneeling beside her cot I prayed for the Spirit of God to impress this teaching upon her soul. I implored for unbounded mercy into her precious soul for God's forgiveness. When I left she appeared calm. When I came back to visit, her mind appeared clear and her faith became resolute, the shadow of doubt removed. Though she lingered a bit longer, she died in peaceful faith.

In this line of work, I always understood that there was an element of risk. Some worried about the fears of an erupting riot, such as the bloody, violent riot of several months prior in May 1866. A Union woman who lived close by our Mission House said she endured sleepless nights on our behalf because of frequent threats. She heard such nonsense as, "Nigger teachers should be cleared out, as well as free niggers." Overly concerned, she expected to hear of our death or demise at any time. Whenever she heard the shot of a pistol, she would look in alarm towards our home.

One day I finally said, "I don't believe we shall have any more riots. I believe in the God of Daniel, who was and is willing to protect us. My confidence is in Him!"

"But you don't know these people as I do," she whined," for I have always lived here. I wasn't going to tell you, but thought perhaps I should so you could be more cautious. They are threatening now just as they did before that awful riot a few months ago."

My co-workers countered, "No. There's nothing to fear with so many soldiers close at hand." Though they, too, had heard the same threats, they believed we were safe with a strong Union presence.

While there, I worked to alleviate the suffering of many families. Traveling to old Fort Pickering Freedman's Hospital, I met Esther Jane. Inquiring her age she quipped, "I's goin' on 200. Massa's book say I's 108, an' dat is eight years for another hundred ain't it? I was sole at sheriff's sale for debt to Massa Sparks. In do ole war Massa George Washington was a mighty kind man. He boarded wid Massa Sparks four or five weeks. He wore short breeches an' knee-buckles an' a cocked hat I dep' his room clar'd up." There were younger folks who could not see as well as 108-year-old Esther Jane, yet her skin was full of lines and very deep wrinkles with an ashen hue. I gave out sugar and crackers to her and to all the others I could muster to eat them.

While at Ft. Pickering, a colored man who had just escaped from his old master came looking for me. His master lived in a time warp with no concept that the war was over and the slaves freed. The ex-slave stayed to take care of his dying wife. After she had died, he planned to leave the plantation with his two small children. Attempting to escape, the old master caught him, took the children and burned his bundle of clothes. He told me it had been his best suit and he only owned one shirt and one pair of pants. Laying out a number of garments, I had him go to the storeroom and select the suit that fit him best. Then I accompanied him to Colonel Palmer's office, where he retold his whole pitiful story. The colonel asked him if he would be able to care for the children if he could get them.

"If you'll be so good as to help me get my children, these hands," he replied holding them out, "shall take as good care of them as they do me." His eyes filled with tears.

I left him with the colonel, who told him he would send an escort of soldiers with him the next morning. "Your old master will dare not refuse giving up the children after reading the note I shall send him," The colonel replied.

One day as I was passing the soldier's barracks that are now used for freedmen, I heard loud sounds of groaning. Calling out, I found "Uncle Philip," a 97-year-old man in great distress. "How long have you been suffering like this?" I asked.

"Only two years, "he replied.

"Two years must seem a great while."

"Oh no, it's only a little minute, compared with the eternity of rest in glorious mansions Jesus went to prepare for me; for I knows I's got a home thar', missus, I knows it, 'case I's seen it, an I feels it."

Providing for his physical needs, I was blessed by the spiritual strength he shared with me. Uncle Phil was definitely green with old age, yet his mind clear and his ability to share memories excellent. He told of the cruel beatings and torture from his owner for living out his faith when he was a mere lad of eleven. A young Phil had been mercilessly beaten, hung, scoffed and ridiculed by a cruel master. The physical and mental torture almost drove him crazy. For several years Phil remained in a trance, until the prayers of his dear mother were answered and he awakened. Scenes of suffering continued for him over many years and were particularly clear and vivid in his mind. Reading a psalm or chapter from the Bible to him from time to time, Uncle Phil would refer to these passages, as he had meditated on them between my visits. Sharing his story of being beaten to the point of death for not renouncing Jesus, he would often shed tears. His elbows would rest on his knees with his face buried in his calico kerchief, and he would cry until the kerchief was drenched.

One day when I came for a visit, he was just raising from that kneeling position and he said, "I's jus' bin prayin' for you," he said. "I did't know as you's so near, but I felt your spirit. It sort o' lifs me up to talk wid you. I prayed dat de good seed you's sowin' 'among our people may lodge in good groun' an' bring a hundred fol'. You' doin more for our poor, ignorant people dan you knows."

He lived a year after I left Memphis. I enjoyed sending him a couple of dollars now and then. Friends often called upon him to make sure his needs were supplied. I heard that the last words he uttered were from the lines of a favorite hymn, "Give me wings." His happy spirit took flight. Always impressed with Uncle Philip's faith, he hid the words of the Good Book in his heart. Though he had never been able to read, God used him as an instrument in the lives of many, pointing souls to the truth and love of Jesus Christ.

Chapter Twenty-Two

"Bless the children!"

Arriving home In May 1867, I found to my dismay a letter from the County Superintendent of the Poor, Mr. Burton Kent, with the following notice:

> MRS. LAURA S. HAVILAND – Many persons transported by you last year have become a county charge, and it has become an intolerable burden to the tax-payers. Any person bringing a child or indigent person into this county, who is not legally indentured, shall be prosecuted to the full extent of the law.

Outraged by this charge I immediately visited the Lenawee County Poor House, three miles outside of town. Taking a mental inventory and asking questions of the house matron, I could hardly believe there was not a single colored child there. Out of 51 residents there were only three refugees. One immigrant only, Mr. Morris Brown, had come to Adrian the previous summer. Discharged after two and a half months might be a *burden,* but it certainly was not "intolerable to the tax-payers."

Researching all of these facts, I wanted to set the record straight. How much had our immigrants cost the tax-payers? Calling Mr. Helms, our grocer, I asked him his cost for supplying a widow with several children who had been sick for at least two weeks. He said he had provided a load of groceries and food. But when I asked the total cost, he could not supply the figures needed. He promised to find them for me when I returned on the following Tuesday. On my return Helms remembered helping another family that had lost a loved one. There was a burial cost involved. Helms said he also helped with an armful of wood, a small sack of flour and other groceries. I asked if he had supplied the family more than once. "No," he said, "the wife was able to provide for the rest of the family." The cost for her totaled $8.96! After calling on Mr. Helms three appointed times, he was still unable to give me the other precise totals. So, I calculated all of the supplies and services at their highest rates. From my research these expenses were $35.

Writing an article for our newspaper, the Adrian *Times* I included these figures in my defense of the orphanage. I informed citizens that our orphanage was operated by the American Missionary Association (AMA), who was in charge of its support. I found a mathematician who was able to provide me the exact fraction of a mill that each taxpayer paid rather than an "intolerable burden upon the tax-payers."

This article finally led me to a face to face confrontation with Burton Kent. He responded incredulously, "Really? Do you mean to say that an organization such as the American Missionary Association is supporting the orphanage? Well, how were we to know this?"

I grimaced through my smile and replied, "Perhaps we should allow the facts to dictate our actions rather than the prejudices of one or two influential statesmen who obviously neither care nor have a heart for these children!" It became more and more obvious to me that these threats had sprung up from prejudiced parties.

I remained close to home for a while until our public relations were in good standing once again. I worked diligently to raise funds for renovations and repairs to the home for over a year. As our orphanage was found to be in good order, and our matron Mrs. Edgertona greed to continue in this capacity, I finally felt free to serve elsewhere.

Receiving word from General Howard that my work was needed in Charleston, South Carolina, I headed to Charleston, via Washington D.C. Stopping over in Toledo on January 29, 1869, I spent the night with dear friends, missing my original train and catching a later one the next morning. Traveling through the mountains, we passed the wreckage of three rail cars, which were still burning. I noticed an injured woman being removed from the train on one side of the snowy embankment. Hearing that several were killed and many injured, I was stunned to realize that this had been my original train. Had I not decided to visit with friends in Toledo, I could have easily been among the dead and dying on this train. For the third time in my many travels by rail and river, I felt that I had providentially missed a fatal accident. I was thankful for the Guiding Hand that protects and preserves in fulfilling the plan of our lives.

Arriving at the Washington depot, I met my wonderful brother Harvey Smith and his son. It was such a joy to spend time with him and see his work teaching in the freedmen's schools there. Catching up on the times, "old" and "new," we treasured our time together. On the Sabbath we attended the Colored Methodist Episcopal Church. I was asked to speak at this large meeting, and so I shared Uncle Philip's story of walking with the Savior for 97 years in the midst of his persecutions and sorrows of slavery.

As I spoke of his beatings, how he was whipped until he lost consciousness, several in the meeting wept. Following the meeting many came to share with me their stories. Several of them were also whipped for praying. One woman remembered fainting while she was still being whipped. Another man was kept in stocks, in addition to being whipped for hours, and almost died. His master used the same exact words that Uncle Philip's master used with him. "He would whip the praying devil out of him." Thank God that neither master was able to whip the Spirit of God out of these faithful men. Their prayers had helped them persevere and survive the horrors of slavery.

Preparing to travel on to South Carolina, Dr. Reynolds, the Surgeon-in-Chief, asked if I would stay and help him in Washington D.C. with relief work. He felt certain that this would be fine with General Howard. The next day General Howard called on me and concurred that I was needed most in Washington, at least until the winter season was over. He asked me to visit soup kitchens and investigate this work.

Sharing with me the duties that he and Dr. Reynolds wanted me to fulfill, I responded. "General Howard, I have a special request of you."

"Oh," he paused, leaning in and looking over his spectacles.

"Yes," I continued. "I would like for my authority to remain a secret."

"Really?" he asked in surprise.

"That way no one will suspect me, and I can investigate these services and projects from the best advantage."

General Howard agreed to my condition, but also asked that I investigate other aspects of the charitable programs for freedmen. "Mrs. Haviland, we need you to examine the condition of those applying for our charities, as well as the manner in which the charity is given."

Agreeing to his requests I was given room, board and a furnished office at the Freedmen's Campbell Camp Hospital. Visiting Josephine Griffin's relief office before mid-morning on my first day, there were sixty to seventy persons who called on her to find work. From a distance I followed a number of folks home who applied for soup kitchen tickets. I visited with twenty families that day and found many of them living in wretched squalor. One poor sick man I found had a very high fever, and on occasion lost consciousness. His bed was a pile of rags in the corner of a room. In this condition he couldn't get out to apply personally, and there was no family to intercede on his behalf. We saw that he was given food and suitable bed-clothing. The Bureau physician, who we called, said he would have died within a couple of days had he remained in that condition.

One Irish woman, applying for relief, was renting all of the rooms in a fine brick house, except for the back room where she and her family lived in fine style. This situation revealed a great deficiency in our system. Those who suffered most often lacked the self-confidence or courage to ask for help, while those who needed no help took advantage of the system and even profiteered as this Irish woman.

Overall, I found that soup houses were well managed. One day, however, I met an exception to the rule. I decided to enter the "Savage Soup-house" as a curious spectator in a motley crowd. I was treated to a sip of fine soup. It was so delicious that it might tempt the "palate of an epicure," yet the other caldron looked horrible, even too forbidding for human consumption. I soon understood the method of this soup-house. The good soup was served to white applicants first, while the colored people standing in the yard biding their time were served the soup of death!

As I was watched, an unacceptable situation arose. A policeman told a shivering black man he should go inside and place his pail on the farther block for the good soup.

"I'll be sent out," he weakly responded.

"I tell you. Go in," the policeman ordered. "I'll see about that."

The black man had barely gone in when the manager shoved him out the door saying, "You know better than to come in yet. Another thing, this soup is for white folks. The other is for niggers."

The policeman walked in and reprimanded the manager. "I have seen fish made of one and flesh of another long enough. Here are women and children standing out on the ice and snow, waiting all this afternoon for you to serve the white people first. Another thing I'd like to know, why is their difference in the soup? That black stuff is hardly fit for pigs to eat, Mr. Savage, and you know it."

"Our citizens furnish the ingredients for this soup," Mr. Savage rebuffed the officer, "and our citizens shall have it."

"Doesn't General Howard furnish a hundred pounds of beef and two hundred loaves of bread each day? And on Saturday this number is doubled. And by the way, are these not our citizens?" He gestured to all of the black citizens standing in the long line outside freezing.

"There are ten thousand too many of 'em, and it's none of your business. I shall do as I please," Savage raged back while one Irish woman walked in and out with four quarts of soup, three loaves of bread, and a large slab of meat.

"I shall make it my business to report you to General Howard," The policeman rallied.

Cursing at the kindly policeman, Mr. Savage grumbled, "I could care less about your reports to General Howard. Get out of my kitchen!"

After all white and colored persons had received their soup, the policeman left. I was tempted to cheer him for his outspoken bravery, but thought my silence was the better part of valor.

Instead I followed him, and as I passed him, I said in a low tone, "I thank thee for thy words to Mr. Savage."

"Stop, do you live here?" he asked.

"Temporarily," I replied.

"Go slowly till I get my club, so I can catch up. I want to talk to you."

Soon he caught up and introduced himself as Officer Ross. He inquired whether I was one of the visiting inspectors. I told him that General Howard had authorized me to inspect soup kitchens.

He asked, "Are you going to report Savage?"

"I am on my way now for that very purpose," I stated.

"I want to visit with you more," he replied. "I am on my way to see the police lieutenant about this." Giving me his badge number he said. "Let's meet in a few minutes at Pennsylvania Avenue." Then he was off.

Wanting more information on that pathetic soup, I called at the cabin of the poor black man who had been pushed out of Savage's kitchen. He showed me his quart of "an excuse for soup." He had it on the stove cooking, boiling the raw half bits of turnips and potatoes. The man let me taste it, and I fully agreed with Ross's description. "It was hardly fit for pigs." The man told me he always had to cook it again, or it made the family sick. He had been recuperating from pneumonia, but his mother was still suffering from it and he was caring for her yet. I rushed to the closest grocery store, where I bought them bread, tea, crackers, rice, sugar and mustard for a plaster to place on the mother's side. The soup kitchen had given him but one slice of bread with his quart of soup to feed the seven in his family, four of whom were sick.

Later I met Officer Ross at Pennsylavania Avenue. Breathless from his duties and running to catch up with me, his lieutenant had sent word that if need be, he would call General Howard himself in order to confirm my report. Thanking him, I made my report to General Howard.

As a result of this day's encounter, Mr. Savage received a notification from General Howard's office stating:

> Mr. Savage, there must be no difference in quality or quantity of soup served between rich or poor and black or white. The notification identified a report of such a distinction had been made. This pandering must stop immediately!

Mr. Savage angrily denied any difference between soups given out to customers. As such notifications were also printed in local newspapers, Savage asserted this denial to the *Daily Chronicle,* and even accused the reporter of being a liar.

Using Mr. Savage's own words in his conversation with Officer Ross, I submitted a counter rebuttal in the *Daily Chronicle* that was printed the next day. Dr. Reyburn, the Surgeon-in-Chief of our relief work, included a preface to the article. I also received approval from Officer Ross for printing the encounter and using his name.

Savage was in an uproar. He swore and raged that he would press charges against me for defamation. He verbally attacked the police officers, as well. This caused the D.C. Chief of Police to call me in and check-out my official credentials, as they were missing from the *Chronicle* article. Officer Ross met me at the station and was quick to say the chief was not questioning my authority. He was just curious, as the station was receiving bad press over Mr. Savage's rants.

Opening my portfolio I presented my credentials to the D.C. Chief, repeating my original request of General Howard. "I ask only that my position remains confidential, as I have much better luck doing my work anonymously."

Taking a few moments to look over my portfolio, he remarked, "Mrs. Haviland, I think you are authorized to inspect all of us. I see in these remarks that you have diverse experience in working with the post-war reconstruction efforts. We may in some cases be able to render assistance to you."

Thankful for this positive encounter, I found their police assistance most helpful in several situations. Savage made empty threats against all of us, the police department, as well as our non-profit relief work, but nothing ever came from them. And no other word was printed in reference to the editorials in the *Chronicle.*

Yet there still seemed to be a lot of grumbling on the streets. Surgeon Reyburn overheard comments from a group of Rebels at a street crossing. "Why don't Savage do something about that soup-house affair, and not be a numb-head and let that woman wind him around her finger like that?" Another asserted, "If I'd lied once over that old soup-house, I'd lie again before I'd hold still and take all that."

Savage actually did change his soup-house policy in the short run, but his white customers and secession friends wailed too loudly and before long he had gone back to his old ways. Fortunately the kitchens were closing for the summer and Savage's Soup Kitchen was not reinstated for the fall. I was released from this task with Savage and continued on with my work of helping the sick and suffering.

Campbell Camp's physician, Dr. Cook, informed me that a child had frozen to death in the Kendal Green Barracks. Neither one of us knew who was in charge there, so I went to the barracks and found a ten-month-old dead child who looked to have died of a chill. The dead child's mother had just returned empty-handed from the difficult task of finding a coffin for her baby. Her shoes were worthless. Wading through melting snow, her shoes and feet were frozen to the bone and the bottom of her dress soaked. Crying, she said, "My chil' was the fourth in my row of cabins that froz' to death!"

I called on the other families in her neighboring cabins to find that the mother's story was true. No one in the camp was allowed to have more than "two four-foot sticks" of firewood in 24 hours. None had fire. All told the same sad story. There was no coal and a great lack of wood. I also observed that there was not adequate bedding or clothing for a single family to feel comfortably warm.

Inquiring, I was informed that Major Thompson was in charge of the Kendal Green Barracks. Making a visit to his headquarters I found that the major had taken his family to the capital to observe President Johnson's impeachment trial at the Capitol.

Returning to General C.H. Howard's office, I reported on the dreadful conditions for these poor families. General Howard sent me with fifty loaves of bread, quilts and blankets for the destitute and a coffin in his ambulance for the dead child. He instructed me to give one loaf to each of the families I had visited and the rest to Major Townsend, not Major Thompson. The general was shocked to find these families under Townsend's care in such a destitute condition. He asked me to continue on with a thorough investigation of this camp and barracks.

The next day I visited forty families. Of these I found twelve sick and in desperate need of supplies. From the hearsay among Major Townsend's police guards at Campbell Camp, it sounded as though there had been much suffering in these camps all along. Two cross police guards approached me and insisted, "Ma'am you must come immediately to the major's head-quarters."

I asserted, "I am calling on these camp residents per General Howard's request, and I will not stop unless I receive orders from him." Finally, after they realized I would not be deterred, they left me alone. I heard later that the major had charged his police guard to bring "that woman" to his office immediately and keep her there.

It finally dawned on me that this Major Townsend was an acquaintance of mine. Working diligently alongside his wife and daughters in Sunday School, these women were excellent in their Christian spirit of self-sacrifice. Major Townsend called on General Howard, where he learned that I was the inspector. Making a quick about face he promised the general he would assist me in any way to support the poor. Yet, while he spent his day at my office and going to see the general, I spent mine visiting the barracks attending to needs of people. Not long after this, Major Townsend was dismissed from his duties for a sundry of small misdemeanors.

President Johnson's impeachment trial spewed sparks of drama and excitement throughout Washington. On May 16, 1869, the news spread like wildfire that the President had been acquitted in the trial, but his power would be curtailed. Here's my journal entry from that day.

> Johnson has turned his back on our soldiers, who bled and died to save the nation's life, and made no serious effort to put an end to the Ku Klux outrages in the Southern States. For this reason many demanded that he be removed from his office. With these people his acquittal foreboded ill, but we still hope for the best.

A great buzz at Campbell Camp surprised everyone. Uncle Dodson, a 65 year-old "plantation preacher," had been torn away from his wife twenty years earlier by his unrelenting slave master. They begged their master to sell them together. Kneeling at his feet, the only response they received was a lash and a kick in the gut before they were torn apart.

One day during my stay, a woman showed up in Uncle Dodson's front yard crying out, "Oh Ben Dodson, is dis you? I am your own Betty." She grabbed and clasped him closely.

Stunned beyond belief, he pushed her back to get a close look and cried out, "Glory! Glory! Hallelujah! Dis is my Betty shua."

"I foun' you at las'. I's hunted an' hunted till I track you up here. I's boun' to hunt till I fin' you if you's alive," Betty wept.

"Mir'cles of mir'cles, God has brought us back together!" Ben shouted ecstatically.

Weeping great tears of joy, Ben cooed. "Ah, Betty, we cried harder'n dis when da sole us apart down dar in Egyp'." Soon they were living happily together once again in their own cabin. Their joy brought a needed smile to everyone's face in this camp of gloom.

"Bless the children!"

Uncle Dodson always had a way of bringing a smile to my face. A self-professed plantation preacher, he was not always accurate. He quoted in a prayer meeting, "Adam called his wife's name Eve because she was the mother of all evil." Often Uncle Dodson would ask me to read a chapter from the Bible in chapel meetings "an 'splain it to us." So, I felt I should take this occasion to read Genesis chapter three. When I got to the part, "because she was the mother of all living," Uncle Dodson called out"ebil, ebil, sistah Hab'lin, ebil."

Since Uncle Dodson was learning how to read the easy words in the first grade reader, I placed a Bible in front of him and pointed to the word "living."

"Dat is so in dis place," he conceded, "but dat 'evil' is some place in de Bible."

"Father Dodson," I patiently replied, "I have read every word in this Bible a number of times, and there is no such sentence between the two lids that Adam called his wife's name Eve because she was the mother of all evil."

A smile ran from face to face throughout the entire congregation. I often said, "It's a miracle these poor folks do not misquote Scripture more often, as most of them had never been allowed to read."

Turning to a brother, Uncle Dodson declared, "Brodder Davis, I've labored in de Gospel mor'n forty years wid de white ministers and de black ministers, an' I neber foun' one so deep in de Scritpur' as sistah Hablin." Then we continued on in our services with great joy and satisfaction.

Folks testified to being punished severely for learning the letters of a "little white boy." One man agreed, "Oh yes, well do I 'member when I was punish', too." Another concurred, "for tryin' to learn to read."

"It's a wonder thee all have passed through such trials and deprivation and still survived as very intelligent people." I replied.

Receiving a shocking note from Mrs. Edgerton, dated May 14, 1869, it read: "Mrs. Haviland, Rev. Shipherd and the American Missionary Association (AMA) will close the doors of the Haviland Home immediately. An auction has been slated for May 14, and the children will be placed in homes before this day."

With an aching heart I knew my life course was about to change again. The startling fact was that May 14 was also the day I received the telegraph. It would be impossible to place forty children in homes so quickly. I wrote J.R. Shipherd with a proposition reminding him of our verbal agreement and proposed new terms to reopen the orphanage until all could find suitable homes.

Meanwhile I received the disconcerting news that four orphans were placed in the county poor-house, and others would be there soon. Four younger children were left on the streets of Adrian to find their own homes. Another four had been left with a poor colored family who had been paid to care for them until better accommodations might be found. Four others were left with a Palmyra white family. They were also promised payment until other arrangements could be made. One ten-year-old girl was left with a woman of ill repute, and the little girl had been seen on the streets drunk.

I wrote to Rev. E.M. Cravath from the AMA Cincinnati division, and my old friend Levi Coffin, seeking help and support for these children. I learned from Levi that eight children had been left sitting on the stone steps of the AMA office in Cincinnati with a note in a ten-year-old child's hands.

The note read: "These children were sent by you to the orphanage near Adrian, Michigan. It has closed. You must take care of them."

Word was that Mrs. Edgerton had sent them from the orphanage on the express wagon. Arriving at 6 am the office had not opened, so the driver simply left them on the steps with a note. Levi Coffin fed them breakfast, as they had eaten nothing during the night. Rev. Cravath paid $100 to a Cincinnati orphanage to take them.

An open letter from Levi Coffin in the Adrian paper read:

What ails Michigan? Why can they not care for thirty or forty of these poor little homeless orphans, when we have had a few thousands to look after in this great thoroughfare? Where is the Christianity and philanthropy of thy great State? Why send these children back to us, who took them from those crowded camps, where there was so much suffering and dying, for the purpose of their being properly trained, and fitted for usefulness, amid humane surroundings?

After seeing my appeal and letter to the AMA, both Coffin and Cravath joined me in my efforts to reopen the orphanage. I wrote several letters to the AMA in New York. Including an account of the deplorable treatment of these children, I also included a copy of the letter from Levi Coffin. I sent a telegram asking this question: "How could thee allow these little ones to be turned back into harm's way on the streets?"

Their reply, "Mrs. Haviland, this is the first we have heard of this unacceptable behavior. We had no knowledge of this activity. We have telegraphed Mr. Shipherd to dispose of nothing more connected with the orphanage. How long would it be before it could be reopened should we place it in your hands?"

I responded, "It shall be re-opened as soon as I receive official authority from thy association to do it, and I will resign my position in my current work."

Rev. Smith and Mr. Whipple, members of the AMA New York, visited me in Washington and authorized me to reopen the home for the orphans and serve as its general superintendent. Arriving in Cincinnati I took the abandoned children home with me.

Mr. Whipple informed me that everyone expressed concern for me in behalf of the orphanage except for Mr. Shipherd. Shipherd said, "I have done nothing for which Mrs. Haviland or anyone else should have any reason to complain."

Shipherd, whom I never saw or spoke with again, was ordered to send 23 boxes and packages of goods back to the orphanage. I bought back what furniture I could find. Unfortunately, much of it had been given away at a great loss to the orphanage. The AMA sent me $50 for supplies. I was able to gather 30 of our children who had previously lived at the orphanage. My whole time and energy were now devoted to this work!

Certainly, I was up to the task! Here we were a third time trying to pull this orphanage together. Yet, the burden seemed light when considering its importance. Providing the necessary support was not easy, but we would find it. We had already bought a horse, repaired a buggy and hired one ex-soldier, Charlie Taft, who had been left impaired from his service in the war. Charlie agreed to spend the winter helping us with whatever projects we deemed necessary for his room and board. Excitement prevailed as our prospects looked brighter now than at any time since the Raisin Institute had been transformed into an orphanage. Our goal was to help these little folks receive training, support and kindness. Our hope was that these innocent little ones would become useful citizens rather than inmates or tramps.

Unfortunately a major challenge to our progress lurked close by. After a busy sewing day I moved quickly to place some sewing patches in their box in the hall room. It was twilight outside. Not carrying my lamp, I mistakenly walked through the cellar door rather than the hall door. Stepping into midair I plunged eight feet headlong, hitting my head against the edge of a hard-wood beam. Lying unconscious on the cellar floor, I was first presumed dead. But as signs of life appeared, a physician was immediately called. The orphan children took up a vigil of prayer day and night. Prayers from many across the country went up on my behalf.

Rev. Cravath of the AMA in Cincinnati sent a letter of concerned inquiry to which my daughter Laura Jane responded, "Mother is unconscious from a dangerous fall, and we (her children) are earnestly praying for her restoration. If our

Heavenly Father sees fit to grant our petition, thee will receive a reply from her when practicable."

His immediate response: "You may rest assured our All-wise Father will restore your mother if he has further work for her to do. You may also be assured that her friends in this city are uniting in prayer with her children for her recovery."

My condition was very odd. They said I was unconscious. Yet, I could hear what people were saying, but I couldn't respond. "She will never speak again." I heard one say. Yet, I believed I was getting better. Was I really sick? I also remember thinking that my children might be sad at the thought of losing me. I would try to say, "I am going to get well." As hard as I tried, I could not speak a single syllable. At times I would painstakingly listen to hear if my children were in the room with me. It seemed as though I must be off somewhere floating in the ethereal blue sky, lying on a soft, tranquil white cloud. The next thing I knew, three day and nights had passed without my realizing it. Then suddenly the beautiful white cloud disappeared, and there were my three beautiful daughters looking down on me.

One of the girls said excitedly, "Mother looks as if she knows us!"

"Well, of course I know thee! Thee are my daughters," I thought. "But what are thy names? Okay, not so fast. What is my name?" I wondered while looking around the room assessing the wallpaper. There were maps, pictures and even furniture that looked familiar. "Where am I? Am I in a large city or in the country?" The one thing I could remember was that I was advanced in age. "What have I done in my life?" Yet, nothing would come.

While thinking these turbulent thoughts in my own mental soliloquy, suddenly it dawned on me, "I'm Laura Smith Haviland! I'm in the Haviland Orphanage."

"Dost thou know me, mother?" asked my daughter Jane.

It took me some time to speak, but I finally said, "Yes!" and then it took longer to say "Jane," and later, "Mira" and finally, "Esther." Each time required a great amount of effort and recollection on my part. There was great laughter and joy at my accomplishment.

Finally Esther said, "Don't have the least anxiety or care about the orphanage, for friends have brought grain, flour, meal and groceries in abundance." Those words flowed over me like a heavenly balm—what relief! Surely the Lord is the Father of the fatherless.

Rubbing my head and trying to find the right words, I stuttered. "Wha-What is the ma-ma-matter?"

"Mother, thee fell into the cellar and were badly hurt!" Jane spoke.

I must have looked so surprised because I just said, "Really?"

"Yes, it was a bad fall." Mira continued, "Thee fractured the bones and artery at the base of thy skull."

"Oh! That's why my head hurts!" I lamented, rubbing my head, but the words came easier. Looking at my daughters and thinking of the various cities in which they lived. I asked, pointing to them individually, "How did thee know? When did thee get here?"

They began to share all of the details. My son-in-law had telegraphed each one of them. Prayers and gifts had come in from all of our friends and loved ones. Their animated talk continued, but I must have been overwhelmed or stunned by the bruise on my head and the many other bruises and concussion incurred. I fell asleep during the conversation. I think I might have slept all my senses away. Yet, I was blessed to receive tender nursing from my four daughters, and I praise the One who alone is the prayer-hearing God.

For six months I was ordered to complete rest, the worst punishment I could have received. Yet, I spent luxurious time with family and friends, thinking of "absolutely nothing." That's what the doctors had prescribed. It was two years before I made a complete recovery.

Through these years it was "hit and miss" for me as I experienced several spells of unconsciousness during which I simply had to lay my work "at the cross." The accomplishment in reopening the Haviland Home came from the prayers and support of many friends after my fall. In spite of my health conditions, we also eventually presented, and succeeded in passing, a proposal for the Michigan State Legislation to create the Coldwater State Orphanage. Asking God to help me complete the work of creating an orphanage in Coldwater, Michigan, I spent these two years working towards this cause. Accepting each day as a gift and an opportunity to serve the children, I was blessed.

My episodes of unconsciousness reminded me that life could be snuffed out at any moment. The words of the poet would come to mind during my spells, and I meditated on the promise of my Heavenly Home

"Tis a glorious boon to die, A favor that can't be prized too high"

Ah, such peace and tranquility. . .was I dead? Where was I?

Chapter Twenty-Three

Jolt!

Ah, such peace and tranquility...was I dead? Where was I?

Suddenly the train jolted! The women in the passenger cabin were rudely awakened from their sweet sleep. "Oh my!" Laura's voice echoed with the impact of the halting train. Her body jerked into foggy consciousness with the choppy stop. Sojourner's arms were wailing in the air and she stammered, "What, what's happenin'?"

Still half asleep, Laura suddenly jerked awake as well. "How long have I been asleep?" she asked. Laura opened her eyes in dazed astonishment. She couldn't get her bearings. Ah, yes, she thought. She had been dreaming, dreaming about her life, and what she would write in her life-story.

Sojourner said, half muttering, "Huh? I dunno. Uh, I think we're in Columbus." Opening her eyes, she looked about the cabin and noticed that Elizabeth had stepped out.

"Laura, Sojourner, Wake up! Hurry!" Elizabeth called to them through the window. She had already departed the train car with her bag.

Laura stretched trying to gain a sense of equilibrium. She felt completely discombobulated. Yawning, she asked. "What? What did thee say, Sojourner? Where's Elizabeth?"

"She's probably already met up with her daughter," Sojourner quipped sleepily.

"But of course," Laura remembered. She was on the train with Elizabeth and Sojourner. They had just arrived in Columbus to meet Elizabeth's daughter. Laura sat up and said with a sleepy smile, "And so would we if we were in her shoes."

Suddenly, Elizabeth opened the passenger cabin door and said in a glad tone, "Ladies, come, come! Our chariot awaits!"

"Elizabeth, hast thou seen Caroline?" Laura asked, still trying to shake herself awake.

"Yes. I've seen both Edwin and Caroline from a distance. Girls, wake up. Thank goodness we have a little bit of time. We're not supposed to get off until the train comes to a stop."

The wheels of the train were continuing to churn slower and slower. Finally the halting, squealing brakes on the train slowed the big metal locomotive to a complete stop. While they waited, the ladies quipped about their unbelievably long nap.

"How long have we been asleep?" Sojourner queried.

"I don't know, but it seemed like eternity to me," Laura reflected.

"Laura! How could thee speak of eternity in such a trite manner?" Elizabeth quipped half-laughing.

"Seriously, I feel like my whole life swept before my very eyes in the last few hours," Laura confessed.

"Yes, my dear, the two of thee must have slept for at least three, maybe four hours. I was too excited! I just couldn't sleep." Elizabeth continued, "But I did rest."

"Hmm. I can't imagine why thee would be excited." Laura smirked as the three of them laughed.

Sojourner and Laura rushed as they scurried to step off the train. They couldn't believe they had slept so long and that their final destination had come so quickly. Of course, Elizabeth was the first to jump off the train.

Laura couldn't shake the feeling that she had just relived most of her adult life in the last few hours. She felt sore all over. Had she dreamed that she had taken that horrible fall on the stagecoach with the stubborn mules or had it actually happened again? Had she dreamed that she had just fallen eight feet from her kitchen hallway onto her cellar floor? No. She could never have lived through those experiences twice!

"I'll just shake it off," Laura thought to herself. As the passengers filed off the train Laura worked to collect her thoughts and mind. It was great to meet Elizabeth's beautiful daughter Caroline. Caroline and her husband, Edwin De Green, were fine English Quakers, and it was a highlight to meet such a dear, devoted couple.

Caroline was thrilled to greet and meet her mother's friends, Laura and Sojourner. "Oh, I've heard so much about both of thee," she gushed as she hugged them both. Caroline chatted nonstop about the exciting work of the Columbus Training Institute. Elizabeth was the financier of their joint effort, and Caroline was the brains behind its work. Caroline begged the ladies to take a tour of the school still that night.

Laura told Caroline, "We are perfectly fine with a tour as we have just spent the better part of three hours napping. I think I must have slept in the wrong position. My neck feels as though I slept in the wrong position, and a walk will do me good."

Sojourner responded. "No, it was probably that lurching of the train as the brakeman kept pressing on the brakes. But Laura is right; we had an absolutely delicious nap. I'm ready for a tour."

"Well, I'm sure that thee needed some extra rest," Caroline responded. "I know the long hours and days thee spend in serving the needs of others."

Edwin, Caroline's husband, courteously loaded the ladies bags onto the covered wagon and helped them all on board. They were thankful for the extra protection of the cover as rain drops turned into a straight line of wind and rain. They wrapped Edwin in blankets and covered his poor wet head. Caroline even held an umbrella over him. Upon their arrival, however, poor Edwin was completely drenched. Gallantly, he helped his female attendants into the Columbus Institute facility under a huge umbrella.

The ladies were greatly impressed with the school training rooms. They arrived just as an evening class was dismissed. The Columbus Institute offered industry and agricultural classes for the men. Classes in cooking, canning, and sewing were available for the women. Sojourner and Laura were adequately impressed with the school's work.

Laura's eye caught sight of the sewing room and said to Caroline.

"Caroline, dost thou need another sewing instructor?"

"Always," Caroline quipped with a gleam in her eye. "And Mrs. Haviland, I hear thee is one of the best seamstresses we could enlist. I'll add you to the teaching schedule."

"I'll be glad to work with such a class. We have several bolts of gingham and cotton with us that we can use for that very purpose," Laura added.

"Thank thee, Sister Laura. The Lord knows we need all of the material and clothes we can find. Shall we begin tonight?"

They all laughed heartily and Laura demurely asked, "Dost thou think, Caroline, that we can wait at least until morning?"

"Yes, yes! Tomorrow will be just fine," Caroline replied with a big smile.

The ladies' task was to gather necessary supplies and funds needed for students to complete their education. Sojourner and Laura began writing to friends in the Freedmen's Bureau as well as local merchants for these supplies. The response was rewarding as the school was having such a positive influence on both indigent white and black refugees.

Sojourner and Laura also worked with the women day after day. Many of them knew exactly who Sojourner was, and they would come ask for her autograph. She loved her students and handed out her autographed shadows, a black and white postcard with Sojourner's silhouette. Sojourner's height and robust figure, voice and preachy sing-song venue were well known by many. She was a welcome speaker for churches and civic groups. Though this trip west to Kansas was the dream of a lifetime for Sojourner, unfortunately her health began to take a turn for the worse. She cherished each moment and would exclaim at the end of each day, "Laura, look at what a great life our brothers and sisters of color can find in this state! Here is land, opportunity and educational classes for both men and women to learn a trade, to farm the land and to start anew."

"Yes, sometimes we are so busy meeting the immediate needs of Exodusters, we lose sight of the bigger picture-their future." Laura sighed.

"Laura, these folks don't know how to make decisions. Sometimes, I wonder if they'll ever completely be able to soak up, enjoy and bask in their freedom. Many of them keep lookin' over their shoulders thinkin' the other shoe's goin' to drop and someone will chain them up as their slave," she moaned.

"Yes, Sojourner, I understand," Laura sympathized.

"I wish there were more I could do to help them see their way, to see the light of freedom, 'freedom's holy light.'" Sojourner wistfully echoed.

"We've worked hard to break the chains on their bodies. Now, they have to break the chains on their minds." Laura chimed in.

"Oh yes, yes! I hate to leave at this critical time," Sojourner lamented.

"Sojourner, thou should think about the wonderful support thee has already been to the Exodusters," Laura comforted.

"Perhaps?" She faltered. "I am truly blest to have made this journey, to have seen this hope for my people to be fulfilled to this point," Sojourner concluded.

"Yes, thou is just like Moses, with one exception," Laura declared.

"Whatever cou'd thee be thinkin', Mrs. Haviland?" Sojourner questioned with a half-smile creasing into the corner of her lips.

"Well, Moses never stepped over into the Promised Land. But Mrs. Sojourner Truth, thee hast traveled through it, encouraging the children of promise to lay down their claim and to build new lives for their families, providing hope for generations to come," Laura exclaimed.

"May it be so, Sister Laura. May it be so." Sojourner whispered as if in prayer.

Within two weeks, Sojourner felt the need to return to her home in Battle Creek, Michigan. Walking with her to the train depot, Elizabeth and Laura carried her belongings. There was not the usual bantering, but they spent their moments sharing caring thoughts that would carry them all through the days ahead.

Elizabeth mothered Sojourner tenderly. "Sojourner, don't forget to apply this hot pack of spices before thee goes to sleep. I'm sure the train attendant will heat it on the iron for thee. It will be good for thy cold."

"Oh, thank thee, Elizabeth. I think once I get on the train I will sleep well. I will miss the two of thee so dearly. Thanks for all thy tender care and help."

"Sojourner, thee is so easy to help. I can't imagine what we would have done had it not been for thy service," Elizabeth responded.

"It has been a joy to work with thee," Laura added.

Sojourner took both of their hands with tears in her eyes and said a little prayer. "May the Lord bless the good work from these hands and keep my sisters safe."

Elizabeth and Laura both responded, "And may He be with thee as well."

They laughed and cried. It was time for the sun to rise, but the day was rainy and dark. As they waited at the train station in Columbus to send Sojourner home with lots of love and warm clothing, they huddled together under the awning at the train station.

As Sojourner began to walk towards the train, Laura cried. "God be with thee, Sister Sojourner!"

"And with thee, Sister Laura. If I don't see thee again on this side of eternity, I'll be looking for thee on the other side, my dear sister."

They hugged tenderly one last time and would never forget their beautiful trip of the last few weeks and this time together. As Laura turned away, wiping tears from her eyes, she waited for Elizabeth to say her good-byes.

Waiting until the wheels of the train began to move and the whistle started to blow, they stood at the train counter and waved and waved, not even sure if Sojourner could see them. Elizabeth and Laura were both strangely sad and quiet as they headed back to the Columbus Institute.

What a legend! Sojourner Truth towered over everyone not only in height, but in her service. Her suffering made her tender, and her disappointments could never snuff out her light of hope.

In the early spring Laura decided to travel back through the state, revisiting the old places she had traveled on her Leavenworth, Wyandotte, Quindaro, and Fort Scott circuit fifteen years earlier. The trip served a dual purpose: revisiting these communities and raising funds for the Columbus Institute. It was rewarding to see those she had helped fifteen years earlier in 1864. Many of the freed families whom she had found shivering to death, without a roof over their heads at that time, were now in homes, diligently working the land or in trades that provided for the needs of their families.

As Laura made her rounds many would rush out to warmly greet her. One of these was Amy Bethel, Green Bethel's daughter, whose family had lost so much in Quindaro. Laura remembered Amy leaning on her shoulder, crying over the loss of her mother. And now she was a mother of three beautiful children herself. Amy introduced Laura to her children and they shared many heartwarming stories.

Then there was Agnes Everett. She greeted Laura with two healthy children by her side. Agnes said, "Children, this is Mrs. Laura Haviland. She is the reason you are both alive!"

Laura meekly replied, "Oh no. I just instructed thy mother on how to feed thee."

Shyly, they smiled and both said, "thank you."

"Oh my, it is so good to see how thee both have grown into healthy young people."

Of course, there were other "not so happy stories" of families that didn't survive. Some of these froze to death, others starved. These were heartbreaking, yet most could have been predicted.

One of the most serious concerns for the Exodusters in Laura's mind was the group formed after the war by previous slaveholders called the Ku Klux Klan. These wicked men covered their faces with white sheets, sneaking out in the middle of the night and burned crosses in the yards of black families. More often than not they burned the house down as well. Such hatred sent shivers down Laura's spine.

Hatred and ignorance did not end with the changing of laws. A law cannot change the heart of individuals, and many times it does not even change the action. However, this is no time to give up. Perhaps the love of a friend—caring, sharing, the giving of a life to serve—this alone can change hearts. How many lives must be lost before prejudiced hearts will change?

Laura returned to Columbus after two months of travel. Elizabeth met her at the depot, having just returned from Washington D.C. Her welcoming words were full of hope.

"Oh Laura, I'm so glad thee is back. I have so much to tell thee," she said ecstatically as she greeted Laura at the railway station. As Laura climbed into the wagon with her bags, Elizabeth could scarcely wait to share her exciting news.

"Laura, I have only been back for two weeks myself."

Laura replied, "I knew thee had planned a trip to Washington D.C."

"Yes, two weeks ago to this very day, I sat in the oval office with President Garfield," She quipped happily.

"Do tell!" Laura gasped. Elizabeth had her attention now.

"Yes, President Garfield has not only promised to fund our work from the past year, but he also promised to provide support for the next two years as well!" Elizabeth almost shouted out the words.

"Wonderful!" Laura clapped her hands for joy. "God knows we need it."

"Yes, indeed. Our funds have certainly been drained. " Elizabeth sighed.

"Well," Laura said, "I guess since the influx of freed families has practically stopped, people do not realize there is yet a great need. They just don't understand we're still helping a lot of these people."

Elizabeth sighed. "Yes, but this gives us hope. Think of it seriously, Laura. President Garfield has promised that he will send his support for our funding of supplies to the destitute Exodusters in Kansas."

"Yes, I heard that the first time thee said it!" Laura's voice contained a tinge of orneriness.

"Laura Smith Haviland!" Elizabeth cried out.

Laughing, Laura replied, "I think it's simply marvelous, Elizabeth." Then she commented rather soberly, "Elizabeth, it is difficult to imagine that that thee has raised close to $70,000 single-handedly for this life-saving cause. And to think that now thee has found a way to cover all of our expenses. That is truly marvelous. Thy gift of fund-raising has helped tens of thousands of people, over and over."

"Thanks be to God, Laura. It was not me. Thanks be to God," she said, reflecting a thoughtful smile.

"Yes," Laura smiled. "And, thou hast continued to support this work with thy own funding. That's another gift from God."

Elizabeth nodded, looked at Laura and spoke in a serious tone. "Yes, but Laura I will need these funds before long, which is why the President's promise is a wonderful blessing. Please do not say anything about this to Caroline and Edwin."

"Mrs. Comstock, what is thee saying? Art thou dipping into thy personal savings to pay the way for the Columbus Institute?"

"Shh. . .Please do not make a fuss about it! I just do not want Caroline and Edwin to worry."

"Elizabeth! What was thee thinking?" Laura asked raising her voice in concern.

"Please, Laura, thee must promise to keep my secret!" Elizabeth begged.

"As a friend, I will always be true," Laura quietly responded.

"Thank thee," Elizabeth responded simply.

Laura could sense her friend breathing a sigh of relief. Trying to lighten her spirits, Laura said, "Well, Mrs. Comstock, which one of thy three Quaker dresses dost thou plan to wear to the big gala event in Congress, escorted on the President's arm."

Elizabeth laughed. "Well, as all three dresses look much the same, does it really matter?"

The ladies laughed. And Laura could tell Elizabeth was feeling a bit better.

Laura said, "How exciting for thee, and what a blessing!"

"Yes, it is a blessing! The President gave me his personal word. He said he will meet with me in January and we will attend the Congressional sessions together. Can thee imagine it? I will be attending a Congressional Session with the President of the United States!" she giggled.

Laughing at her dramatic expression, Laura had to say, "That is noteworthy. A Quaker abolitionist will attend a special session of Congress as the guest of the President."

Elizabeth blushed and smiled, "Nonsense, It's all in the line of duty."

Laura, with a twinkle in her eye, just smiled.

Arriving at the Columbus Institute, Elizabeth helped Laura carry her bags as they continued to chat about the happenings in Columbus and Elizabeth's upcoming adventure to the country's capitol.

These were exciting days for the Columbus Institute. Governor St. John, who deeply appreciated the leadership that Elizabeth and Laura had given over the past two years in implementing the relief efforts of the Kansas Freedmen's Bureau, chose to honor their work. In a May 1881, letter Governor St. John stated his choice to honor the work of the Kansas Freedmen's Bureau and the Columbus institute. A special statewide event would be held on the premises of the Columbus Institute on Saturday, July 2, 1881. It would be a public open house to recognize their work as an example of service during this era of the state's reconstruction.

Governor St. John would make a special trip to the Columbus Institute with several dignitaries. One of these would include the ladies' dear friend and St. John's sister-in-law Susan B. Anthony. Laura was excited as this would be a great opportunity for her to return Susan's kindness with a festive gala at the Institute for them. The female students prepared an exquisite dinner of baked halibut, creamed peas, fluffy homemade rolls and chocolate mousse crepes that was shared together before the main festivities of the afternoon.

Visitors from Columbus and across Eastern Kansas rallied to make this event a great one. All of the spring housecleaning and cooking had been done. There were plates of homemade cookies of all kinds and fruit crepes made by the members of their cooking class stacked on trays in the kitchen for all of the many guests that were to arrive. Students arrived first to welcome all of the guests, serve the food and park their buggies. The American Flag was flying proudly in front of the Columbus Institute on the grand day of Governor St. John's arrival. People lined the walkways and were directed to the back of the Institute where tables and chairs were lined up under the half-grown trees. The crowd continued to grow until it was too difficult to get an official count. There was standing room only. Some of Laura's old friends—Dr. Speck, Dr. Woods and Lawyer James from Lawrence—were in the crowd. And there were freedmen and women everywhere who wanted to say "thanks" in their own special way.

Then a reporter from the *Columbus Daily* arrived. No one had given their presence a lot of consideration. Finally, Governor St. John's coach arrived. A flatbed trailer had been draped with a banner welcoming his arrival. The Governor was surrounded by men on the look-out for imposters or anyone who might try to cause trouble. It was a sad thought, but ever since the assassination of dear President Lincoln, extra security for all leaders had become a reality.

On that day the back lawn of the Columbus Institute was filled with hundreds of people, both black and white, cheering the Governor. It was not just any day that the Governor of Kansas made a special appearance in a small town of Kansas.

Elizabeth and Laura had both donned their best Quaker dresses. Laura's dress had embroidered white-eyed lace on the front of her Quaker gray, and the bustle in the back was outlined with the same beautiful lace. This was truly an extra luxury a good Quaker did not need. As she was teaching these young women the intricacies of sewing, it seemed to be a perfectly worthy project for one of her students. Elizabeth, too, had added a special look to her wardrobe for the day, wearing a distinguishing black Quaker dress beautifully highlighted with a white collar, waistband and trim on the hem.

Edwin, Caroline, Elizabeth, Laura and other distinguished local officials sat on the flatbed trailer turned into a platform. A podium had been provided for the Governor's speech. There was a megaphone, a unique round instrument that carried the sound of the governor's voice throughout the crowd. As he arrived, there were soldiers dressed in their Yankee blue playing a trumpet rendition of "The Star Spangled Banner." Governor St. John made his way to the chair on the platform with us and the event began. Such fanfare was not normal for the Columbus Institute.

It was a hot July Saturday afternoon, and everyone was thankful for the breeze that brought relief from what seemed to be a hundred-plus degree temperatures. Beyond the people and the horse-drawn vehicles, there were patches of sunflowers mixed with the purple, red and orange wildflowers spread throughout the pastures. It was such a beautiful sight from the platform.

Laura leaned over and whispered to Elizabeth, "Look at our beautiful view."

Elizabeth solemnly nodded and added, "Canst thee believe this is happening to us, Laura?"

Governor St. John gave a moving speech, "The Faith and Freedom of our Founding Fathers." Laura kept the flyer of the event as a memento and reminder to pray for our country's President and other leaders.

Next, Governor St. John introduced Edwin and Caroline DeGreen. Everyone applauded their hard work in establishing and operating the Columbus Institute. It sounded like thunderous applause with the many hundreds of people facing the platform clapping for the work of the Institute.

The fine governor then called Elizabeth and Laura to stand by his side at the podium. Governor St John stood between them, grasping a hand from each one, lifting their hands into the air. He said, "I do hereby ordain these two faithful women, tireless leaders of the Kansas Freedmen's Bureau, as the 'Two Most Noble Women' in the State of Kansas on this day, July 2, 1881. I hereby verify that today will be recognized as the Elizabeth Comstock and Laura Haviland Day of Honor. Let's spend this day celebrating their sacrificial work among us."

Again there was thunderous applause, and as this honor was quite out of the ordinary for a Quaker's humble experience, the women stood there not knowing what to do. Elizabeth and Laura were both speechless, something that rarely happened to either one of them during their times of service. They were unaware that he was planning to shower them with such praise. He handed each a plaque that cemented these words into a life-long treasure. All Laura could say was a simple, "thank thee."

After the ceremony, everyone was invited to partake of the cookies, crepes and iced lemonade. Though the crowd was gathering around, Governor St. John had his security guards place Edwin, Caroline, Elizabeth and Laura in a receiving line next to him in order to shake hands and greet all of their guests. Meanwhile the members of the *Columbus Daily* had surrounded the party and asked how to spell names, along with a myriad of other questions about the work, the home town and state of each in the group.

As the hundreds of guests made their way through the line, Laura and Elizabeth entertained their questions and kind accolades. It was a day to remember. People sat at the tables and stayed for hours talking about the excitement and energy of the accomplishments of the reconstruction efforts throughout the Eastern part of Kansas. On a national scale there was much talk of President Garfield. He was attempting to balance some southern sentiments with that of the government reconstruction efforts in the hopes of holding the Union of our United States together. Such deep, heady conversations continued while all seemed to enjoy the beautiful afternoon. The Columbus students proved to be great servers and workers throughout the day's event.

Following this special event, as Governor St. John took his leave, Laura and Elizabeth thanked him for such a special recognition. They still found it almost surreal. It had come totally unexpected on their behalf. The good governor tipped his hat and said, "My dear ladies, an army of men could never have accomplished the amount of relief and support that the two of you have been able to manage in such a small amount of time." St. John, a gracious leader, seemed to really appreciate the ways their non-profit work had taken up the slack of the government in working with those lost, freed souls during the Exoduster era.

After the governor and the rest of the guests had gone, Elizabeth and Laura finally had the opportunity to relax. It had been a day to remember. Looking at one another after the clean-up, they burst into gales of laughter. Elizabeth and Laura loved to laugh together. "Ms. Laura Haviland, Thou art a noble woman!" Elizabeth exclaimed with a twinkle in her eye. Responding with a gasp of subdued mirth, Laura concluded, "No, no, my dear Mrs. Comstock, thou art a noble woman!" And so the bantering went back and forth. Finally they collapsed into the blue velvet high backed chairs in the parlor of the Columbus Institute. They took such accolades in stride, and laughed with joy over the beautiful day. These women would never be disrespectful. It's just that they knew it was not the compliments or the accolades that energized or motivated them to do the things they did.

As they watched that big, red beautiful sun set over the horizon and paint the sky with beauty, they knew it was God who deserved their trust, honor and praise. It seemed as though nothing could disrupt the fulfillment and joy they had experienced on that special day.

    Little did they know the joys and peaceful spirit of this day would be draped by the coming of tragic news.

Chapter Twenty-Four

Tragedy & Triumph

Life in Columbus, Kansas, would have returned to some sense of normalcy after the grand celebration had it not been for the news. Edwin came in the following morning with the *Columbus Daily.* There at the top on the front page, in large, bold print,

President Garfield Shot!

This message had come straight from the telegraph wires. As Edwin cried out the news, everyone came running into the parlor as he read the article to everyone.

President James Garfield was shot at Washington's Baltimore and Potomac railway station on July 2, 1881. Garfield was shot with a .44 British Bulldog in the abdomen. He is surrounded by the best doctors of Washington D.C., along with inventor Alexander Graham Bell. All are working desperately to save our President's life. Charles Guiteau, the attempted assassin, is a lawyer who is under investigation for stalking Secretary of State Blaine and the President over the last several weeks.

We all gasped as the story was read. Caroline cried out, "How could someone be so evil?"

Edwin calmly said, "Obviously, John Wilkes Booth had no problem doing evil to our dear President Lincoln."

"Some people seem to justify or rationalize such evil actions to their own cause," Laura replied.

"Oh yes, Caroline. Humans have been justifying their evil ways ever since Cain set the precedent and killed his brother Abel. We must stop for a moment to pray," Elizabeth sorrowfully suggested.

After a circle of prayer for President Garfield's healing, breakfast was served.

Edwin, still reading the paper, found the article that he had planned to share before the crushing news surfaced. Valiantly trying to lift the spirits of those around the table, he read, "Comstock and Haviland Honored by Governor St. John as the Most Noble Women in Kansas." Elizabeth and Laura politely listened while Edwin read the entire article to them line by line. Laura smiled at Elizabeth and she smiled back. But they were all saddened by the tragic news from the nation's capital. And there was really nothing to say.

Laura finally asked, "Well, did they mention the hard work of Edwin and Caroline Greene's work at the Columbus Institute and the honor they also received on Saturday?"

Edwin's face flushed a light shade of red as he said, "Well, I skipped over that part. Our gala just seems so empty in light of the assassination attempt on President Garfield's life."

"Yes, so true. But it still does not disregard thy hard work here at the Columbus Institute," Laura said, trying to muster a smile. "Thank thee, Edwin," Laura replied as she headed next door to the Institute for her first sewing class of the day!

Everyone carried the sadness of yet another President shot, whose life was lying in the balance. Each day they gathered to hear the news. The President's condition was of great concern to everyone, but in particular to Elizabeth. Garfield had given her his personal word that the Columbus Institute project would be paid for in retrospect. Now, with his life in the balance, Elizabeth knew Garfield's verbal promise stood in the balance, and at this point there was no way to intervene or intercede.

In a moment of deep reflection, Elizabeth asked, "Laura, what shall I do if the President dies and no one will know of his promise to me of needed funds? Certainly one cannot hold a dead man to a promise."

"Of course not," Laura responded. "But thee knows the Lord will provide."

"Yes," Elizabeth smiled. "That is right."

In September word came to us President Garfield had indeed passed away due to the severity of wounds from the assassination attempt two months prior. All of Elizabeth's hopes for reimbursement of her savings had now vanished.

Life returned to somewhat normal. Elizabeth and Laura continued the work, sharing opportunities, providing supplies and clothing for the Exoduster families that had moved from the South during the cold winter season in Kansas. Laura continued to teach sewing classes and she also began to teach a Sunday School class each Sunday at the Columbus Institute. Elizabeth continued to raise funds for these projects.

The Logan Anti-slavery society from Adrian, as well as many others, continued to supply the work with blankets, clothing and other staple products needed for survival. Laura was very thankful for the many women from Michigan who stayed up late nights and rose early in the morning hemming, mending and sewing clothes for women, men and children. Sometimes, Laura could picture them in their sewing circles working their fingers to the bone, but laughing all the while. They knew that every garment sent to Kansas was needed. These clothes were sent in boxes on the railcars by the Freedmen's Bureau Association of Michigan and Kansas.

During the New Year of 1882, the Exoduster migration subsided. Just as quickly as the influx of people into Kansas had begun in 1879, so it stopped in 1882. Though their hard work of providing for people's needs continued steadily, the fervent pace slowed down to a steady, methodical pace. Laura was thankful for the time to catch her breath. Life settled into a routine, teaching and serving the school, and traveling to help settlers only upon request.

Unfortunately, by the middle of September Elizabeth was struggling with her health. After returning from a weekend of travel, Laura met Caroline at the door. With a heavy heart Caroline explained, "Oh, Laura, I'm so glad thee is back. I don't know what to do for Mother. She's just not herself, and yet she still wants to be out working and fundraising for the school, but I dare not let her go."

"Caroline, I'm so sorry. What can I do to help thee?"

"Would thee be willing to serve as her nurse for a few days? Keep an eye on her, keep her resting and tell me what thee thinks! She's rambling words I don't understand," Caroline concluded.

"Of course, I will be glad to do that. Has a doctor come to check on her?" Laura asked.

"Oh yes, Dr. Flannagan is the best in the city. He says we can treat her physical symptoms, but all we can do is pray for her mind." The words tumbled from Caroline's lips as the tears began to fall down her face.

"Oh, my dear," Laura attempted to comfort Caroline by wrapping her arms around her. Caroline began to cry uncontrollably.

Giving her time for a good cry, Laura finally responded, "Caroline, dear. Don't worry thy heart now. She in is the care of the Almighty. He's watching over her. He's also watching over thee and thy work here." Caroline smiled and nodded her assent through the tears.

As Laura walked up the stairway and down the hall to Elizabeth's room, she heard groaning and moaning. Upon her entrance, Elizabeth's weak little voice called out, "Laura is that thee?"

"Yes, Elizabeth, I am here."

"Oh, thank God! My dear friend, Laura! Please stay with me."

"Yes, I will, but Dr. Flannagan wants thee to rest. So I will only stay if thee promises to rest," Laura said taking her hands and sitting on a bench beside her bed.

"Oh, thank thee. Yes, of course I will," she said.

After a prayer for healing and comfort, the two sat in silence for a long period of time as good Quakers do. Laura could tell by her breathing that finally Elizabeth was asleep. Then she made her way in the dark to the room next to Elizabeth's and crawled into bed.

Laura's task was to daily sit beside the bed of her dear friend, watching and praying for any sign of recovery. While Elizabeth slept she would mumble and moan words that didn't always form phrases or sentences. She kept saying, "No President Garfield, no money, no supplies." And of course it made perfect sense to Laura, as she knew of her meeting with the President who promised to provide resources and funds for the supplies. Yet, of course, she had to be faithful to her dear friend and not reveal her secret. Elizabeth was not losing her mind as her daughter and doctor feared.

Thank goodness, Elizabeth's recovery came after several weeks of rest. Dr. Flannagan returned periodically and he was most pleased with her progress. He warned her that if she tried to return to a tedious and stressful regimen, her health problems would certainly resurface.

The decision was made that Elizabeth and Laura return home in mid-November 1882. The rigors of the journey were very difficult for Elizabeth, and her cough and fever returned before they reached Michigan. She was taken to the sleeping car for rest and Laura sat with her, listening to her groaning ramblings about President Garfield. Laura thought aloud, "Poor Elizabeth, dear friend." This made the journey home very difficult. Laura tried hard to keep Elizabeth comfortable all the way home.

Reaching Elizabeth's home, Laura promised her that she would address Congress when they reconvened in January 1883 regarding the Columbus financial burden. Elizabeth's gravest concern was to continue with the fund-raising efforts of the Freedmen's Bureau to support the relief efforts in Kansas.

"God be with thee, Sister Laura. Don't worry about me. President Garfield is gone. A dead man cannot be kept to his promise, and who else would take up our cause?"

"Elizabeth, thou knows very well there are many in the Congress that will support thy cause. Now, stop worrying! I will do my best for thee. God be with thee." And with these words and a hug, Laura left her bedside and returned to her little cottage in Adrian. Elizabeth was transferred the next day to New York City to recuperate in a sanitarium.

Poor Laura was to leave sadness to greet sadness. Having felt very sad for dear Mrs. Comstock, Laura was soon to discover her own deep personal grief. Laura's youngest son, Joseph Haviland, had been elected the Lieutenant Governor of the State of Michigan. He had asked his mother to meet him at his new office in Lansing for a celebration. Arriving at his office in great anticipation, she was met sadly by his clerk and the governor of Michigan.

The governor had received a telegram informing them of Joseph's illness. Rushing to his home Laura found her young son extremely ill. "Joseph! my Joseph!" Laura cried, cradling his head in her arms.

"Oh, my dear Mother," Joseph barely eked out the words in a whisper.

Finding her son close to death filled Laura with sadness upon sadness. Laura cried out to God. "Lord, please take me. I'm close to 75 years old. My son is too young, so full of important work to do in the state. Lord, ist Thee listening? Lord, ist Thee there? This is a big mistake. Take me instead. Please, I beg of Thee. Look at his dear young family." Laura cried out this prayer over and over in her heart. The pain throbbed in her heart wildly beyond control. She spent four tragic, yet beautiful days embracing his dear familiar face burning with fever; and there was nothing that could be done to stop the angel of death from taking him to the other shore.

On the third day it was Joseph himself who became Laura's comfort. Perhaps he heard her pleas to God or he just knew that his mother and family needed to know. He pointed to a Bible and thumbed through it, finding the Scripture II Corinthians 5:1. He motioned for Laura to read aloud, his throat burning too fiercely to speak. Clearing her throat she read the words: "For I know that if this earthly house of this tabernacle were dissolved, I have a building of God, a house not made with hands eternal in the heavens." During those precious days, Joseph made it clear to his mother his precious hope for moving into eternity with this promise. After reading these words, his beautiful wife, two daughters, siblings and Laura surrounded him with love and support. They prayed, sang hymns and shared their love with him. At the end of the fourth day, Joseph simply fell asleep in Jesus's arms with such a peaceful and beautiful passage, leaving the shores of time for eternity.

Though God gave such a beautiful benediction to Joseph's life, Laura still struggled deeply with this loss. What a blow! She had wanted to jump into his body. Why would God take him rather than her? She was old. He was young. Staying with his dear family for several weeks, she finally needed to give them their space and fulfill her promise to Elizabeth Comstock. It was time to head to Washington, D.C.

Almira ('Mira) Laing, Laura's youngest daughter, accompanied her on January 27, 1883, to Washington D.C. They were met and escorted by a page of the Honorable Thomas Ryan of the United States Senate. He directed the ladies to a hotel where they found comfortable accommodations. The page handed them a list of addresses of congressional officers. The young page also informed them they were to meet with Judge Ryan early the next morning in the hotel dining room for breakfast. As the page bowed and walked out of the hotel, 'Mira quickly pulled a coin out of her purse and called after him to return. As he courteously responded, she handed him the coin and thanked him for his information. When he was out of sight and earshot, she said, "Mother, do you not know that we are supposed to tip pages?"

Looking at her in surprise and with a sheepish smile, she simply said, "No, I guess I'm not aware of these things!"

"Oh, Mother! I'm so glad I'm here for you. You definitely need me!"

Laura's modern daughter rarely used their old Quaker pronouns these days. Yet, 'Mira reminded Laura of her archaic ways, reminding her that she came from the "old school."

"Yes, what would I do without thee?" Laura dryly responded. "I have only been navigating my own affairs for the last seventy plus years," she said with a wryly smile.

'Mira knew better than to say another word. The ladies moved onto the brighter prospect of a light dinner before they retired to their hotel room. Laura had to confess that she absolutely loved the time she spent with her youngest daughter. Laura feared that she had neglected 'Mira at times while she pursued her work with the Underground Railroad during her earlier years. 'Mira had never complained nor communicated to Laura that she felt that way. On the contrary, Laura remembered how little 'Mira would greet her eagerly and beg her to tell the stories of helping the slaves escape to freedom. They shared great times. But Laura was not always sure that they made up for the special events that she had missed in her life.

The next morning the ladies received Judge Ryan in the parlor and he escorted them into the hotel dining room, where he informed them concerning the activities of Congress for the day. Judge Ryan had checked the names of the House and Senate members that he wanted the ladies to visit. Of course, Judge Ryan also discussed the legislative bill that was currently being debated, the Pendleton Civil Service Reform Act. This was very interesting to 'Mira. The bill was supported by President Arthur due to the public outcry following President Garfield's assassination. Charles Guiteau, Garfield's assassin, had been bitter for not receiving a consular position as ambassador to Paris that he had aggressively pursued. It was the belief of Congress that a civil service system should be in place so that appointees would be chosen for these positions on merit rather than politics. This was at the core of the new reform act. 'Mira was duly impressed as they sat in the balcony of the Capitol building, listening to legislative leaders as they debated this very important act. The ladies listened with eager interest to the pros and the cons of the reform.

The Capitol was an ostentatious place. Laura's memories flooded back to her earlier days when she contacted legislators to free Thomas Lean and free the

3,000 prisoners. As they walked through the Capitol, 'Mira insisted she would never forget the granite walls and marble pillars. Suddenly her mother's life-work took on an even more interesting intrigue for her.

Late in the afternoon the Honorable Thomas Ryan, M.C., of Topeka, Kansas, introduced the refunding bill of favor for Elizabeth L. Comstock. Laura and 'Mira called on a number of senators and congressmen while there in order to explain the importance of obtaining this funding for Elizabeth's supplies for the Columbus Institute, and the aid for several families who were at risk of losing their farms.

Two days later Haviland heard the great news that she had been successful in her bid. President Arthur and the Congress approved to give the funding retroactive for the year, and also for two years in advance. Laura and 'Mira were ecstatic! Laura also had the satisfaction of knowing that President Arthur, the General Arthur who first secured her transportation and passage of supplies during the Civil War decades earlier, signed this refunding bill into law.

Yet with the good news also comes the bad. It actually took two and half years longer before the funding for Elizabeth was received. Laura said to Elizabeth, "My experience with 'red tape' during war times continues on with the United States Congress twenty years later." And though it came late, when she finally arrived at Elizabeth's home with her funds they had a great celebration. Elizabeth was well enough to celebrate. The first words out of her mouth were, "Laura let us sing the 'doxology!'" Of course, this was their joke as good Quakers of their era did not sing, even if it was a song of praise to their God! That night Elizabeth and Laura sang it heartily in the room with the doors and windows closed. They were sure that God enjoyed it! They even considered opening all of the windows and doors and singing it again, but instead just laughed at the thought.

The following two years brought great times with family and friends, as well as the sorrows of loss within her family. In 1885 Laura lost two brothers; Dr. Sala

Smith died in the spring of 1885, and Harvey Smith, a teacher for fifty years, died the next fall. Sala had provided health care for the family for years, and her dear Harvey had sacrificed much in order to educate the children in his classes. Laura loved Harvey dearly for his role in selling his farm land and donating it to the Havilands to begin the Raisin Institute. Her heart grieved over losing these loved ones. Once again Laura had to remind herself that she, too, was headed along the same path to their heavenly destination. The loss of her Joseph, Harvey, Sala and others reminded her of the deep sorrows of 1845.

But Laura also had many opportunities to speak and share the needs of Kansas indigent families during these years, as well. Elizabeth and Laura had planned to make one final trip to Kansas, as Elizabeth had secured $3,000 designated to support families of refugees who had been slaves or children of slaves. Elizabeth had worked on this project for years, and now it was time to fund the right project. Once again Elizabeth was severely ill and unable to make such a difficult journey. She wrote Laura and insisted that she go, transferring the "power of attorney" to her in order to carry out the instructions within the will.

In 1886, Laura boarded a train, once again heading to Kansas to help those in need. Working with the lawyer, A.B. Whiting of Topeka, Kansas, with the $3,000 from the estate, 240 acres of rich, dark soil were purchased and divided into ten acre lots available for 24 worthy families. Now 24 families could establish a small acreage farm, build a home and a life.

While in Kansas, Laura traveled over 500 miles across the state. She found vast improvement among the freed families of the Great Exodus whom they had served from 1879-1881, though it had just been four years earlier. It was a rewarding, memorable trip!

Laura found a mission that she committed to support and serve called the "Half-Acre Mission," and later renamed the "Samaritan Mission." Planted in the midst of 'Hell's Half Acre,' it has been said. "No tongue or pen can describe the wretchedness that existed in 'Hell's Half Acre.'" Much agony and suffering continued to prevail. Many refugees had no way to provide for their families. Laura's heart went out to these families who had been dropped off at the junction of the Missouri and Kansas boundary line seven years earlier. Some of those 60,000 Exodus refugees were still struggling to survive.

During this last trip through Kansas in 1886, Laura met many new settlers traveling west to find land that they could call home. She remembered that time in her own life when she and her husband had "pulled up roots" and headed to Michigan to place their stake on their own homestead; what a memorable time for her young family. It was exciting for Laura to meet so many young families traveling in search of the same opportunities her family had found many years earlier.

One evening about dusk, six covered wagons pulled into the Ft. Leavenworth Camp where Laura had made her home while there. Laura was packing her bags, preparing to head home to Adrian the next day. Her work was complete. The weary Quaker travelers were fatigued from their long journey, and as the colonel in charge was not present, Laura sought to assist them. They were Quakers from Indiana, just south of Michigan. Laura had a great time visiting with these Quakers about the Northeast. Some of them were already a bit homesick, and it was a treat for them to visit with an old Michigan grandma!

Once they had received permission to stay in the fort that night, they settled in to make a fine meal. The Indiana Quakers insisted on sharing their supper with Laura, while Laura insisted on providing rations for them. As the women folk were visiting, Laura shared some of her experiences in the Kansas area.

Then one of the men, Caleb Davis, asked his wife.

"Does thee know who this dear little woman is?"

Laura looked at him in surprise as if he thought she might be a spy. She said before anyone had a chance to respond, "Why, I have always been the same little woman! I am Laura Haviland," She plainly stated.

"Really?" a sweet little wide-eyed girl, Mary Albertson, asked, peeking out from behind her mother's skirt.

"Yes," Laura calmly replied. There was total silence. Laura began to fidget. She could never remember a time when a group of Quakers questioned her identity. She was beginning to think they might request her official papers at any time.

It was sweet little Mary who broke the silence. "Why, that's wonderful! What an honor it is to meet thee!"

"Yes indeed! The privilege is ours, Mrs. Haviland!" A young Josiah Binford reached forward to shake her hand.

Another lady, Miss Theodore Pickett, ventured forward to take Laura's hand and said, "Thee must know that we have heard so many stories of thy work and labor of love for the cause of freedom and humanity along our way."

Deeply moved by the warmth and admiration of these kindred spirits, Laura felt the tears well up in her eyes. Little Mary came running over and asked if Laura would tell her and the other children stories about the slaves escaping to freedom in the Underground Railroad. All of the children circled round her as they sat near the campfire with their wagons surrounding them. She began to share with them some of the stories of Willis & Elsie Hamilton, John White, Maria, and George & Eliza Harris. They were so quiet. As Laura retold her life experiences from decades earlier, the only sound that could be heard besides her voice was the peaceful crackling of the embers on the campfire. When Laura looked up, every eye was upon her. Simply stunned and amazed at their genuine interest, she suddenly became self-conscious and responded, "Oh dear, I must be boring thee with all of these old stories."

"Oh no!" was the response with a resounding cry.

Little Mary came running to her and said, "No, please don't quit. We want to hear thy stories. Thou art the 'Underground Angel!'"

Bursting into laughter, everyone enjoyed Mary's sweet spontaneity and innocence. No one had the heart to correct her theology. Laura smiled and said, "Thank thee, child!"

Then their spokesman, Mr. Davis, courteously replied, "Mary, we are certainly keeping Mrs. Haviland from her chores and duties."

"Actually, I've really enjoyed this," Laura had to confess. So, after a few more tales, and a promise that she would tell them about Uncle Philip the next morning, they all headed to bed.

Laura's visit with the Indiana Quakers was so delightful, a memory to treasure. As they parted ways, she gave Miss Pickett her address to stay in touch. And so they did. It was delightful to hear of their arrival to their new colony on the Kansas prairie. The adventures of an Indian scare, a tornado and prairie fires threatened to devastate the small Quaker town. But in spite of it all they built a community and started an academy to teach their children. Yet, Laura was deeply honored when the new Kansas Quaker School was named after her, the "Haviland Academy." Miss Pickett informed Laura that she was the first teacher in the "Haviland Academy." Then several years later Laura, learned that her sweet "little" Mary Albertson had grown into a teacher for the academy, as well. Further, she could hardly believe that they would name their new town after her later in 1886

Truly this was a treasured honor. Having a child, a school and even a town named after her was unexpected. Laura was not a wealthy woman, and though many viewed her as a philanthropist, she was not. Yet Laura shared a great wealth, the riches of her Savior. But the truth of Laura Haviland's work is that she simply enjoyed helping those in need and sharing all she could on their behalf.

This included the sacrifices of many and the wealth of some. Most of the time the supplies she disbursed came from ordinary, everyday people who wanted to give a little, and when "the little" from these folks multiplied, it became very great indeed!

Young people today, living close to the turn of a new twentieth century, dangerously think that life is about "what's in it for me?" or "what can I get out of it?" Oh yes, Laura had dealt with many such entitlement "pigs" or "clay-eaters." She believed this entitlement mentality started at the beginning of time with Eve in the Garden of Eden and "the Apple!" What a thought! Perhaps good, ole Uncle Dodson understood this unique concept after all about Eve, the mother of all humanity. Laura had to simply laugh aloud at the thought of Uncle Dodson and his blunt scriptural interpretations, and in particular this one, "Eve as the mother of evil." Yet, the Scriptures clearly state, "All have sinned and fallen short of the glory of God," Romans 3:23.

Laura recognized the greatest joys of her life have been in service to God and others! The truth of the matter is "we are most blessed when we give and serve others." Oh, that the current generations of young people will not miss this truth!

Sitting once again on a railcar winding back north and east to that beautiful state of Michigan, Laura had time to ponder all of these thoughts. Sojourner Truth had gone ahead of her to the other side of eternity. How Laura missed her in these moments! And then there was her dear friend Elizabeth Comstock, who continued to recuperate with her daughter in New York. Heading home, she needed to check on her orphanages, the Coldwater School and the Haviland Home.

Laura sighed deeply and wondered, "Could I still have a few good years of service left in this old body? After all, I'm only a mere seven and a half decades down the road of life." Still Laura missed Charles, her baby Lavina, both of her Harveys, Joseph, Sala, her parents and other loved ones "on the other side."

Laura said to all whom she met. "I'll just keep looking for my Savior in those I meet along the way. The ones who will one day say, "I was hungry and you fed me. I was thirsty and you gave me a drink. I was homeless and you gave me a room. I was shivering and you gave me clothes. I was sick and you stopped to visit. I was in prison and you came to me" (Matthew 25:35-37).

Pulling into the Adrian rail station, Laura strained her eyes and was delighted to see her dear children and grandchildren waiting for her. The children from the orphanage were there, holding signs that said, "Welcome home, Aunt Laura! We love thee!" It was then that she knew there was still another chapter "in the bones" of this old Underground Angel.

"Thine for the oppressed!"   Laura S. Haviland

Postscript

Laura Smith Haviland lived another thirteen years, dying at the ripe old age of 89 in 1898. She has been commemorated in her hometown of Adrian with a life-size monument of her in front of the Lenawee County Historical Museum at Adrian, Michigan. Mrs. Haviland's statue is an exact life size replica. In this monument she is sitting, reading her autobiography *Laura S. Haviland: A Woman's Labor and Lifework*. A special room is also dedicated to Laura Smith Haviland in the Lenawee County Historical Museum. Mrs. Haviland was inducted into the "Who's Who in Michigan Women's Hall of Fame" in 1983, at Lansing, Michigan. Another community, Haviland, Ohio, was also named for Mrs. Haviland.

About the Author

Dr. Sheryl White has served as the Director of Lay Ministries at the First United Methodist Church in Pratt, KS for eight years. Sheryl received her Doctorate of Ministry degree in 2004 from Houston Graduate School of Theology. The dream to create *Underground Angel* arose from her dissertation, *The Haviland Heritage Foundation: Extending the Life of Laura S. Haviland in 21st Century Haviland and Beyond* through her dissertation director, Dr. Carol Vaughn. Sheryl lived and served the community of Haviland, Kansas for twelve and a half years serving as an instructor at Barclay College and Minister of Christian Education at the Haviland Friends Church. She is a graduate from Anderson University School of Theology with two post graduate degrees, a Master of Divinity (1989) and a Master of Arts in Theology and Ethics (1995).

CPSIA information can be obtained at www.ICGtesting.com
Printed in the USA
BVOW08s1530201214

380037BV00005B/70/P